Paper Tiger

A big cat overthrows the Indian state and establishes a reign of terror over the residents of a Himalayan town. A welfare legislation aimed at providing employment and commanding a huge budget becomes 'unimplementable' in a region bedeviled by high levels of poverty and unemployment. This book provides a lively ethnographic account of how such seemingly bizarre scenarios come to be in contemporary India. Based on 18 months of intensive fieldwork, the book presents a unique explanation for why and how progressive laws can do what they do and not, ever-so-often, what they are supposed to do. It reveals the double-edged effects of the reforms that have been ushered in by the post-liberalization Indian state, particularly the effort to render itself more transparent and accountable. Through a meticulous detailing of everyday bureaucratic life on the Himalayan borderland *Paper Tiger* makes an argument for shifting the very frames of thought through which we apprehend the workings of the developmental Indian state.

Nayanika Mathur holds a British Academy Postdoctoral Fellowship at the Department of Social Anthropology, University of Cambridge. She is additionally a Research Fellow at Cambridge's Centre for Research in the Arts, Social Sciences and Humanities.

CAMBRIDGE STUDIES IN LAW AND SOCIETY

Cambridge Studies in Law and Society aims to publish the best scholarly work on legal discourse and practice in its social and institutional contexts, combining theoretical insights and empirical research.

The fields that it covers are: studies of law in action, the sociology of law; the anthropology of law; cultural studies of law, including the role of legal discourses in social formations; law and economics; law and politics; and studies of governance. The books consider all forms of legal discourse across societies, rather than being limited to lawyers' discourses alone.

The series editors come from a range of disciplines: academic law; socio-legal studies; sociology; and anthropology. All have been actively involved in teaching and writing about law in context.

Series Editors
Chris Arup, *Monash University, Victoria*
Martin Chanock, *La Trobe University, Melbourne*
Sally Engle Merry, *New York University*
Susan Silbey, *Massachusetts Institute of Technology*

Paper Tiger

Law, Bureaucracy and the Developmental State in Himalayan India

Nayanika Mathur

CAMBRIDGE
UNIVERSITY PRESS

University Printing House, Cambridge CB2 8BS, United Kingdom

One Liberty Plaza, 20th Floor, New York, NY 10006, USA

477 Williamstown Road, Port Melbourne, VIC 3207, Australia

314-321, 3rd Floor, Plot 3, Splendor Forum, Jasola District Centre, New Delhi - 110025, India

79 Anson Road, #06-04/06, Singapore 079906

Cambridge University Press is part of the University of Cambridge.

It furthers the University's mission by disseminating knowledge in the pursuit of
education, learning and research at the highest international levels of excellence.

www.cambridge.org
Information on this title: www.cambridge.org/9781108458177

First published 2016
First paperback edition 2018

A catalogue record for this publication is available from the British Library

Library of Congress Cataloging in Publication data
Mathur, Nayanika.
  Paper tiger : law, bureaucracy and the developmental state in Himalayan India / Nayanika Mathur.
    pages cm. -- (Cambridge studies in law and society)
  Summary: ""Provides a unique explanation of the often-paradoxical effects of progressive
legislations in India"--Provided by publisher"-- Provided by publisher.
  Includes bibliographical references and index.
  ISBN 978-1-107-10697-0 (hardback)
  1. Rural development--Government policy--India--Chamoli District. 2. Wildlife conservation--
Government policy--India--Chamoli District. 3. Bureaucracy--India--Chamoli District.
4. National Rural Employment Guarantee Scheme (India) 5. India. Wildlife (Protection) Act, 1972. 6.
Chamoli District (India)--Politics and government.
  I. Title.
  HN690.C463M37 2015
  307.1´412095451--dc23
  2015014740

ISBN 978-1-107-10697-0 Hardback
ISBN 978-1-108-45817-7 Paperback

For Ravi and Tishya

Contents

List of figures

Glossary

adamkhor	human-eater
asli	real
atank	terror
avashayak karyavahi	necessary action
bagh/baghin	(male) leopard or tiger, (female) leopard or tiger
bhrashta/bhrashtachar	corrupt/corruption
chai	tea
Collectorate	The District Magistrate's office
farzee	fake or fraudulent
jaloos	procession of people
janta	the People
kachcha	temporary/raw
kanoon	law
krit karyavahi	action taken
kaghaz	paper
kursi	chair
maidani	plainsperson
neeche	below/down/down-there
paisa	money
pahar	mountains
pahari	mountain-person/s
panchayat	lit. council of five
Pradhan	village headperson
prarthana patra	lit. prayer letter; petition
pukka	permanent
rozgar	employment
sarkar	state/government
sarkari	adjective form of *sarkar*. State-like/government-y
shikar	hunting/the hunt

shikari	hunter
upar	above/up/up-there
vibhag	Department
vikas	Development
-wallah	an indication of the human/animals association with the prefix
yatra	travel/voyage/pilgrimage
zindagi	life

Acronyms

BDO	Block Development Officer
CDO	Chief Development Officer
CM	Chief Minister
CWW	Chief Wildlife Warden
DDO	District Development Officer
DFO	Divisional Forest Officer
DM	District Magistrate
DPO	District Programme Officer
FD	Forest Department
GP	*Gram Panchayat* (Village Council)
GPVA	*Gram Panchayat Vikas Adhikari* (Village Council Development Official)
IAS	Indian Administrative Service
JE	Junior Engineer
MoRD	Ministry of Rural Development, New Delhi
MR	Muster Roll
NREGA	National Rural Employment Guarantee Act, 2005
NREGS	National Rural Employment Guarantee Scheme
OG	Operational Guidelines
RTI	Right to Information Act
WPA	Wildlife Protection Act, 1972

Acknowledgements

My deepest gratitude shall always be reserved for the people who appear as acronyms in this book. Though I argue against the concept of the nameless, faceless bureaucrat, I have had to, for obvious reasons, deliberately render them thus here. I could not, however, resist 'initializing' my office-mates in Gopeshwar in the text, who initiated me into the art of government with infinite kindness and patience. In Chamoli district, the members of DGSM, HARC, *Janadesh*, *Aniket*, *Dainik Jagaran*, *Amar Ujala*, and the Bamboo Board were always ready for a *chai* and chat. Ramesh Pahari, in particular, was always warmly welcoming. The affection of Vimla, Golu, Raja, Vinod, Chochoo, Aarti, Meena, Sheroo, Rumi, and baby Cheeni sustained me during my time in Gopeshwar and made it home. In Dehradun, Sanjay Bahti, Ravi Chopra, Vibha Puri Das, P. C. Joshi, S. T. S. Lepcha, and, especially, R. S. Tolia were extremely generous with their time, suggestions, and encouragement. I have lost count of the number of people in Uttarakhand who exhorted me to complete my research and propped it up with acts of inexpressible care. I am not sure they will ever encounter this book, and if they do, will almost certainly find it other than they had imagined. Should they happen upon it, I hope they will recognize the world I describe, even if only in glimpses, and know it as their own.

I was impressed and inspired by the assortment of people I have grouped together as the NREGA interpreters. Once again, I do not name any of them, other than Jean Dreze, whom it would be futile to anonymize. I fear they might not agree with all my arguments, but I do hope they will see that I share in their struggle.

All the events I describe are faithful representations of what transpired and are true to life. I have, however, scrambled places, names, acronyms, official designations, and times. The real-life identities of the people who inhabit this book have thus been rendered untraceable and unverifiable.

The research and writing of this book has been generously funded by various bodies. My PhD was made possible through a Gates Cambridge Trust scholarship held in conjunction with the Overseas Research Students Awards Scheme (ORSAS). Fieldwork in India was additionally supported by the Smuts Trust, the Williamson Memorial Fund, a New Hall travel grant, and the Leverhulme Trust. Sections of this book have previously appeared in *Journal of the Royal Anthropological Institute (JRAI)*, *Modern Asian Studies*, and *Political and Legal Anthropology Review (PoLAR)*. They are gratefully reproduced here with permission. I am grateful to Dayanita Singh and Sarnath Banerjee for letting me use their photograph and drawings respectively.

Friends have accompanied me at different stages of this Himalayan trek that began with my PhD in 2005 and now, almost exactly a decade on, culminates in the publication of *Paper Tiger*: Ross Anthony, Mirjana Bozic, Liana Chua, Rohit De, Shumita Deveshwar, Charlotte Faircloth, Jessica Johnson, Chris Kaplonski, Rekha Konsam, Nick Long, Ella McPherson, Nomfundo Xenia Ngwenya, Evelyn Ofori-Koree, Annabel Pinker, Branwyn Poleykett, Hulda Proppe, Surabhi Ranganathan, Lavanya Rajamani, Mishka Sinha, Alireza Taheri, Catherine Trundle, Alice Wilson, Umut Yildrim, as well as other inmates of the 'Soc Anth basement' and participants in the writing-up seminars at Cambridge. Perveen Ali, Chris Beckman, Franck Bille, and Mi Zhou have – each in their unique way – pushed me to believe that *Paper Tiger* would one day come to be. Megan Rivers-Moore continues to show that academia can be done, politics and ethics intact. Sara Abbas, Sirisha Indukuri, and Subhasri Narayanan have been the best of friends during the hardest of times.

Many people have read/heard bits of this book, invited me to present from it or indulged me in fruitful conversations about it: Yamini Aiyar, Arjun Appadurai, Chris Bayly, Susan Bayly, David Gellner, Holly High, Matthew Hull, Pamela Kelley, Annemarie Mol (for that 'street supervision') Madeleine Reeves, Nikolai Ssorin-Chaikov, Sara Shneiderman, Soumhya Venkatesan, and Thomas Yarrow. I want particularly to thank Francis Cody and Kregg Hetherington for their brilliant reading of drafts of this manuscript. This work has also benefited from being presented at American Anthropological Association (AAA) panels in Montreal and San Francisco, Association of Social Anthropologists of the UK and Commonwealth (ASA) panels in Auckland and Edinburgh, European Association of Social Anthropologists (EASA) panel in Tallinn, European Association of South Asian Studies (EASAS) panel in Zurich, British Association of South Asian Studies (BASAS) panel in Edinburgh, and at workshops in Cambridge, Manchester, the London School of Economics, Sussex, and the Centre for Studies of Developing Societies (CSDS) in Delhi.

From the University of Edinburgh, where I taught for a year, I am grateful for the collegiality of Gerhard Anders, Adi Bharadwaj, Barbara Bompani, Jacob Copeman, Sidharthan Maunaguru, Jeevan Sharma, Jonathan Spencer and, especially, Richard Baxstrom, Lotte Hoek, and Tobias Kelly. My co-conspirators at Cambridge's superlative Centre for Research in the Arts, Social Sciences, and Humanities (CRASSH) probably delayed the completion of this book with all those late pub nights, but then they did also make the return to Cambridge such a pleasure: Hugo Drochon, Alfred Moore, and Andrew Mckenzie-Mcharg. I am extremely grateful to the directors of our superb 'Conspiracy and Democracy' project at CRASSH for freely allowing me the time and space I so desperately needed to finish this book: Richard Evans, David Runciman, and John Naughton. I thank my students at Cambridge and Edinburgh for sitting through my lectures on development bureaucracies, economic anthropology, and the anthropology of politics and for their somewhat alarmingly critical reading of texts in our seminars.

I have been very fortunate in the enthusiasm of Finola O'Sullivan and Qudsiya Ahmed, my editors at Cambridge University Press, and in the support of the series editor, Sally Engle Merry. I thank the three for their belief in this book. The rigorous reports of the three anonymous reviewers for Cambridge University Press were instrumental in tightening the final presentation of this book. Different avatars of *Paper Tiger* have been marvelously proof-read by Valerie Rivers-Moore and Sumati Dwivedi. Jose Santos very generously worked his magic on the book cover.

There is a delicious poignancy in the fact that this book is being published simultaneously in Delhi and Cambridge, for these are the two Universities that have centrally shaped my thinking and writing. I have learned what is termed Social Anthropology in the UK at the extraordinary Department of Sociology at the Delhi School of Economics. Andre Beteille was my first teacher of Sociology, and he will always retain this pre-eminence. Amita Baviskar's sparkling lectures triggered my interest in the anthropology/sociology of development and economics. My tutors at the Delhi School deserve a special mention for the intense brilliance of their sessions: Rita Brara, Deepak Mehta, and Harish Naraindas. Further back, at Hindu college, Ujjwal Kumar Singh and Anupama Roy, shone through as exemplars of committed teachers, writers, and activists. My intellectual debt to Veena Das will be clear in the pages that follow. What remains hidden, though, are the many incredible conversations we have had, which have helped give me the courage to write what I truly believe in and made this the most honest book it can be. At Cambridge, Barbara Bodenhorn, James Laidlaw and Sian Lazar have cheerfully supported me in myriad ways and through many stages. I greatly value the mentorship of Laura Bear, Harri Englund and Yael Navaro-Yashin and draw inspiration from their engaged scholarship. I owe a profound debt to David Sneath for his unflinching support. He has read every bit of this book many times over, starting with its earliest, coarsest iteration. Somehow, he always managed to respond with characteristic incisiveness and meticulousness to those fragments of writing that have coalesced into *Paper Tiger*. Needless to say, all the shortcomings of this work remain mine.

Quite apart from the wonderful care Binod Kumar took of me in Dehradun, I have him to thank for our delightful *pagal kutta* Cinnamon Bun. Gaurav Ahluwalia, Manika, and Saurabh Endley remain supremely supportive siblings even as Saharsh, my darling Hootycat, remains true to his name(s). My *Dadi*, the late Shakuntala Devi, encouraged me ever since I can remember to do *padai-likhain*. My *Nani*, Sarla Coomar, has, happily, been recently issued with a 'life certificate' by the Indian state that serves to prove she is still alive, and hence eligible to continue receiving her pension. Given her adorable buoyancy, we can safely say that in this instance the *sarkari kaghaz* is mapping onto the real with a high degree of precision. This book invokes the memory of my much-missed grandfather, B S Mathur, from whom I have most keenly learnt the need to care for language; to weigh and value every word. My little sister, Tapsi, makes life navigable by enabling – amongst other things – hair-braiding, sari-draping, door-unlocking, music-downloading, car-driving, and firstbook-writing. My mother, Tishya Mathur, and my father, Ravi Mathur, have lovingly helped me find my way in this world and laughingly comforted me when I have got lost. With deep love, this book is dedicated to both of them.

Map of Uttarakhand

Map not to scale

Prologue

Yahan tumko kuch nahin milega, 'you won't find anything here', said the kindly senior bureaucrat. It was the September of 2006 and we were sitting in his large office, located in the Secretariat at the heart of Dehradun, the capital city of the State of Uttarakhand in northern India, which had recently (in 2000) been carved out of Uttar Pradesh (UP) as a separate political entity. I was dismayed. After weeks of petitioning, phone-calling, and waiting, I had finally managed to get 5 minutes with the topmost development bureaucrat in this new Indian state. I had just breathlessly reeled off my spiel about being a doctoral student desirous of studying the 'inner functioning' of the development wing of the state of Uttarakhand. To accomplish this, I had requested his permission to sit in his office for 12 months and follow through their implementation of the brand new and much-celebrated National Rural Employment Guarantee Act of 2005 (NREGA). He was taken aback by this request to access, and participate in, office life. To think it through, he called in his 'Number Two', i.e., his immediate junior in the Rural Development Department. Both of them together puzzled over my request, again and again asking me why I would want to spend a year in their office for, 'there is nothing here other than papers and files', 'you won't understand anything of development by sitting here in Dehradun', where 'we are involved merely in routine business'. The 'real work' (*asli kaam*) of development schemes happened in the districts, according to both of them. They were not, I could plainly see, averse to my sitting in their office if that was really what I wanted to do, but they genuinely did not see any point in it. They gently suggested that I might want to have a look at the districts before I made a decision. If I did decide to work out of a district then I must, they said, give them a 'report' on what exactly was going on there for 'God alone knows what those chaps get up to'.

I was slightly unnerved by the incredulity with which the two senior bureaucrats had responded to my request. Further, the dull grey offices I saw in Dehradun did not seem particularly conducive to unearthing the 'state's scandalous life' (Aretxaga, 2003, p.401) as I so hoped to do. I discussed possible field sites with other people in Dehradun – NGO workers, academics, bureaucrats, journalists – and they all told me that I would 'find nothing' (*kuch nahin milega*) in Dehradun for the 'real' (*asli*) things happen in the districts. Increasingly swayed by this near unanimous recommendation of moving down to a district, I decided to visit Chamoli district.

I chose Chamoli for many reasons.

First, NREGA, at that point, was operational in only three out of a total of thirteen districts in Uttarakhand, Chamoli being one of them. The district reported high levels of rural poverty and unemployment, which had put it on the Indian Planning Commission's priority list as one of India's 200 'most backward districts'. Secondly, the district shares a long border with Tibet, which brought to my mind the growing anthropological literature on territorial borders and frontiers that seems to imply a peculiar quality to these spaces on the edges of states. Finally, and most crucially, another senior state official I met soon after – the Chief Information Commissioner (CIC) – offered to introduce me into the district administration. The CIC concurred that I would 'find nothing other than paper just sitting here in offices in Dehradun', and eagerly encouraged me to go see the 'real situation' in a 'remote and backward' district such as Chamoli. As it happened, the CIC was going to be in Chamoli in early October to evaluate a project aimed at improving the livelihoods of bamboo basket weavers. Before I could even venture a suggestion, the CIC had peremptorily ordered me to meet him there so that he could 'fix matters'. I was to precede him up to Chamoli bearing a letter of introduction from him, to make the acquaintance of the district officials.

The district office

Armed with my introduction, I made the 12-hour drive up to a small government-run tourists' rest house in the village of Pipalkoti, where the project evaluation was to take place. The letter was printed in Hindi, on the CIC's official letterhead, a thick cream-coloured sheet of handmade paper with the logo of Uttarakhand glossily embossed on it. It listed, in bullet points, the facts that I was a student of Cambridge University, was doing PhD research on poverty alleviation in Uttarakhand, and had chosen Chamoli district as my field site due to its 'backward status'. Therefore, 'full assistance' must be provided to me. It was signed by the CIC and stamped with his official seal. As we jolted our way up and down mountains and valleys, I wondered at the archaic officialese of this piece of paper that I was so carefully carrying.

The town of Gopeshwar, administrative headquarters of Chamoli district, is located about 25 km away from Pipalkoti. Though I had arrived a couple of days before the CIC, the government rest house was already humming with preparations for the upcoming evaluation. The very first morning after arriving at Pipalkoti, I drove up to Gopeshwar to request an appointment with the top state representative in the district, the District Magistrate (DM). The DM's Personal Assistant (PA) did not even glance at me before telling me that the DM was too busy and I should come back after a 'few days'. At this point I silently produced the letter from the CIC. As if by magic, the PA instantaneously sat up and took notice of me. I was quickly ushered into the DM's office with the hushed announcement that I had 'come on CIC sahib's recommendation (*sifarish*)'. The DM glanced through the letter, said, 'Of course we shall provide you with every assistance you could need as CIC *sahib* says', and promptly rang up his subordinate, the Chief Development Officer (CDO), whom he ordered to meet me immediately. The DM told me the CDO was the one who directly handled all the development work of the district, and would be able to 'give me' what I was looking for. I was escorted out of the DM's office by a peon who walked me down to the CDO's office where, again, I was immediately shown in.

The CDO was struck dumb by my request to spend a year in his office. He immediately called in his 'Number Two' – the District Development Officer (DDO) – for a consultation. The CDO and DDO understood my objective of studying the implementation of NREGA, but kept asking me how I would be able to do that by sitting in an office all day, that too for an entire year. Both of them assured me that it was pointless to work out of the district office for the 'real work' (*asli kaam*) on NREGA actually happened in the blocks (a block is an administrative unit comprising a cluster of villages with each district containing a certain number of blocks 'under' them). I would, they told me with total certainty, 'find nothing here' (*yahan kuch nahin milega*) for 'we are just tied up in files and routine'. The CDO suggested that I look at Dasholi block, which was not only nearby but, 'if the reports they send up are not *farzee* (fake/fraudulent)', was performing well. Like their senior colleague in Dehradun, the two officials also told me that I could make myself useful by telling them what – if anything – their juniors in the block office were doing. The CDO, somewhere between seriousness and jocularity, said that I could, in fact, function as their 'spy' (*guptachar*) in the block, for no one would ever suspect a young female student of espionage. Before I had time to react to this rather alarming suggestion, the CDO had telephoned the Block Development Officer (BDO) of Dasholi and informed him of my impending arrival. I was then given instructions on how to get to the BDO's office, which was in Chamoli town, located at a distance of 12 km below Gopeshwar.

The block office

The BDO was uncomfortably officious, obviously taking the CDO's verbal orders to provide me with 'full assistance' very seriously. He, too, said he would be happy to have me sitting in his office observing NREGA for as long as I wished, but felt obliged to inform me in advance that:

'You really won't find anything here...We just simply follow orders issued from the district and the work really happens in the villages. Why don't you choose some villages to do your research in?'

He then pulled out a map and pointed out villages close to the main road, so that I wouldn't have any difficulty climbing up to them. I was beginning to tire of this litany of 'you won't find anything'. I heard him out, thanked him for his advice, and left to ponder what I should be doing.

The village office(r)

On my way down to the main road from the Block office, I paused to catch my breath and admire the startling blue of the river Alaknanda, snaking between the sheer brown mountains on her way down to meet the Ganges. A man came up behind me and initiated a conversation. This gentleman turned out to be a village-level development officer. I explained my project to him. His instantaneous response was:

'Then why are you here? You should be in New Delhi to see how they make the rules that they send down to us here. We just try to follow orders from above. You won't find anything here in the villages'.

This line – *yahan tumko kuch nahin milega* (you won't find anything here) – had been repeated to me at every single office I had been to so far. Now, even functionaries positioned at the absolute end of the delivery chain were authoritatively declaiming it at me, and on the road at that. Was it a platitude to get rid of me, a mechanism to absolve themselves of responsibility, or something these officials really believed to be true? What was it they thought I was looking for, anyway? With my pre-planned research methodology in ruins, where and how was I ever going to locate 'the developmental Indian state'? The state, it appeared, was always elsewhere, never here.

On reaching my little rest house in Pipalkoti, I was greeted by its manager, a waiter, and three young men who were involved with a bamboo basket weaving co-operative. They, like everyone else, were most curious to know what I was doing gadding about the district. Over a cup of *chai* I explained my research-student position and my interest in studying *sarkar* (the state). On a hunch, I asked them – five men in all – where they saw the state (*aapko sarkar kahan dikhta hai*). Instantly, a couple of them pointed up in the direction of Gopeshwar. Pipalkoti lies in the valley while Gopeshwar is atop a large mountain, out of sight from where we sat, but the men gestured in that direction and one said

'Gopeshwar *mein virajman hai*' (the state is seated in Gopeshwar). The hotel manager said, 'but, you are coming from *sarkar's gaddi*' (the throne of the state) i.e. New Delhi, and the waiter noted, 'Here it is at DM-*sahib's*' (*yahan par to DM sahib ke yahan hai*).

I was deeply struck by this very physical and literal location of the state in administrative headquarters, spaces, and bodies. The instinctive gesture towards Gopeshwar and the mention of DM-*sahib* were in stark contrast to the bureaucrats who had consistently pointed to 'elsewhere' as the place best suited to study the state, or the 'real work' of state-led development. At long last, here were tangible and definitive directions. That night, I decided the most sensible course of action at the moment would be to begin by working out of Gopeshwar and see where events took me. The next morning, I marched back to the CDO with a request to be allowed to work in his office. Once again, the DDO was summoned and informed of my decision. Both officers appeared bemused by what they, no doubt, saw as the fundamentally flawed research strategy of a wilful young elite woman, who had little idea of how the state works and how development is made to happen. They were both certain that once I had found 'nothing here but paper, files and routine', I would, of my own accord, relocate to a village or even to the block office. But to pander to my whim, they smilingly agreed to 'post' me in their office in the best location possible. This was adjudged to be with a 'staff of subaltern officials and scribes of all sorts' as Weber (2006, p. 50) might have described them, the members of the National Rural Employment Guarantee Scheme (NREGS) cell. This little cell had been created especially to operationalize NREGA in its schematized form as the NREGS.

I was inducted into the cell with the designation of 'Researcher' through the means of an official letter ordering the same.

The pages that follow describe what I went on to 'find' in this little cell and the wider world it connected to – the town of Gopeshwar, the Himalayas, development policies and rationalities, bureaucratic instruments, artefacts and rituals, and, even, hungry big cats.

Introduction

The title of this book is drawn from a fieldwork episode during which the Indian state was adjudged, loudly and angrily, to be nothing but a paper tiger (*kaghaz ka bagh*). The episode was the arrival of a human-eating big cat in Gopeshwar resulting in multiple deaths and injuries and the commencement of what was popularly described as a 'reign of terror'. The big cat's reign appeared to, perplexingly, go unchallenged by the Indian state for well over 2 months. This period was defined by paper and tigers – in the most literal sense. The papers required included the all-important hunting permit that would allow the district authorities to legally kill this state-protected species. The feline in question was a leopard, a species that has the same legal protection in contemporary India as tigers do, and in addition is called *bagh* in Hindi, as the tiger also is. More generally and beyond the individual case of the human-eating big cat of Gopeshwar, 'paper tiger' is descriptive of the series of sophisticated plans and laws drawn up by the developmental Indian state, which consistently underperform, if not collapse outright.[1] My intention in this book is to provide an ethnographically derived, situated analysis of this paper tiger-like nature of the developmental state. This I do by focusing on precisely those repetitive, mundane, banal, and seemingly innocuous practices of local government offices that the bureaucrats I met adjudged as amounting to 'nothing' (*kuch nahin*). I show the consequences of these practices to be far reaching, ranging from the provision of employment and the payment of basic wages to the protection of humans from predatory animals. Ultimately, I propose that in the evaluation of the developmental Indian state, we refocus our critical attention on hitherto neglected sites and devise languages to express the truths that they produce.

My focus is on the process of enforcement, as well as the particular effects, of two widely commended laws: the National Rural Employment Guarantee Act of 2005 (henceforth NREGA) and the Wildlife Protection Act of 1972 (henceforth WPA). The NREGA was the original object of my anthropological attention. The WPA, on the other hand, I stumbled onto. This statute was invoked, with profound consequences, during the big cat's reign of terror. This excursion into the field of human – animal conflict and relations now forms the lynchpin of my explanation for why laws can do what they do and not, usually, what one would think they should be doing. In the final chapter, I focus on big cat protectionism to discuss a perennial complaint against the Indian state: its staggering slowness and propensity for making people wait endlessly even when swift, decisive action is desperately required. The section on NREGA focuses on affective bureaucratic labour and materiality while the one on WPA on bureaucratic temporalities. All through, I am concerned with how law is translated into practice. I use 'translation' in two senses. First, I follow the conversion of a text authored in Delhi in the English language to a subject much-talked about and mulled over in Hindi, in the Himalayan borderland (Englund, 2006). In particular, I focus on how words on which the NREGA's legitimacy crucially depends – transparency, accountability, audit, participation, guarantee – were interpreted, understood, and acted upon by lower-level bureaucrats. Secondly, I use 'translation' to refer to the tracing of the labours of a heterogeneous group of actors and, especially, the marshalling of things in the process of making a law real (Latour, 1996; Mosse, 2005). There is a material – specifically, a paper-y – tangibility that laws must acquire as they painfully inch their way towards legitimate official proclamations of enactment. I find translation as an analytic device particularly appealing due to its 'critical openness' and, hence, 'its productivities as a nondeterministic act of meaning and value creation' (Turem and Ballestero, 2014, p. 8). It is in the ethnographic elucidation of the process of translation that this book locates its contribution and, simultaneously, makes its case for shifting the frame through which we comprehend and analyse the developmental Indian state.

Paper Tiger, in the perusal of laws as they move through state bureaucracy, shows why certain laws do not work as they ought to and how they are capable of producing absurdity. This focus on the translation of law leads me to dwell on the struggles of state functionaries to read, understand, communicate, and execute laws. We know that citizens are often befuddled by state law. What has attracted less comment is the extent to which state officials themselves have to overcome what Das describes as the 'illegibility' of the state, the very 'unreadablity of the state's rules and regulations' (2007, p. 168). Crucially, this struggle with illegibilities emerges not from some deficiency in the capacity of subaltern staff to comprehend law, but rather from the very practice of making a law real. As Das notes, illegibility is not an exception but very much part of the way in which rules or laws are implemented (172). In the presentation of the contemporary Indian state as constantly entangled in the erasure of illegibilities, this book inverts Scott's (1998) now-famous thesis on modern statecraft as an exercise in legibility. In Scott's conceptualization, the practice of making legible through the use of state simplifications is problematic due to its profound misrepresentation of complexity. Scott's thesis begins at the point when legibility, with all its attendant problems and potentially catastrophic results, is achieved via modern state practices and rests on it as a fundamental assumption. The focus of this book, instead, is on the practices and things whereby legibility is *believed to have been achieved* in the eyes of the Indian state. Accordingly, I show how the NREGA was endowed with official reality on a piecemeal basis by the Uttarakhand state bureaucracy through slow and careful translations of the authoritative texts, letters, meetings, sedimented institutional knowledge of preceding rural employment schemes, and the incessant production of a variety of documents. The NREGA, I argue, never reached a legibility of the sort its framers anticipated and expected; rather, aspects of it were made more or less officially real through the daily labour expended on it. Agents of the state know that rules can never be followed to the letter. Their energies are directed instead at making it appear *as if* the illegibilities have been overcome, *as if* orders have been followed, *as if* the NREGA has been made real. And the primary means through which this occurs is by the production, circulation, reading, and filing of the correct documents – through the assembling of what I study as the paper state.

The paper state

The Indian state is known to be an inveterate writer, its paper obsessions commented upon in film, novels, newspapers, everyday chatter and complaints, and various academic writings. Moir (1993) traces this form of governance, called the *Kaghazi Raj* or government by paper, to the operations of the East Indian Company in India as early as the seventeenth century. It was through an incredibly complex and comprehensive system of writing and reporting that the home government's ruling authority was maintained in India. That the post-colonial Indian state has, in crucial respects, retained the British colonial state's institutional structure and wider legal and cultural practices of rule, has been said many times in different contexts (e.g. in Chatterjee, 2004). In post-1947 India, the expansion and bettering of what Ludden (2000) has described as a 'Development Raj' has been effected through the installation of a gigantic development bureaucracy through which development plans, programmes, projects and, more recently, laws flow. Development has been absorbed not only into the institutions of the state, but also into what my informants describe as its '*sarkari* culture' (government/state culture). This absorption is most materially obvious in the Indian state's obsession with paper (*kaghaz*). The *Kaghazi Raj*, I argue, has not merely been inherited by the post-colonial Indian state. This book aims to show that contemporary neo-liberal dictums of 'transparency' and 'accountability' (Mathur, 2012a) are exacerbating the fundamentals of this supposedly antiquated system of the distant past: through an explosion in paperwork and an ever-expanding reliance on documents as constituting concrete evidence of the expending of state labour and production of 'results'.

While the Indian bureaucratic state's marked obsession with paper cannot but be linked to its particular colonial and even pre-colonial past,[2] I believe this is not a uniquely Indian story. A profound reliance on paper/documents/files is the constitutive feature of bureaucracy, as Weber has noted and the fiction of Kafka, Gogol, and Orwell has illustrated. Ethnographies of institutions and organizations (Harper, 1997; Riles, 2006b), states (Stoler, 2009; Feldman, 2008) post-war polities (Navaro-Yashin, 2012), and increasingly globalized auditing regimes (Hetherington, 2011) demonstrate the ubiquity of documentary practices and the manner in which paper underpins action and constitutes proof. Against this backdrop, while *Paper Tiger* is rooted in the interplay of law with bureaucracy and with the concomitant assemblage of the contemporary developmental Indian state, its implications for the three intertwined categories of law, bureaucracy, and the state extend further afield.

South Asia has generated an impressive regional literature on paper and documents, which is unsurprising, given their omnipresence as well as their power to alter lives.[3] My own study of the processes whereby laws are 'made real' (Latour, 2002 p. 85) by the state leads me to focus on the social and affective lives of documents as they circulate within the labyrinthine Indian bureaucracy (Appadurai, 1988). In writing an ethnography of Indian state bureaucracy I cannot but describe its domination by the documentary: the overwhelming desire to have everything in writing (*likhit mein*), a tendency and capacity to paper over things, the employment of an 'on paper' doublethink under which officials thunder at their juniors for working only with paper (as opposed to with some form of the real, the *asli*) even as they state that the only thing that matters is that the papers be in order. My conceptualization of the paper state is not restricted to attaching an adjective to the state in order to highlight an aspect of this entity, namely its obsession with paper. Paper is not just a thing that bureaucrats work with, and documents do not only make visible a particular state-endorsed developmental reality. Rather, I highlight the centrality of this thing, paper, – to the composition, maintenance, and assemblage of the Indian state.[4] As Hull concludes in a review of the burgeoning literature on bureaucracy and texts, 'documents are not simply instruments of bureaucratic organizations, but rather are constitutive of bureaucratic rules, ideologies, knowledge, practices, subjectivities, objects, outcomes, and even the organizations themselves' (Hull, 2012b, p. 253). To dismiss paper as mere bits of official matter, as *just* paper, or even to restrict oneself to highlighting its capacity to create 'paper truths' (Tarlo, 2000) would be, then, to underestimate the life-endowing powers of paper, which are vital to the state.[5]

The state, I believe, is best understood as a relational set of practices (Sneath, 2007; Berdahl, 1999; Chatterji and Mehta, 2007).[6] The set of bureaucratic practices that this book describes – reading, writing, lettering, filing, producing and circulating documents, holding meetings and conducting audits – allow the developmental Indian state to come into being. As anthropologists of the state have emphasized, our task is to understand *how* an it-ness is attributed to 'the state', not to assume 'it' exists as 'an a priori conceptual or empirical object' (Sharma and Gupta, 2006, p. 8; Mitchell, 1999). The bureaucratic practices that go into composing the Indian state are charged with contingency, uncertainty, coercion, and affect; there is a precarious nature to their unfolding. They do not occur mechanically despite that oft-repeated metaphor of the machine of the state, which, with all its connotations of a unitary system working on automatic, is highly misleading. The intentionality that is often attributed to the state-as-monolith collapses once the ethnographic black box of a *sarkari daftar* (government office) is opened up to reveal, in all its greyness and haplessness, the movement of law through the bureaucratic everyday.

The law and its interpretation(s)

While bureaucracy has remained relatively understudied (Bear and Mathur, 2015), the primary law under scrutiny here – NREGA – has generated a substantial corpus of analytical work. Given the wealth of work on NREGA, two points are worth outlining: first, the harvest to be reaped from an ethnographic approach to law in its localization within the everyday world of lower-level bureaucracy. Second, the differences between such a study and others are not only methodological but also, more importantly, epistemological. I therefore provide a brief reading of NREGA and touch upon its varied interpretations before proceeding to situate *Paper Tiger*. NREGA is one of India's most well-known welfare attempts in recent years. It guarantees the right to work (albeit for only 100 days in year and as unskilled labour) for 67 per cent of 1.3 billion people (the rural population of India). This makes it a legal gesture of Himalayan proportions by the developmental Indian state. In a period of states being advised to 'cut back' or 'retreat' from direct welfare-related activities, NREGA stands out due to the vast financial investments it requires of the state. In August 2005 when it was unanimously passed by the lower house of the Indian parliament, estimates of its cost ranged from anything between 0.5 and 4 per cent of India's GDP.[7] In 2009, it was renamed the Mahatma Gandhi National Rural Employment Guarantee Act (MGNREGA). I continue to refer to it as NREGA not just because that was how I knew it during my fieldwork, but also because I am loath to participate in the project of appropriating a law to a particular political party or person.

Various authors have described and analysed how this bill was conceived and approved with total consensus in the otherwise fractious Indian Parliament (see Lakin and Ravishankar, 2006; MacAuslan, 2007). I do not rehearse the process of NREGA's conception and passage but, instead, touch upon the vocabulary employed in the English language and in the national capital of Delhi by NREGA activists and advocates. The narratives woven around it and the adjectives and metaphors employed possess in and of themselves clues to how the law was subsequently translated. The law is often ascribed in the press and particularly by the Congress party to their President, Sonia Gandhi.[8] Gandhi herself has more than once located NREGA within the larger politics of her husband and mother-in-law – Rajiv and Indira Gandhi – who had also initiated similar public works and rural employment schemes. On the other hand, politicians and academics associated with the various Communist parties would inform me repeatedly in my interviews with them that NREGA is a product of the Left's historic pressure on the Indian state to constitutionally enshrine the right to work. Thus, the Left stressed the rights-based character of the law as opposed to Congress highlighting its patrimony. One activist giddily described the movement for the NREGA, which featured bus rides around the country and signatures on saris that were subsequently strung from lamp posts outside Parliament, as a '*nasha*' (a high). A member of the Communist Party of India (Marxist) (CPI-M) memorably converted the law into a verb by speaking of 'the NREGA-ing we have been doing for so long.' There were plenty of plays on the name itself – NREGA is pronounced as *naregaa* in Hindi and English alike. It rhymes quite well with *marega* or 'will/to die' in Hindi, allowing for phrases and slogans such as 'without NREGA one will die' (NREGA *nahin to marega*), and so on. A very prominent narrative form emerging in particular from people associated with the influential Peoples Action for Employment Guarantee (PAEG) linked NREGA to the Maharashtra State's well-regarded employment guarantee scheme (MEGS) and to the pressure from local organizations in the State of Rajasthan to 'see official records' of famine-relief works. The narratives from civil society activists showed, clearly, that there was heavy emphasis on the visual aspect – of seeing, inspecting, transparency, witnessing, publishing, and publicizing. This emphasis on being able to see, and forcing the state to disclose records and facts is the most prominent aspect of the design of the NREGS, one that is continually celebrated by activists as a singular achievement. This book shows that the effects of this turn to transparency are double-edged. While they upset previous manners of welfare delivery, they are not, I claim, revelatory of the real (*asli*) workings of the state. Rather, they lead to an enhanced focus on the production of what my informants described as the *sarkari zindagi* (state life) of NREGA, a life that, more often than not, does not readily map onto its *asli zindagi* (real life).

In the English language and the cosmopolitan centres where NREGA commands a particular discursive framing, the many supporters of the NREGA describe it variously as a 'progressive', 'historic', 'flagship', 'productive', 'revolutionary', 'empowering', 'radical' legislation/programme. In Uttarakhand, however, the vernacular press coverage has moved away from such normative accounts to a much more descriptive coverage of the prosaic practicalities of the scheme. Accounts of this type appearing in the media at the time of my research were, invariably, highly critical of NREGA's performance. Strongly worded headings dominated its coverage in Chamoli: 'thousands of rupees spent but not a road in sight', 'plenty of progress in official figures but none at the ground', 'people continue to tolerate corruption in government schemes, nothing has changed', 'tired of empty promises by *sarkar*', 'another regime, another scheme, same result', and so on. In Uttarakhand, agents of the state did not consider NREGA revolutionary – rather, the word they used most often to discuss it was, in English, 'unimplementable'. For lower-level officials, this law and the operational guidelines that govern its implementation were products of a crazed imagination and of an elite disconnection from the labours of real implementation. This programme, they said, could only be authored by people who work out of 'air conditioned offices in Delhi'. In the state spaces of Uttarakhand, I found a profound cynicism towards NREGA, one that was enfolded within a wider narrative of critical deconstruction of the state-led project of development (Mathur, 2012b). Puzzlement with the varying and discrepant portrayals of the NREGA encouraged me to work my way backwards to study its conception, passage into law and rationale *after* I had completed fieldwork in Uttarakhand. A central claim of this book is that these discrepant portrayals of a single legislation are not the product of a lower-level bureaucracy that is slothful, corrupt, or simply incapable of understanding the law. Rather, I argue and demonstrate in the pages that follow that these discrepancies in everyday chatter arise because the lower-level bureaucracy is all too aware of the difficulties intrinsic to the implementation of this new legislation.

Another point of difference between my informants in Uttarakhand and the hegemonic discourse emerging from the metropoles such as Delhi is that the former are not invested in the project of stabilizing a 'particular framework of interpretation' (Mosse, 2005, p. 168) that was essential not just to bring NREGA into being but also to ensure its continued existence. NREGA in India has managed to recruit a huge coterie of advocates, practitioners, and lobbyists, forming what Mosse terms an 'interpretive community' (2005, p. 9) and what I gloss together as 'NREGA interpreters'. These include politicians from all shades of the political spectrum, bureaucrats, certain academics, activists, and groups ranging from small grassroots NGOs to large international organizations such as the United Nations Development Project (UNDP). All of them celebrate NREGA as a singular achievement of the developmental Indian state. A rhythmically catchy, egalitarian political slogan is attached to the NREGA – *har haath ko kaam do, kaam ko saheen daam do* (give work to each hand, and give the correct wage for all work) – which is shouted out as a preamble to public meetings and is printed on posters and T-shirts distributed among students and activists. Equally arresting are advertisements the government of India often runs for its own work with the NREGA, which prominently feature similarly self-laudatory exhibitions. For instance, a full-page advertisement, which appeared in all the major English-language newspapers, shows a pretty, young, smiling woman dressed in bright pink with silver jewellery. The setting is distinctly rural and the young woman, evidently the village belle, stands before a pool of water, bearing a surprisingly light load on her daintily covered head. Behind her, other men and women are seen hard at work. On the horizon one sights a long single file of people with loads on their heads, marching purposefully in one direction. The caption reads, 'Towards a Republic of Work'. Underneath the photograph, the sub-heading states, 'National Rural Employment

Guarantee Act connects rural India to work opportunities'. Another popular image accompanying write-ups on the NREGA is shot from an angle well above a labouring group of veiled women in brightly coloured saris, diligently engaged in kneading mud (Figures 1 and 2). A strategic utilisation of such imagery and the constant references to the NREGA in speeches, newspaper articles, scholarly analyses of development in rural India, workshops and activist meets, and in other such forums allowed this law to acquire a particular life – one that endowed it with legitimacy as the 'flagship programme' of the former ruling coalition in power, the United Progressive Alliance (UPA).

India's 2009 general elections returned the Congress and the UPA to power, which was widely attributed to these parties' so-called 'inclusive growth' policies, of which NREGA was a primary example. In the afterglow of the election victory,

Figure 1: Full page newspaper advertisement for NREGA

Figure 2: Image commonly accompanying write-ups on NREGA

Congress Vice-President Rahul Gandhi (son of Rajiv and Sonia Gandhi) made his very first public appearance on national television and declared: 'the people of India' have seen that the Congress stands for the development of 'All of India ... which is why we have schemes such as the NREGA'.[9] After the decimation of the Congress and the UPA in the recent 2014 national elections, NREGA has all but vanished as an explanatory trope. This overnight disappearance of what are now-dismissed as tokenistic measures that are unable to meet the aspirations of the rural poor or as mere populism serves to show how critical the constant task of interpreting and presenting NREGA was in the first place and how this labour was what allowed – for the time the UPA was in power at the centre – to keep a particular imagination of the law and its effects alive.*

---

* As this book goes to press, speculation on the fate of NREGA continues in India. The day before the union budget of 2015 was announced the Prime Minister described the programme, in particularly stinging terms, as "a monument to the failure" of the Congress party. The day after NREGA was to get one of its highest ever allocations in the budget. The ambivalence towards NREGA as evidenced in its many unflattering descriptions made by highly placed politicians, bureaucrats, and media persons has not – for the time being – resulted in its scrapping. It remains unclear if it is simply a fear of electoral losses or a backlash by the rural unemployed and/or other, unknown factors that has prevented the present dispensation from getting rid of it or squeezing it dry of funds. Whatever the future holds, the heated debates and incredibly diverse interpretations of this developmental law's performance and utility serve as a mirror on the many ideological and political rifts in contemporary India.

NREGA, for the 18 months I followed it around India over 2006 – 2008, had a palpable aura of importance round it. On the one hand, this was very useful for me as an ethnographer since it produced vast amounts of activity: meetings, construction and circulation of documents, training workshops, awareness-generation events, audits of all sorts, constant talk, posters, media reports, documentaries, research by students like myself, conferences, articles in leading journals like the *Economic and Political Weekly*, and so on. In my otherwise unfathomable fieldwork, the only bit that made sense to everyone was my focus on NREGA. On the other hand, there did exist a key issue that I consistently faced in my attempt to undertake an ethnography of what one of my informants used to call the Shah Rukh Khan of developmental legislations (Khan is a Bollywood megastar). This superstar law brings with it an intense polarization of opinion. This polarization partly stems from the fact that it enjoins state interventionism, a position that invites a powerful backlash in the contemporary moment. It is for this reason that the NREGA interpreters had to, as a collection of essays by a leading group of them entitles it, 'battle for employment guarantee' (Khera, 2011). The battle is real enough and the genuineness of its good intentions is also unquestionable. However, given the sense of embattlement that the NREGA interpreters felt and believed in, coupled with their relatively powerful presence on the national scene and their stranglehold on the English-language media and research centres, there is a distinct absence of nuance in debates and studies around it. I identify two broad avenues that have so far emerged for a critical engagement with the law in India. I analyse both in order to, first, demonstrate the epistemological and political framings from which they emerged and, secondly, to more clearly spell out how my methodological reliance on ethnography allows for a different analysis.

Neoliberals anti-NREGA and NREGA anti-neoliberalism?

The first avenue for NREGA critique is one whereby one (i.e. the commentator) is immediately branded a 'neo-liberal' or as an academic at the Jawahar Lal Nehru University (JNU) in Delhi put it to me, a 'World Bank-IMF baby'. The NREGA does appear, on the face of it, to be opposed to what is conventionally understood to constitute neo-liberalism. Standard neo-liberal thinking remains deeply opposed to centralized state planning given that the state has only 'imperfect knowledge', unlike the market which is automatically able to pick up signals (Ferguson, 2006). Neo-liberal political regimes are, typically, believed to enact policies that reduce benefits to the unemployed (Rose, 1996, p. 59), resulting in the downsizing of welfare bureaucracies (Sharma, 2008, p. xvi); processes that are described as the 'shrinking' and 'retreat' of the state. In India, the favoured euphemism utilized to describe the post-1991 liberalization of the state is 'reform'. Mainstream neo-liberal theory positions itself in opposition to Keynesian state interventionism (see Harvey, 2005, pp. 20–21), rendering a rejection of Keynesianism central to many definitions of neo-liberalism (e.g. Larner, 2000). In discussions with politicians, bureaucrats, academics, and activists/NGO workers marshalling around or against the NREGA, such a commonplace definition of neo-liberalism is explicitly articulated. The adjective 'anachronistic' is often deployed to refer to this statute – critically by its detractors and proudly by its interpreters. The Act is widely regarded as the insertion of something that does not quite fit, which does not appear in the correct order of chronological time, into the policy framework of a rapidly liberalizing state.

I, however, strongly question the extent to which NREGA stands as some sort of an Indic response to neo-liberal policies. Theorizing on the rationalities of government has deflected attention away from 'expansion' or 'shrinkage' of the state as indicators for levels of liberalization, enabling the argument that neo-liberalism 'involves less a retreat from governmental 'intervention' than a re-inscription of the techniques and forms of expertise required for the exercise of government' (Barry et al., 1996, p. 14). If one were to think of neo-liberalism, as I choose to do, as 'a pervasive form of political rationality' (Collier and Ong, 2007, p. 17), which 'while foregrounding the market is not only or even primarily focused on the economy; it involves extending and disseminating market values to all institutions and social action' (Brown, 2005, pp. 39–40), then one would have to re-examine the somewhat romantic characterization of NREGA as Third-World resistance to the global march of advanced capitalism. The political rationality of neo-liberalism – its way of thinking and acting – seeps, I argue, into the discourse of the NREGA, which places it not entirely outside the realm of the post-liberalization Indian state's ideological commitment to the market as the central organizing principle of life.

Let us look more closely at what the NREGA is, what it is trying to do, and, most importantly, *how* it plans to accomplish its objective. It is a sophisticated technical programme which is attempting to include the rural unemployed into the game of the economy and it plans to do so, in the statute's own words, thus: by creating a regime of rights, through processes of empowerment, transparency and accountability, by bringing neglected populations into the warm embrace of the national economy, by opening up the rural market and imparting financial literacy to the rural poor. The law clearly identifies the state as a purchaser of labour power on the basis of demands voiced by its empowered citizens who are, simultaneously, the suppliers of labour as well as the state's customers in a transparent transaction conducted by the law. The transparency – accountability – participation – empowerment linkage is strong, if often confusing as these various techniques melt into each other. The NREGA contains within itself the presumption of the mechanism of 'self-selection', which much like the invisible hand of the market, automatically slips into operation. This 'self-selecting' character of the NREGA distinguishes it from earlier rural employment programmes, which were 'targeted' ones in the sense of being tailor-made to a particular community and operated on the basis of planned financial allocations decided in New Delhi or the state capital. This is yet another indication of what Jean Dreze describes as its 'new-age' character (2009, p. 7).[10] The assumption is that given the nature of the work – manual, unskilled, and compensated at minimum daily wages – only the neediest will actually appeal to the state. Through its enactment, the NREGA allows for the discharge of the state's responsibility not to let anyone absolutely drop out of the economy and the larger social system. Were the NREGA to function in practice as it is intended to on paper, it would enfold the rural unemployed into a market wherein the state becomes 'purchaser' and the labourers the 'providers'.

The guidelines and other social audit manuals linked to the NREGA meticulously lay down how the state is turning a scrutinizing gaze on itself. Every single document and process can be and should be inspected – audited – by the citizens on the basis of this empowering law. This aspect, of auditing and what is considered to be the resultant transparency and accountability of the state, is widely celebrated by the NREGA activists. The very same auditory practices have been described by others as intrinsically linked to neo-liberal political rationality (Strathern, 2000; Powers, 1999). In Foucault's posthumously published lectures at the College de France, which discuss the nature of neo-liberalism, he has made the critical point that the 'scrutinizing of every action of the public authorities' is not 'just a political or juridical criticism; it is a market criticism, the cynicism of a market criticism opposed to the action of public authorities' (2008, p. 246). The romance of resistance that NREGA brings, largely due to its charismatic and canny interpreters, has inhibited a critical reading of the very body of the law. I want to be clear that my argument is not that NREGA is something we can term 'neo-liberal', if such a thing does ever exist in its pure form anywhere.[11] What I do maintain though is that if one follows closely the vocabulary and the framing of NREGA texts, one can see that the law bears testimony to a neo-liberal political rationality. So seductive is neo-liberal rationality and so pervasive has it grown that one need not overtly preach its values to reproduce much of its language (cf. Wacquant, 2009). While my central objective here is to ethnographically demonstrate the life that the NREGA acquired in the high Himalaya, it is important to begin with a deep reading of this ambitious developmental legislation. And while indulging in such a reading, one may well be tempted to resist the celebratory narratives that the NREGA interpreters constantly re-establish through multiple means and to the detriment of more far-reaching critiques.[12]

The vexedness of implementation

The second and more widely used avenue for analyses of the law directly implicates the state bureaucracy. It does this by bemoaning a process that is easily derided but almost never described: implementation. This book closely follows the implementation of both the NREGA and WPA. I show that the NREGA met with limited acceptance and the district bureaucracy struggled to implement it. In the face of a human-eating big cat in Gopeshwar, the existence of the WPA actively impeded the district bureaucracy's capacity to manage the animal and protect human lives. This in turn led to an extreme anger against both the state and the predator, feeding into a growing and more generalized animosity towards wildlife conservationism in the Himalaya. In the context of the NREGA, then, I present a picture that surprises: a region with high levels of poverty and unemployment appears seemingly incapable of implementing a programme that is aimed at overcoming precisely these ailments. The high level of distress out-migration from the mountains to urban areas in the plains, especially by young men, is one of the most noticeable trends in the upper Himalaya, a region whose visible emptying-out is contributing to an ever-growing spatial inequity within India. In the context of the WPA, I describe a situation that is feeding an anti-conservationist position. This is evident in the rising incidences of murders of big cats in Uttarakhand, often in a particularly brutal manner. There is also a silence amongst residents on the issue of poaching and trafficking of big cats, due to a growing apathy linked to a perceived anti-human bias in the collection of wildlife laws and policies.

Having set forth the depressing outcome of NREGA as well as the paradoxical effect of the WPA in Uttarakhand, my argument is, emphatically, not rooted in the familiar one of bad or weak implementation. Precisely as Gupta has argued, 'this position [of poor implementation], ubiquitous in the discourse of many middle-class, urban Indians, reproduces both a colonial complaint of the incompetence of the natives and a class bias towards subalterns in the bureaucracy. If the problem is poor implementation, the blame falls inevitably on lower-level officials who, for reasons ranging from corruption to poor training and education, are deemed incapable of implementing the wonderful programs thought up by metropolitan experts' (2012, p. 25). My focus, too, is on the everyday enactment of bureaucratic practices (*ibid.*). However, my ethnography leads me away from Gupta's elegant argument, which foregrounds structural violence as the outcome of bureaucratic practices. What interests me is understanding why and how what happened *happened*. Instead of proposing or modifying a pre-existing theory/ theoretical apparatus, my intention in this book is to make sense of certain situated issues that arose over the course of my fieldwork: why did bureaucrats struggle to expend the massive NREGA budget in Chamoli district? Why was this new welfare legislation widely considered to be 'unimplementable'? How come residents of the Himalaya could tell me with such certainty that the Indian state is more concerned with protecting the life of one big cat than of several humans? Ultimately, the questions this book wrestles with are how come 'paper tiger' appears such an apt descriptor of the Indian state? Why is it that a breezy and persistent difference continues to be upheld between that which is considered 'real' (*asli*) and that which is only 'on paper' (*kaghaz pe*) and is sarkari (*state like*)? A singular - and merely theoretical or anecdotal - focus on violence, a position most clearly assumed by Graeber (2012), would not only not provide empirical answers for these pressing issues but might also end up obscuring precisely those specificities of bureaucratic actions that are so vital to capture and have recently been accomplished to great effect by Feldman (2008), Hetherington (2011), and Hull (2012a).

For the sake of analytical clarity, let me again divide up the manner in which implementation surfaces, again and again, as the answer to why India's exquisite laws, plans, and policies fail with an almost predictable regularity. One prominent manner in which the Indian state's failings have been studied is through the invocation of a 'gap' arising from difference between elite policies and subaltern interpretations, or from weak institutional capacities that are unable to convert policy into practice (see Fuller and Harris, 2000; Mosse 2005).[13] *Paper Tiger* disagrees with this conceptualization of a chasm between law and its practice which arises from weak or poor 'capacity'/'capability'. For, what comes to the fore in this book is not so much the poor capacity, capability or skills of lower-level state agents for understanding and implementing laws. Rather, I ask and then illustrate what it means to obey a rule; how and through what material substances one exhibits the pursuance of ordained procedure; how progressive laws result in unforeseen consequences; and if, in fact, some laws can ever be executed in practice. In other words, I move away from the disjuncture between the plan and its realization to elaborate the process through which this realization happens. It is within this process with its varying personages, materialities, temporalities, and affectivities that this book locates the explanation for that which is widely perceived as a 'gap'.

The other prominent manner by which the vexedness of implementation has been studied is through recourse to what is believed to be the state's intrinsically predatory nature. This approach speculates on the basic character of the Indian state and names it, for instance, as a 'shadow state, private status state, state of last resort and spinning state' (Harris-White, 1997), a state that has been captured by elite interests or particular caste configurations, or one that is subjected to unrelenting corruption. The arguments related to systemic corruption find a particularly popular acceptance (Wade, 1985). I had a range of people telling me all through my fieldwork that the NREGA, like other government development schemes, would never work because all involved parties are only interested in 'eating' state money, as the popular metaphor for corruption goes. The systematicity of corruption within the Indian state comes across well in the former Prime Minister Rajiv Gandhi's much-cited statement: 'If the central government releases one rupee to the poor only ten *paisa* reaches them'. Twenty-five years after this statement, in 2009, a study commissioned by India's primary planning body, the Planning Commission, released results that claimed Gandhi was not very far off the mark. According to this report, only 16 *paisa* out of each rupee was reaching the targeted poor from the Public Distribution Scheme, a programme to deliver subsidized food grains.[14] P. Sainath's (2000) superb coverage of the usurpation of funds in rural India as described in his book *Everybody Loves a Good Drought* is a journalist's account of what is widely – in policy and academic circles alike – considered the root of the failure of the developmental Indian state: structural corruption that impedes if not entirely negates the state's capacity to deliver development.

Empirically it remains unclear what is and what is not a 'corrupt' practice (Sneath, 2006), and the very act of labelling something as such needs to be explored further, especially in the Indian context where the practice is considered to be rife. Narratives of corruption in India have been shown to constitute key dynamics of colonial knowledge, which juxtaposed despotic, oriental forms of governance against a rational, disciplining British system that could counter the hopelessness of Indian traditions and customs (Gould, 2012, p. 4–5). This is not to deny that corruption is almost built into most interactions with the state that it is exploitative, exclusionary, and debilitating. As the popular anti-corruption uprising in 2011 in Delhi led by the activist Anna Hazare showed the experience of corruption provokes intense anger against the state. This book, however, eschews treating corruption as an explanatory trope for the failure of development. Corruption, I believe, is the lazy person's answer to why the Indian state fails with a startling regularity, much as discursive critiques in the Foucauldian vein allowed for answers to the failure of development to be provided sans empirical detailing (Yarrow and Venkatesan, 2012). There is, first, the very real problem of obtaining reliable empirical data on corruption in India, as opposed to its discourse and perception, as captured by indices that are constructed through rather dubious methodologies by organizations such as Transparency International and the Planning Commission. Over the duration of my 18-month-long fieldwork, the spaces I worked in were saturated with 'corruption talk' (Lazar, 2008), but it was only rarely that I directly witnessed corruption-as-practice. Of course, it is to be expected that these transactions would not be undertaken in front of me and that, in general, they take place 'under the table' as the popular euphemism goes. However, the paucity of such experiences has led me to consider more seriously just how closely talk of corruption equals its practice. This is not a question I have an answer to, but I do want to pose it before moving onto my far more central problem with the corruption literature in India. I find an excessive focus on corruption detracts from the core issues of how the Indian state actually functions, what it does, when, how, and why.

During the period the man-eating leopard was active, residents would often link the paper-tiger character of *sarkar* (the state) to its predilection to 'eat', i.e., indulge in corrupt practices. However, as I argue in the final chapter of this book, the big cat was asserting its sovereignty over us all and had managed briefly to displace the local state due to conflicting social times, legal assemblages, and their associated material practices (Mathur, 2014). The bizarre incompetence of the state, in the case of the maneater, was not because officials are only interested in eating money. In the case of the NREGA, the situation is somewhat different. I show in this book that a long-standing system of functioning that can be and often is termed 'corrupt' did, in fact, impede its implementation, but in an entirely surprising and counter-intuitive manner. In brief, the transparency clauses built into the NREGA have allowed for a new system of documentation to be introduced into an arrangement (*bandobast*) that was considered traditional (*paramparik*). Referred to colloquially as the Contractor Raj and the PC system, this is a mode of operation in which a private contractor oversees the execution of public works and rural employment schemes. The contractor gets this overseer position by giving a 'cut' or a percentage (hence the 'PC' of the colloquial title) of the total value of the project to state functionaries. The precise cut that the bureaucrat gets is directly commensurate with his rank and position in the state hierarchy. The contractor who then employs the labourers and oversees the construction work, makes his own profit by doctoring accounts, controlling *kaccha* (temporary) muster rolls, underpaying the labourers, using substandard materials, and other creative accounting practices. I show how some astute designing in the NREGA interrupted this system, with the result that the law struggled to take off in Uttarakhand. Contractors were not keen to pick up works under the NREGA, and having ample alternatives, chose to avoid this programme, at least temporarily. In consequence, the entire public works system came to a grinding halt.

At first glance, my entire discussion of the Contractor Raj and its partial disruption by the transparency-demanding NREGA would appear to attest to the fundamental 'corruption' that bedevils the Indian state. This would contradict my overall claim that corruption is not the answer to the question of why laws/ development programmes struggle to be realized in letter and spirit. However, I stand by my original argument and want to take this opportunity to think more deeply about what corruption is and how it is analysed. In Uttarakhand, the Contractor Raj and the associated PC system is not considered – if we use the same moralizing language that NREGA interpreters, development experts, policy wonks, and the media do – a good thing *per se*. But then neither is the state or state-led development (*sarkari vikas*) or anthropology or big-cat conservationism. So let us, for a brief period, suspend moral judgement and stop thinking of this 'corrupt' practice through the dichotomy of virtue and vice, instead focusing only on what the contractors were enabling. And that is the execution of a rural employment programme, albeit at reduced wages for the labourers, and with the very real possibility of the elimination of a range of eligible beneficiaries just because they did not fit into the contractors' social networks. Thus, the situation was not ideal, and the drafters of the NREGA recognize this only too well and therefore are keen to eliminate it. But in a region where the state commands extremely low material resources, the Contractor Raj did allow for work to take place. My informants felt a direct animosity to the local contractors and described them as *goondas* (thugs) and *badmash* (rogues). Yet they, too, thought that the Contractor Raj enabled something to happen which the state on its own was struggling to accomplish. Furthermore, even in places where the contractors were absent, a similar process operates whereby state agents disallow certain communities or individuals from benefiting from the welfare programmes. These state agents, similarly to contractors, 'eat money' by cooking figures and keeping *kaccha* muster rolls. The distinction between the state and the non-state in villages is hard to maintain and, for all practical purposes, does not really matter.

Beyond the fact of overworked and underpaid state employees, there is a more crucial aspect of the developmental state that is pushing me to reconsider the effects of the Contractor Raj. This is linked to what is considered the 'real work' of the (paper) state by its employees, which is keeping the *sarkari zindagi* (state life) of the law alive. I focus on everyday bureaucratic life and labour in this book precisely because I want to make clear how and through what substances the developmental performance of the state is birthed. While the agents of the state are busy making sure that the state life of law keeps going, by working on their papers, files, and participating in state rituals like meetings, someone has to go out and do the more gritty, hands-on work that a scheme such as the NREGA demands. The contractors were in possession of the time, motivation, savvy, and social relations to handle this. I also find it telling that the most comprehensive analysis of the performance of the NREGA thus far, undertaken by the Comptroller and Auditor General of India (the CAG), points to the difficulties in expending the budget and making the programme implementable. Covering a period from April 2007 to March 2012, the CAG report notes that in fourteen States and one Union Territory, only 30 per cent of the annual plan budget was utilized, thus indicating 'significant inefficiencies in implementation of annual plans (Government of India, 2013, p. 7)'.[15] Even in States that are held up as exemplars of NREGA implementation (such as Andhra Pradesh), studies have shown a 'deepening of the corruption syndicate' and a shift in the manner in which money is pilfered, which allows for the programme to be executed (Aiyar and Mehta, 2015, p. 16). My point is not one of crass instrumentalism in which I am arguing for corruption as the grease to the squeaky 'wheels of the state'. Rather, I am describing an ontology; the prosaic realities of the developmental state in the Indian Himalaya. Here the papery worlds of bureaucrats and the existence of the Contractor Raj is a 'social fact' in Durkheim's sense of the words. My position is very similar to the subtle arguments put forward by Anjaria (2011) and Jauregui (2014), both of whom show that everyday corruption in India opens up, if briefly, what Anjaria describes as a 'space of negotiation' and which I, like Jauregui, think of as the practical capacity to get things done. While these two works come to their conclusions through an ethnography of corruption, I have arrived at a similar place from a different direction – the everday life of law and state bureaucracy. It is my hope that on seeing what this particular world looks like and how the developmental state in India is produced and kept alive my distancing of this work from the hegemonic corpus that focuses on corruption and bad implementation will become clearer. So will, I hope, my argument that we need to rethink what we are so quick to recognize – and deplore – as constituting corruption. I argue for putting aside the normative, morally laden baggage around the concept of corruption, that not only has a disturbing colonial history in India but is also deeply entangled with the primitivism of the international development apparatus, which consistently characterizes states in the global South as, somehow, lacking and aberrant (Mathur forthcoming). In lieu of joining the large chorus that spends its time bemoaning what is popularly described as the 'cancer of corruption' in India and dreaming up ever-expanding auditory and punitive measures to somehow control the truant state, *Paper Tiger*, instead, concentrates its attention on the much harder task of articulating the bureaucratic everyday.

Sarkar and the everyday

A rhythmic routine was central to the everyday life of the bureaucracy in the Indian Himalaya. The seven or so hours of daily office time were devoted to meticulously labouring on and with documents, filing, attending meetings, and, occasionally, breaking for *chai*. Paperwork permitting certain functionaries would periodically summon their official vehicles to inspect a village or an office located lower down in the hierarchy. These excursions out of the office, too, possessed a replicable form and were very much part of the routine of everyday life. The monthly and annual calendars were punctuated with particular dates when meetings and inspections were slated to take place, or reports and balance sheets expected to be produced. Winter came and went, bringing with it a human-eating big cat, heavy snowfall, and the closure of the nearby Badrinath temple. State elections were held in February, leading to the replacement of the incumbent Congress party with the Bharatiya Janata Party (BJP). Spring slowly crept up, bringing the blossoming of wildflowers, and of jacaranda and pine trees. In her wake came Summer, marked locally by the elaborate ritual of flinging open the hallowed portals of Badrinath temple, and by the subsequent arrival of hordes of pilgrims. A minor earthquake occurred in the dead of the night when, as a local newspaper headline described it, 'along with the earth, our hearts quaked'. The monsoon burst upon us suddenly and furiously, cutting off the district from the rest of the country for days on end. Right through the flow of seasons and local events, the government offices remained quietly immersed in their paper-y activities. Only the sounds of the slurping of *chai*, the shuffle of files, and the rustle of paper would, on occasion, break the silence. Days melted one into the other, months came and went, but the routine of everyday life remained.

How, then, does one write of the 'everyday', the 'everyday state', and 'everyday life', terms that are often utilized in anthropological work with a taken-for-granted quality (Highmore, 2002). De Certeau makes a case for taking everyday practices seriously so that they 'no longer appear as the obscure background of social activity' and to do so, ways have to be found of 'penetrating this obscurity, to make it possible to articulate them' (1988, p. xi). But how exactly does one articulate the realms of everyday bureaucratic practices that are characterized by mundane repetition within a sharply context-specific field? In recent years, some innovative anthropological works on bureaucracy have highlighted the form and aesthetics of bureaucratic practices (Riles, 2001, 2006b; Strathern, 2006), affect (Navaro-Yashin, 2012), materiality (Hull, 2012a; P. Harvey, 2005) and the 'psychic life of paperwork' (Kafka, 2012). Outside anthropology and in the Indian case, there has been a recent explosion in the genre of memoirs by retired bureaucrats, which has acted as a series of exposes of public secrets (Baru, 2013) and more general musings on life in India's corridors of power (Subramanian, 2004). In many ways, these writings mimic accounts from the Raj such as Philip Mason's famous and painfully paternalistic *The Men Who Ruled India*. There is some quite lovely fictional writing such as Chatterjee's (1988) semi-autobiographical novel *English, August* and the recent dystopian, time-travelling *The Competent Authority* by Chowdhury (2013). An increasing interest in the everyday worlds of lower-level bureaucracy is evident in arenas as different as blogs, visual exhibits, and texts produced by NGOs, activists, and think-tanks. One of my personal favourites is a graphic novel called *The Harappa Files*, authored by Sarnath Banerjee. It opens with a meeting of the Greater Harappa Rehabilitation, Reclamation & Redevelopment Commission (GHRRR) (Figure 3). 'GHRRR is a secret think-tank of elite bureaucrats, historians, ethnographers, social scientists, law enforcers, retired diplomats, and policy makers'. In short, the colonels and admirals of society who operate from the nether regions of the 'government's subconscious' (2011, p. 11). The GHRRR is meeting to decide how the findings of their decade-long commission, called 'the Harappa files', are to be made public. On the basis of recommendations from various experts, they come to the conclusion that they will employ Banerjee (the author) to disclose the contents of these files through a combination of images and text for, as the communication wing puts it: 'to tell new stories one needs new languages' (2011, p. 12). *Paper Tiger*'s attempt is to use the language of ethnography to capture the everyday life of Indian state bureaucracy.

At the centre of this work stands '*sarkar*', which as Fuller and Harris note (2000, p. 15), is 'the commonest Indian vernacular term' that can be translated 'indifferently' into 'state' or 'government' in English. The fact that the Hindustani word *sarkar* does not make the government/state distinction that exists in English is to be noted, for it indicates an expansive notion of state power and government. *Sarkar*, in my reading, is best understood as an intimate repository of state power. Thus, it can mean just the government but also, as the prologue indicates, a person (DM *sahib*); further, certain objects such as official documents (*sarkari kaghaz*) and places (such as Delhi, Gopeshwar, Dehradun, an office) can be infected with its magic. The East India Company, during its period of rule in the Indian sub-continent, was referred to as Company *Sarkar* or Company Bahadur. This form of honorific continues, and it remains extremely common in Hindi to directly address representatives of the state as just '*Sarkar*' or to say something like 'I am angry with *sarkar*' as if the state were an individual. Not just agents of the state but anyone who is a figure of authority or is seen to wield power, legitimately or illegitimately, can be called *Sarkar* as a sign of respect. The Bollywood film entitled *Sarkar* neatly captures this commonplace personification of the state/authority in India. The film stars the veteran Indian megastar Amitabh Bachchan, whose character bears the given name Subhash Nagre, but everyone calls him *Sarkar*. '*Sarkar*' lives in a well-fortified colonial-style bungalow. He has a large number of gun-toting guards to look after him as well as a series of offices that manage administrative work. Petitioners come seeking justice from him when the egregious legal system fails them, which it does all too often. He hears them out empathetically and ensures justice for them. From the rooftop of his bungalow he gives *darshan* (a viewing or public appearance that carries connotations of the sacred) to his follower subjects. Politicians and bureaucrats who are connected to the legitimized state system are careful to pay homage to *Sarkar* as well, even though behind his back they refer to him as a *goonda* (thug).[16] The eponymous protagonist's self-portrayal as a 'masculinist protector' in the film *Sarkar* (Sharma, 2008, p. 46) is one that the Indian state, too, often attempts to display. However, there is something ambivalent in the gendering of the Indian state, for another commonly used way of referring to *sarkar* is, as Sharma also notes, *mai-baap* (literally mother – father). Das, too, describes instances when the *mai-baap* phrase is uttered and the intimacy of a parental bond with *sarkar* is suddenly professed (2007, 199).

The intimate nature of *sarkar* and its capacity for personification was very much in evidence during the 2014 national elections when the BJP's landslide victory led to the installation of what is popularly described as 'NaMo *Sarkar*'. 'NaMo' is an acronym of the new Prime Minister, Narendra Modi's, name. The projection of a 'strong leader' image and overlaying of Modi's person with the mantle of future *sarkar* were noteworthy – and ultimately successful – electoral ploys deployed by the BJP and their spin doctors during the campaign. Since assuming office, however, Modi appears keen to propagate the myth of the modern state as a monolith working, as he himself puts it, as 'an organic entity' (see Hansen and Stepputat, 2001). In his first Independence Day speech delivered from the ramparts of the Red Fort in Delhi on 15 August 2014, Modi spoke, almost like a new ethnographer, of himself as an 'outsider' to the elite politics of Delhi who was shocked (*chaunk gaya*) when he got an 'insider' view.[17] What shocked him was that '*ek sarkar ke andar darjano alag alag sarkare chal rahin hai*' – inside one *sarkar* you have dozens of other *sarkars* running. 'It is as if', he continues, 'Everyone has set up their own fiefdoms'. Modi spoke of seeing '*bikhrav*' (dispersal) and '*takrav*' (collision or confrontation) within the one *sarkar*, so much so that departments of the same *sarkar* are knocking at the gates of the Supreme Court for relief against each other. That different government departments can be at loggerheads with each other and are in fact fighting it out in the courts is, Modi made clear, problematic for the functioning of the state. Using precisely these English words in his otherwise entirely Hindi language speech, he exhorted that instead of being an 'assembled entity', *sarkar* needs to be an 'organic unity, an organic entity' working in harmony. Of course, the anthropology of the state has long shown that rather than being the organic unity that Modi seems so desirous of producing, it is – to use his words again – all about *bikhrav* and *takrav* (dispersal and collisions), though it tricks us by, somehow, assembling itself together as an entity (Mitchell, 1999). I show in this book both the fundamentally fragmented nature of *sarkar* and the processes whereby it accomplishes the hard act of assemblage. The latter process depends centrally upon, I argue, *sarkari kaghaz* (paper).

To address someone as *sarkar* is normally a sign of respect, unless it is uttered sarcastically in order to signify the pomposity or delusional self-importance of the addressee. *Sarkari* – the adjective form of *sarkar* – is much more acutely context-dependent. Within the apparatus of the state I show, for instance, how *sarkari* or becoming *sarkari* is a deeply aspirational state of being. But outside this particular context, to call someone or something *sarkari* normally carries pejorative connotations. So, *sarkari* can mean empty routine, or a numbed and dumbed-down manner of acting/thinking. Calling someone a *sarkari kutta* or *sarkari* dog generally means the person has no individual mind of his/her own, but mechanically follows orders. *Sarkari* can also mean 'free' in certain contexts. So NREGA labourers often protest at being made to do work as the

Figure 3: Ministry of Hope © Sarnath Banerjee

wages they are being paid comes from *sarkari* money. The food one gets on trains in India such as the Shatabadi or Rajdhani expresses is often described as *sarkari khana* due to its standardization and slight blandness. I remember landing at the spanking new Terminal 3 of New Delhi's international airport and immediately thinking that this archetypal 'non-place' (Auge, 1995) might boast the clone-like brands of globalized consumer capitalism, but the carpet remains *sarkari*. I am not sure what precisely it is about the carpet at T-3 that instantly made me categorize it as *sarkari*, probably its dull brown colour and slightly grubby appearance (cf. Fehervary, 2009). One recognizes something as *sarkari* through the deeply immersive and intimate fact of living within the territory of India and being forced to deal with *sarkar*. *Sarkari* can, thus, be the taste of a potato cutlet on a train; the physical touch of a fading form; the phraseology of public announcements blaring out from a loudspeaker; or the very sight of an Ambassador car or a towel draped onto the back of a large swivel chair. *Sarkari* can refer to governmental practices such as demanding everything be set out on paper in a particular format, or asking for ridiculous details, or making multiple copies of the same document, or finding meaning in a stamp/signature. Another commonplace implication of *sarkari*, which this book explores in detail, is that of untrustworthiness; of being fake/fraudulent. So *sarkari kaghaz* (paper/ documents) or *sarkari* statistics (*aankde*) are normally categorized as that-which-is-not real (the opposite of *asli*). Mody, for instance, notes how court officials in Delhi dismiss civil marriages as false, as mere 'paper marriages' or '*sarkari shadi*' (government marriage) (2002, p. 250). It is worth noting here that the word typically used to describe *sarkari* reports, documents, statistics, and files is *farzee* (fake or fraudulent) and not *nakli*, though the latter is the exact antonym of *asli* and carries stronger connotations of deception and falsity. The constant description of *sarkari* things as *farzee* makes sense within the wider context of *sarkari* culture and its everyday life that this book describes. As a central objective of *Paper Tiger* is to make the contemporary Indian state ethnographically available, all through this book I retain *sarkar* and *sarkari* at moments when the English translations become inadequate to the descriptive task.

An ethnography of *sarkar*

In my attempt to make *sarkar* ethnographically available, I have employed a diversity of literary and anthropological techniques including narratives on space, discourse analysis of government texts and vernacular newspapers, meditations on affect and time, vivid descriptions of office life including state spectacles such as monthly meetings, inaugural ceremonies and evaluations, and a perusal of the affective life of paper as it circulates within the labyrinthine Indian bureaucracy. In the articulation of bureaucratic everydayness, I have, then, adopted an eclectic methodology guided by the vagaries and specificities of my fieldwork.

I worked out of the NREGS cell in Gopeshwar for 10 months starting in late 2006. All through this time, I kept office hours – 10:00 a.m. to 5:00 p.m., 6 days a week – with the rest of the staff, following their schedule in its entirety. Most days would be spent in the same little room going through files, reading the local newspapers, and sitting out on the roof watching the goings-on of the Collectorate (the District Magistrate's office). I would accompany my office-mates and other senior bureaucrats to state events, which consisted largely of routine inspections and inaugurations. In addition, I tried to attend independently as many NREGS events as possible, such as village council meetings and social audits. I made it a point to attend the Block Development Council meetings (BDCs) that are held every 3 months at every block headquarter. Increasingly intrigued by the block offices, from March onwards I also spent 1 day of the week at the Dasholi block office. Officially, I was a non-participant observer in the NREGS cell. However, little tasks were found for me such as translation of the guidelines into Hindi, typing letters in English on the computer, and cross-checking all the reports that were sent out from Chamoli. After an initial few weeks of stilted interactions, I was slowly accepted as a fixture in all the NREGS-related events and had full and free access to its official documents and files in Gopeshwar. The level of access I had surprised even me. In live time, I saw documents and files being created and destroyed. I sat in on series of meetings, some of them very tense and even what could be considered 'sensitive'. What allowed for this sort of fieldwork access other than serendipity needs to be spelled out.

I believe there were a number of reasons I got the 'post', as my office-mates referred to it, of a research student in the district office and block offices of Chamoli. My introduction through a letter and accompanying recommendation from a powerful, charismatic, and well-known state official was a huge factor in opening the gates. Furthermore, this official, the then Chief Information Commissioner (CIC) of Uttarakhand, is my father's former colleague and, perhaps, that contributed to his unhesitating support of my research project. I say perhaps because the CIC is himself a renowned scholar of the Himalayas and has written many books on developmental and governance requirements of Uttarakhand. He is, famously, extremely supportive of anyone doing research on this region. Another PhD student I bumped into in Uttarakhand who is white, male, based in the US and had absolutely no prior connection to the CIC also told me of the many ways in which the CIC had supported his fieldwork, including with recommendation letters and phone calls. Beyond the introductory reference, everyone soon learned—simply because that was the first question that was always asked of me—that my father is also a member of the Indian Administrative Service (IAS) albeit from the Uttar Pradesh (UP) cadre. My own kin relation to the state as well as my upper-middle class, Indian national, elite University-based position not only allowed me into the hallowed portals of the Indian state but also protected me in many ways. This is particularly true when it comes to sexual harassment within government offices, which is rife in Uttarakhand. My young female friends, primarily NGO workers or college students whom I was tutoring in the evenings, related many unsavoury stories of the lewd comments and general harassment they faced when they so much as entered the very offices out of which I was working. While I often felt extremely high levels of discomfort being the only woman in these overwhelmingly all-male spaces, especially at meetings, I was never directly subjected to sexual harassment of a similar form. Strangely enough, I actually think being a young woman helped me in Chamoli, for I was considered 'unthreatening' by most people. Some of the older men, in particular, were quite happy to take me under their wing. When I would accompany them on inspections or general tours, they would patiently explain what they were doing or point out certain aspects of the village or the event that they thought I might have missed or be interested in. I also lived in the same housing colony as the district officials in Gopeshwar so I soon got to know them quite well at a personal level. When their wives and children would visit them from Dehradun or other cities in the plains I would be invited over for dinner or *chai* to meet them. Over time, these officials came to trust me and became convinced that I was not an auditor or a spy but merely a research student.

My complete access was, however, limited to Chamoli district and this, I believe, was for reasons that went beyond my classed and gendered positioning. There was a general belief that given how 'remote' and 'backward' the district is, there is not anything particularly important happening in its government outposts. The crumbling little office in a borderland Himalayan district was not considered of particular import and could be opened up for ethnography, whatever that may be. The more 'important' offices in Dehradun and Delhi were, however, an altogether different matter. When I tried to get permission for a similar stint of fieldwork in the Ministry of Rural Development in New Delhi, my request was immediately slammed down by a particularly autocratic senior bureaucrat. This person told me in cutting tones that the only way I could 'ever even hope' to get any access to their files or proceedings was by using the RTI before summarily dismissing me from their office. The meeting lasted less than 5 minutes and I was never even offered a seat. In the Dehradun Secretariat where I did do fieldwork, I was never allowed to attend the smaller meetings or spend time with the senior officials. I was let into the large, State-level meetings, but then these were also being opened up to the state press, and so were tightly controlled events bordering on public relations exercises. During my time in the Secretariat, I was handed a select few NREGA files to read and, for the entire 3 months I was there, was made to sit in a large office with many clerks and accountants who regarded me suspiciously, despite my best efforts to befriend them. My bag would be checked by security upon point of entry and exit from the Secretariat. I had to get a pass made and renewed every week in order even to enter the large office compound of the Secretariat. I am certain that the files I had been handed were vetted by someone first. The highly circumscribed nature of access in Dehradun and the stonewalling in Delhi made me realize not just how lucky I had been in Chamoli, but also how the state itself constructs hierarchies of stateness and governmental gravitas across its differentiated tiers and spaces.

I spent time in Delhi also to interview bureaucrats, activists, and academics who had been central to the passage and design of the NREGA. As a result, I travelled with the economist-activist Jean Dreze, one of the architects of the statute, and a group of activists to the state of Odisha to evaluate the performance of the NREGS. I then returned to Dehradun where I spent 3 months in the Rural Development Department's NREGA office in the Secretariat and a further 8 weeks in the archives of the Hindi-language newspapers *Dainik Jagran* and *Amar Ujala*. This book concentrates on the time I spent in Chamoli district; the fieldwork that followed it, however, informs central arguments. The time in Dehradun at the Secretariat and the newspaper archives made clearer a particular imaginary of Chamoli district, as well as showing the similar form of bureaucratic practices within the state apparatus. The interviews with NREGA interpreters in Delhi brought to the fore what I think of as the public avatar of the law. The Odisha trip made clearer the way development expertise is produced. The intense immersion in the everyday life of the state in Chamoli had left behind, inexplicably, a lingering sense of unfinishedness. I felt the urge to know more, to follow the actors further afield. Thus, I followed activists, bureaucrats, politicians, newspaper stories, documents such as job cards and muster rolls to other districts of Uttarakhand, Dehradun, Delhi, and Odisha. In the end, I have doubled back to where I began – 'my' office in Gopeshwar – but with an added awareness that has, I like to believe, allowed me to see the world in my grain of sand.

Paper Tiger as it unfolds

I begin this book with a narrative recounting of the space within which it is primarily set. Gopeshwar the little mountain-town and, by extension, the district of Chamoli was almost always described with the adjective 'remote'. Agents of the state, particularly those who had been posted here from elsewhere, pronounced Gopeshwar un-livable, akin to a prison. I dwell in detail on the lamentations of state officials bemoaning what they describe as their 'punishment postings' to the upper Himalayas. This punishment is survived by cocooning oneself off – physically and emotionally – from the town and by constantly seeking avenues of escape from it. The cocooning process leads to a recession into the self, which is made physically manifest in the empty and shuttered buildings in the official colonies or the state-space of the town. Though the physical edifice of an exemplary centre of the state had been constructed in Gopeshwar, it could not engineer an enlivening sociality to match. Instead, buildings remained in disuse, wearing a haunted look. Through an interrogation of the trope of remoteness, this chapter argues that the creation of the new, putatively Himalayan state of Uttarakhand has served, paradoxically, to accentuate the traditional characterization of the mountains as a backward, inferior space within India. Subsequent chapters return to the theme of 'remoteness' and the distance from *sarkar* that was voiced by all, including those who are – within the setting of the district – believed to embody *sarkar*.

Chapter 2 identifies a distinction made by the primary implementers of the NREGA between what they identified as its 'two lives': the 'state life' (*sarkari zindagi*) and its 'real life' (*asli zindagi*). In this chapter, I map out the state life of law, which holds sway in official documents and files. NREGA was said to command a particularly rich life on paper. For its primary implementers, it is Paper and not the Law, as the framers claim, that is the distinguishing hallmark of NREGA. To follow the process by which the NREGA is converted from a text authored in New Delhi to, say, a water tank in a village in Chamoli district is to see clearly the import of having made impressions on paper. Processual observance of the steps laid out in the Operational Guidelines (OG) of the scheme is said to be achieved, in the eyes of the state, when the correct official documents (*sarkari kaghaz*) have been produced in the prescribed form within the stipulated time frame, possessing the ordained signatures and/or stamps and/or seals of approval. Further, these documents have to be made to grow, so to speak, by being transferred between the correct state channels within particular time periods. In this chapter, I work through three ethnographic vignettes located in different villages to show how the state life of law is not just confined to *sarkari daftars* (government offices) but extends out to the 'remotest' of places and touches the poorest of people. The significance of what gets written down on an official piece of paper, of who materially controls such documents, and of how statistics and reports can be 'fixed' before being declared '*pukka*' (final/permanent) is startlingly evident in these three distinct events. Against the backdrop of the quotidian flurry of such paper-based activities, I argue that the law commands a merely spectral presence.

In Chapter 3, I focus on the cries of 'unimplementablity' that accompanied the NREGA in Uttarakhand. Right across the board, in a response that for once collapsed the hierarchies within the state's vertiginous development bureaucracy, all the implementers of the NREGA emphasized its voluminous paperwork as well as the innate impossibility of its implementation. I link the new documentary regimen ushered in by the NREGA directly to its desire to inject 'transparency' and 'accountability' into the Indian state. I argue that the imagination and mechanics of transparency in NREGA and the associated Right to Information Act, 2005 (RTI), can only ever be realized through an exacerbation of the documentary basis of the state. In short, given the manner in which the developmental Indian state makes its operations knowable and demonstrable, transparency has to be materially produced. It is the 'transparent-making documents' demanded by NREGA that were, ironically enough, making the law difficult to implement. I demonstrate this argument by attending initially to the overwhelming volume and forms of labour expected from lower-level development bureaucrats to produce the transparent-making documents. Subsequently, I turn to the kinds of work these papery artefacts were doing, to show how they were posing a hindrance to the regular working of the Indian state. The kind of work that certain documents can do – particularly that innocuous little object, the job card – is highlighted. The unsettling characteristics of the NREGA, I propose, are to be located not in its legality or the discourse of rights and good governance it shrilly proclaims, but rather in its documentary compulsions.

Chapter 4 concentrates on the epistolary practices of the paper state. I argue that just as the job card is a wily little actant, so too is the seemingly most banal of letters capable of acting in a variety of ways. Such missives can introduce, translate, clarify, complain, harass, act as protective shields, exhibit the perusal of procedure or the fantastical nature of state rules/demands, they can be forgotten, lost, or deliberately binned. Their production requires the hard labour of writing, interpreting, reading, drafting, re-drafting, begetting signatures and stamps, packaging, and posting-out. The struggle to interpret rules and the law is evident in the incessant back-and-forth of letters, many of which dealt with attempts to correctly understanding the minutest of clauses. In this chapter, I provide a classificatory grid for the innumerable letters I encountered as they flowed in and out of the NREGS cell. I do this not to mimic the classificatory practices of states but rather to, once again, make ethnographically available the form, tone, affect, and capacity-to-act of these seemingly mundane pieces of *sarkari kaghaz*. Government letters are not just process-generated dull parchments but rather, as I show them to be, affectively loaded and absolutely central to the process whereby laws can be interpreted and translated and the paper state assembled.

Chapter 5 moves from the written to the oral through a recounting of meetings. Special attention is paid to two types of meetings: the monthly evaluation meetings of the district's development bureaucracy, held in Gopeshwar, and the quarterly block development council meetings held in different block headquarters of the district. The transparency and accountability demanded of the contemporary Indian state translated, in this case, into the fact of having convened the stipulated meetings, the oral presentation of statistics present in progress reports, and the upbraiding of junior functionaries. This auditory practice of meetings is also a performance that allows for the local state to physically gather together for a brief, anxiogenic period. Such a performance entails the assembly of agents of the state on the appointed date and time, in the right place, in appropriate dress and in possession of the correct documents. Oral communication takes place between different tiers of the state through which they describe themselves as parts of the same entity working towards common objectives. In the theatre of the state, agents perform 'being *sarkari*'. Central to this competent performance of *sarkari*-ness is the inculcation of an awareness of and respect for the state (*sarkar*). There is a palpable charge, what I describe as *sarkari* affect, to these events, where varied officials physically position themselves appropriately in an enclosed space to discuss matters of state for an extended period of time. Bringing together that which has been ethnographically suggested in the preceding three chapters as well, I end this section by arguing that it is *sarkari* affect that allows for the persistence of everyday bureaucratic life.

In the final chapter, the theatrical meets the exotic. In the quietude of the daily, a human-eating big cat arrived in Gopeshwar and went on to swiftly kill a few people and establish a reign of terror. The state appeared surprisingly incapable of overthrowing the big cat's reign and stymieing the terror. On the contrary, it appeared to be bowing to the big cat with an unseemly servility. Interestingly, the everyday life of the state continued as before albeit with a heightened sense of panic. This was reflected in the nervous demeanours of senior bureaucrats, the large number of emergency meetings that were held, and the frenzied pace with which letters and other assorted documents were produced and dispatched. Another law of the land – the WPA, 1972 – was translated but its unwrittens (Stoler, 2009) and illegibilities disallowed the paper state from holding on to its benign facade. The poverty and unemployment that development schemes attempt, again and again, to address are slow, tragic processes that grind on largely silently while the state is busily immersed in its everyday life. In the case of the attacks by the big cat, death was instantaneous, bloody and public. In an environment of unspeakable terror, subjects were able to unambiguously calibrate the worth of their human lives against the life of a state-protected species. In this remote region of India, the big cat clearly commanded greater bio-legitimacy, attesting to a much wider structure of bio-inequality that shapes the contemporary world (Fassin, 2009). The wait for the sway of the maneater to end was inordinately long, often appearing endless. As time refused to clock on, local residents loudly proclaimed the Indian state to be nothing but a paper tiger. I conclude my study with an examination of the conditions that allow for such a labelling of the state.

Endnotes

1   Mao Tse-tung's piece entitled 'U.S. Imperialism is a Paper Tiger' is probably the proclamation that popularized the phrase. Here Mao provides a useful definition: 'In appearance it [US imperialism] is very powerful but in reality it is nothing to be afraid of, it is a paper tiger. Outwardly

a tiger, it is made of paper, unable to withstand the wind and the rain'. 'U.S. Imperialism is a Paper Tiger', 14 July 1956, from *Selected Works of Mao Tse-Tung*, http://www.marxists.org/reference/ archive/mao/selected-works/volume-5/mswv5_52.htm. Accessed July 2, 2014.

2   Two now-classic papers which are superb studies of the documentary basis of the colonial state in India are Moir (1993) and Saumarez-Smith (1985). In an important recent intervention, Raman studies the early colonial British state in India and demonstrates 'the conditions under which paperwork and political rule came to be so intimately and peculiarly intertwined in the modern colony' (2012, p. 195). See also Ogborn (2007) for his fascinating account of forms of writing and the making of imperial authority in the seventeenth and eighteenth centuries. Hull (2012a) bridges the colonial-postcolonial divide with his focus on semiotic technologies and the materiality of urban bureaucracy in Pakistan.

3   Stoler has argued more generically for studying colonial archives and the documents that lie within them as 'technologies that reproduce states' (2009, p. 28). Most famously Weber (2006) has identified the locus of power in the modern state to reside within the bureau, which in turn is dependent upon files. To touch upon but a few analyses, they have been regarded as central to the experiencing of the state (Corbridge et al., 2005), as modes through which people make themselves visible to the state as rights-bearing citizens (Chatterji and Mehta, 2007), as attestors to the 'illegibility' of the state that also allow for mimicry of state practices (Das, 2004), as 'everyday artefacts of the state' that function as 'paper truths' that can provide insights into the repressed memories of the Emergency in India (Tarlo, 2000), as recruited by the pedagogical project of development that constitutes the act of writing by subaltern subjects to be a form of political agency (Cody, 2009), and as penetrating into and intertwining with the intimate histories and genealogies of Anglo-Indian railway workers (Bear, 2007).

4   My approach is partly inspired by Actor-Network Theory's (ANT's) emphasis on the agency of objects. Latour has made the important point that the social is 'not a substance, nor a domain of reality ... but a way of tying together heterogeneous bundles, of translating some types of entities into another' (2000, p. 113). In this act of tying together, artefacts possess the capacity 'to construct, literally and not metaphorically, social order' (*ibid*). I depart from ANT by not sharing in the underlying anti-humanism of this work and in my descriptions of the affective life of documents, bureaucracy, and the state (Stoler, 2009; Navaro-Yashin, 2012; Bear, 2007).

5   Thus, this work is in conversation with Hull's (2012a) proposal to study contemporary governance as a material practice and follows Gupta in his argument 'for a perspective that sees the state as constituted through writing' (2012, p. 143).

6   As far back as 1940 Radcliffe-Brown could write that, in a sense, the State 'does not exist in the phenomenal world; it is a fiction of the philosophers. What does exist is an organisation, i.e. a collection of individual human beings connected by a complex system of relations' (xxiii).

7   As the NREGA is, on paper, a demand-based scheme it is hard to accurately assess of the exact future costs involved. Even at the time of its inception, there were startlingly different projections in circulation. In a note on the financial cost to the Indian state, prepared by the National Advisory Council, the cost of employment guarantee is anticipated to rise from 0.5 per cent of GDP in 2005 – 2006 to 1 per cent of GDP in 2008 – 2009 (Dreze, 2004). In another prominently cited assessment, economists Chandrashekhar and Ghosh (2004) estimate that were the NREGA to cover one-third of rural households, it would amount to 1.55 per cent of the projected GDP; and should the coverage go up to 40 per cent, it would move up to 1.86 per cent of GDP. In the unlikely event that every rural household in India

were to appeal for work, an appeal that could not legally be turned down, then the cost of the NREGA would move up to Rs 150,000 crore i.e. over 4 per cent of India's GDP. One lakh = 100,000. In the Indian numbering system, after the first three digits, commas are used to divide every two digits. One crore = 100 lakh or ten million.

8   Similarly, Gupta (1998) describes the direct connections made in the village of Alipur in UP, between economic and social reform and the then Prime Minister Indira Gandhi.

9   On the 17 May 2009, the UPA coalition headed by the Congress party won resoundingly in the Indian general elections. For the first time since 1962, a government in India that had served its full five-year term was re-elected under the same leadership. Credit for this achievement was laid, expectedly, at the door of the Gandhi family. Post-electoral analyses – from the Wall Street Journal to radical left publications – of this staggering vote of confidence, conferred by over 400 million voters, seem to agree with Gandhi's assessment that the developmental intent of the incumbent government came through in flagship schemes such as the NREGA.

10 Thus, most of the employment schemes were aimed at below poverty line (BPL) households or those belonging to 'backward' castes or the Scheduled Tribes (STs). The NREGA is 'universal' in its coverage as any rural household can work under it. The targeted nature of previous schemes emerged, further, from the fact that certain financial allocations were made for them by the Ministry in New Delhi. The target for government functionaries, then, was to spend the stipulated budget within the financial year. As opposed to this 'top-down' allocation, the NREGS has a 'bottom-up' financial outlay as, in principle, villagers themselves are to decide how much work they want in a year and make a demand 'upwards' to the state, to grant them this amount.

11 This question of movements or programmes that cannot fully be captured by a monolithic conceptual apparatus such as 'neoliberalism' or 'state welfarism' or 'socialism' has been commented upon by various ethnographers (see Kipnis, 2008; Cody, 2013, p. 11). The NREGA, then, is not unique in being inside, yet also outside, the conceptual rationality of neoliberalism.

12 For a comparable, non-hegemonic critique of NREGA's sister legislation of the Right to Information Act, 2005 (RTI) see Sharma (2015)

13 Mosse describes an 'instrumental view' in international development that views policy as rational problem-solving, a managerial approach that is concerned with 'bringing institutional reality into line with policy prescription' (2005, p. 3). Analyses of the NREGA and its failings are discussed in precisely this vein by its advocates (e.g. by Khera, 2011).

14 'Rajiv was right: Montek says only 16p of Re reaches Poor', *The Times of India*, 14 October 2009, http://articles.timesofindia.indiatimes.com/2009-10-14/india/28097103_1_welfare-schemes-leakage-rajiv-gandhi. Accessed July 2, 2014.

15 'Executive Summary', *Performance Audit of Mahatma Gandhi National Rural Employment Guarantee Scheme*, Report No. 6 of 2013, Comptroller and Auditor General of India, http://saiindia.gov.in/english/home/Our_Products/Audit_Report/Government_Wise/union_audit/recent_reports/union_performance/2013/Civil/Report_6/exe-sum.pdf. Accessed July 2, 2014.

16 In the sequel to *Sarkar*, Amitabh Bachchan takes a back seat and hands over the reigns of governance – *Sarkar Raj* – to his real and reel-life son Abhishek Bachchan. After a complicated series of embroilments with land mafias, political parties, and a London-based multinational company (MNC) that wants to set up a power plant (displacing a large number of villagers), the junior Bachchan is killed. In the final scenes of the film, we see Amitabh Bachchan silently

and deliberately walking into his dead son's office and seating himself on his chair (*kursi*), thus symbolically signifying his return to the throne.

17 'Text of PM's Speech at Red Fort,' http://www.narendramodi.in/text-of-pms-speech-at-red-fort/. Note my translation is directly from the audio version of his speech, which differs slightly from the version presented here. For a recording of the speech see 'PM Narendra Modi's Independence Day Speech', YouTube video, 1:06:27, https://www.youtube.com/watch?v=yOwD2S3oHjU. Accessed July 2, 2014.

1

A Remote Town

Space is space, life is life, everywhere the same.

—J. M. Coetzee, *Waiting for the Barbarians*

Provincialism, or provinciality, is a space recognizable instantly.

—Nita Kumar, *Provincialism in Modern India*

The town of Gopeshwar, the administrative headquarter of the Himalayan borderland district of Chamoli, is the quintessential 'out-of-the-way place' so prized by past anthropologists for the ease with which it could be presented as 'pristine' (Tsing, 1994, p. 282). The town and, more generally, the district was nearly always described to me through the utilization of the English word 'remote'. Gopeshwar is to be found at a distance of 280 km from Dehradun and 235 km from the nearest railhead, Rishikesh.[1] Given its distance from large urban centers, its location on India's border with Tibet, its difficult terrain, and its poor transportation infrastructure, I did not, initially, find the frequent application of 'remote' to Chamoli altogether surprising. However, with time I began to question and further explore this overwhelming discourse of 'remoteness'. Local accounts narrated present-day Chamoli as a place that has, since time immemorial, existed distant from the centre; a distance that remains to be overcome. The trope of remoteness is ubiquitous in all discussions of this upper Himalayan region. It is present in British colonial accounts and in local self-descriptions; in the statehood movement that raged during the 1990s, as well as in present-day quotidian chatter amongst a cross-section of town residents.

The questions I ask in this chapter are how, and why, does a place come to be overwhelmingly defined by its so-called remoteness? What does it feel like to live in a 'remote' Himalayan town? What, indeed, does the attachment of the adjective 'remote' do to a place? Instead of taking the word 'remote' to signify a harmless, geographical fact, I draw upon the now exhaustive work on space, place, and territory that highlights the cultural and political work involved in rendering spaces with a seemingly natural and self-evident geography (e.g. Moore, 2005; Massey, 1994), to argue that this uncritical characterization of Gopeshwar as a 'remote town' contributes to the perpetuation of spatial inequity within India (Ludden, 2012). Beyond the pragmatics of living in and governing a remote place, I describe the experiential aspects of remoteness. Taking these strands together, I make a case for taking the particularities of space seriously in analyses of the workings of law, development, and the state. That thing which we call the Indian state makes itself manifest through a uniform set of practices, things, and relations across its territory. However, the state's operations in remote spaces acquire a distinctive character, which require elucidation in order to highlight their profound consequentiality.

The *Pahar*

At the time of India's independence from British rule in 1947, the regions that were then called the princely state of Tehri-Garhwal, British Garhwal and the Kumaon division of the United Provinces of Agra and Oudh, were incorporated into the large north-Indian state of Uttar Pradesh (UP). In UP, the same Himalayan region was divided into eight mountain districts, of which five were placed under the Garhwal Regional Commission and three under the Kumaon Regional Commission (Rangan, 2000). From 1947 onwards, intermittent demands for a separate hill state had been voiced, but they were largely restricted to urban-based elite groups and individuals (Mawdsley, 1998; Kumar, 2000). In the mid-1990s, there was a sudden flare-up of this demand, for the first time extending to a much larger swathe of the state's population, including its rural residents. The rhetoric that informed this separatist movement was one emphasizing the geographical specificity of the mountains (*pahar*), which required a very different form of developmental effort from the type that is efficacious in the plains (*maidan*). This 'self-evident fact', claimed the agitators campaigning for a new state, was one that the development planners and implementers of UP were quite unable to comprehend, beging primarily plainsmen (*maidanis*) sitting in distant Lucknow, the capital of UP (Mawdsley, 1997, 1998). On 9 November 2000, the Government of India acceded to their demands, detaching the Himalayan portion of UP to create the twenty-seventh state of the federal Indian Union – Uttarakhand. Present-day Uttarakhand consists of 13 districts divided between the administrative divisions of Garhwal and Kumaon.

Residents of Chamoli district had actively participated in this separatist movement, and many proudly told me of their travels down to the big cities in the plains to participate in agitations for the new state. A specifically *pahari* identity coalesced around the rhetoric of discrimination against the *pahari* by the non-*paharis*. The vocabulary of the struggle emphasized the 'essentially secular shared attribute viz, the specificity of belonging to the mountains, and the distinctiveness of mountain society' (Jayal, 2000, p. 4311). Systematic neglect, coupled with exploitation of the Himalayas for their rich natural resources such as timber and minerals, are seen to have begun during British colonialism and to have continued unabated through what is often described as a 'form of internal colonialism' by the post-1947 Indian state (Pathak, 1997, p. 908). The maltreatment of the *pahar* goes hand-in-hand with a stereotype of the *pahari* as lazy and profligate. As *The Garhwal Gazetteer* noted long ago, 'the indolence of the Garhwali and his proneness to falsehood have been insisted upon by all writers' (Walton, 1910, p. 68). Berreman mentions the 'hillbilly' stereotype as well: '*paharis* are thought by people of the plains to be ritually, spiritually, and morally inferior' (1972, p. xxi).[2] The *pahari* identity is, of course, not uniform; differences between Garhwal and Kumaon often crop up.[3] Within Garhwal itself, there is a subtle differentiation. To quote the *Gazetteer* again, 'The Garhwali of the outer ranges is often a miserable creature: abject in poverty: truculent and offensive in prosperity or in the enjoyment of a little brief authority' (Walton, 1910, p. 69). A century on from the *Gazetteer's* observations, the description of remote Chamoli being inhabited by backward, lazy, alcoholic men and long-suffering, hard-working women was commonplace amongst not only state officials but also middle-class residents of Gopeshwar.

Perhaps the one time that the outer region of Uttarakhand ascends to prominence is when considered in its role as the Himalayan bulwark of the land of India (Pathak, 1997; see also Woodman, 1969). China's occupation of neighbouring Tibet and the felt need to better police the Himalayan border regions led to the creation of Chamoli as a separate district within UP. On 24 February 1960, a newspaper advertisement made this news public and named Gopeshwar the new district's administrative headquarters (Pahari, 2005, p. 19). In 1960, however, there was no town of Gopeshwar, merely a tiny village bearing this name located 12 km north east of the small town of Chamoli across the river Alaknanda (Figure 1.1). The district headquarters could not be located in Chamoli proper, due to its unfavorable location along the banks of this river, which subjects it to frequent flooding. Gopeshwar, the village, evidently derived

Figure 1.1: Gopeshwar town seen from afar in the monsoons

its name from the Gopinath (Shiva) temple, which is estimated to have been built between the ninth and eleventh centuries AD. The town of Gopeshwar has grown up all around the temple complex but particularly to its north. What this has led to is the temple serving as the unofficial boundary between Gopeshwar *gaon* (village), as it continues to be called, and Gopeshwar *shehar* (town).

The district headquarters were eventually moved from Chamoli up to Gopeshwar only in the early 1970s, when the new town was deemed fit to serve as the locus of the local state apparatus – in other words, when Gopeshwar was transformed into an 'exemplary centre' of the state, which in many ways is 'not just the nucleus, the engine, or the pivot of the state, it is the state' (Geertz, 1980, p. 13). I utilize the Geertzian term not to suggest that Gopeshwar as the capital is seen to be a 'microcosm of the supernatural order' (1980, p. 13), but rather to argue that Gopeshwar was seen by the residents of Chamoli as an embodiment of the state (*sarkar*) in material terms, looming large over them from its mountain-top location. This perception in turn required this town to function as an exemplar of what the modern nation state of India should and does possess within itself. Through intensive state planning, the tiny village of Gopeshwar was transformed into the district headquarters of Chamoli of today, which come equipped with a hospital, schools, a college, a library, a veterinary centre, sports facilities including a gym for policemen, a petrol pump, a market (*bazaar*), a post-office, a computerized railway reservation centre, an official tourist rest house, a *maidan* (a large, open piece of land for, amongst other purposes, holding public assemblies and conducting military exercises), and spanking new office buildings for every wing of the state that is functioning in the district. Somewhat ironically, the template for the formation of Gopeshwar, this local state's outpost in the nationalist, post-colonial state of India, appears to be none other than the colonial institution of the 'hill-station'.

The hill station versus the mountain town

Hill stations in India were a rather unique urban entity, following neither the traditional pattern of an Asian city nor the colonial one which consisted in the installation of a regimented grid of civil and military cantonments (Kennedy, 1996; King, 1976). Rather their architecture was distinctly anglicized comprising cottages, gardens and orchards, and involved the building of high-quality infrastructure – roads, railways, bridges – from scratch. 'European' institutions such as hospitals, convalescent homes, orphanages, schools, hotels, and missionary headquarters were set up. The British lived in the elevated areas along the ridge crests and flanks, while the native Indian towns were located at lower levels, such as the *bazaar* area and further below (King, 1976). The increasing presence of the British led to a large influx of Indians into hill stations in order to serve them. Physical distancing of one community from another (the British and the 'natives') was much more acute in the mountains than was possible in colonial towns in the plains, because of the vertical layering of the hill station. This racialized segregation is well brought out in Kanwar's (1990) study of Simla, which functioned as the summer capital of the British Raj in India. Simla was divided into two sections: the 'Station' inhabited by the white colonial masters and the 'Bazaar' inhabited by the brown natives. In tracing the gradual development of Simla, Kanwar makes the important point that 'the town was the spatial embodiment of a social system; the process of urbanization expressed the colonial dynamic at the level of space' (1990, p. 250). Within the white Station area, too, houses and offices were constructed along an elaborate layout plan, keeping in mind the rank of the officials residing and working in them. Not only the size and architectural style of the buildings, but also their locations and the views they commanded were privileges to be fought for (see Kennedy, 1996; Kanwar, 1990).

Hill stations are pre-eminently understood as nostalgic spaces where the British could briefly escape 'the three constraining influences of 'the station', 'the heat', and 'the natives'...' (King, 1976, p. 170). This image helped gloss over their increasing importance as sites from which the imperial power, more and more, governed its colony. Kennedy traces the 'shift in the bureaucratic axis of the imperial state from the plains to the hills' (1996, p. 9), as from the second half of the nineteenth century, hill stations became centres of power from where the guardians of the Raj issued political and military orders. He concludes that hill stations in India 'served both as sites of refuge and as sites of surveillance' (1996, p. 1).[4] Under the British colonial state, then, hill stations became places that the ruling elite wished to escape to.[5] Gopeshwar, on the other hand, though also a town in the hills, is a place only worth escaping from, claimed senior agents of the state. Gopeshwar is not termed a 'hill station' despite its location, and despite sharing many of the characteristics of a hill station.[6] Instead, it is just another *pahari shehar* (mountain town). Yet, there are striking similarities in the physical layout of Gopeshwar and hill stations.

The first and most obvious similarity is the physical distancing of the wielders of state power from the 'natives' or the local residents. The agents of the state live and work on the upper crests of the hill on which Gopeshwar is spread out, monopolizing the land, ostensibly, for affairs-of-state. The locals live below, in and around the crowded *bazaar* area. Two-thirds of the way up the town, one comes across a petrol pump constructed at a bend in the road, with a small pavement around it. As the sole petrol pump in town, it is a critical orienting landmark. Directions in Gopeshwar are almost always delivered in relation to it. Hence, such and such office/shop/person is below the petrol pump (*petrol pump ke neeche*) or above it (*upar*). The petrol pump functions as a *de facto* cut-off mark between 'state land' (*sarkari zameen*) and 'non-state land' (*gersarkari zameen*). Only government offices and residences are to be found on the ascent from the petrol pump. The first major office directly after the petrol pump is the Development Office (*Vikas Bhawan*) followed in turn by the Public

Works Department (PWD), the District Court, the Forest Department, and, finally, the District Magistrate's office or the *Collectorate*. On the summit are located the official residences of all the state personnel managing these offices. The District Magistrate (DM), the most powerful government official in the district, possesses a colonial-style bungalow commanding the best view of the Nanda Devi Peak, at 7817 m above sea level, the second highest mountain in India, and the abode of the patron goddess of Uttarakhand.

The second similarity between the colonial hill station and the post-colonial district headquarters shifts beyond a reading of the 'spatial tactics' (Low and Lawrence-Zuñiga, 2003, p. 30) described above to a consideration of the tangible structures comprising the state space of the town. These include an array of offices, residential areas for the officials, a club for socializing, parks in which officials can play badminton and cricket, and a library. Following the model of hill stations, these amenities are built into Gopeshwar too. That is where the similarities end. The club, the parks, the library, and the hospital, with their new-constructed look, stand out significantly in the town. Despite this newness, they remain almost entirely unused, lending them a faintly haunted appearance. In all the time I spent in Gopeshwar, the club was utilized on just one occasion – New Year's Eve – to host a party for the district officials. The library possessed, uncannily, English classics such as the complete works of Oscar Wilde – in a town where almost nobody spoke the English language. Unsurprisingly, then, it too wore a desolate look. While possessing the requisite physical buildings, the space above the petrol pump (*upar*) remained empty (*khali*).

Living in the lake: Residing 'above'

The emptiness of the space above is starkly evident on the very summit of the hill in the residential area called *Kund* colony, which is the exclusive preserve of government functionaries. According to local folklore, there used to be a lake (*kund*) up there which, one fine day, mysteriously dried up. The colony is constructed around and within the dry bed of this mythical lake. Just as Gopeshwar, the town is divided into two by the petrol pump, so is residence in the town partitioned. One either lives 'in Kund' or '*neeche*' (below or down there). To say 'I live in Kund' (*mein Kund mein rehata hoon*) in Hindi literally translates into English as 'I live in a lake/pond'. In Gopeshwar, however, Kund does not denote lake. Rather, it connotes an association with *sarkar* (the state), that small but powerful and prestigious state apparatus in the district, and hence it operates as a mode of distinguishing oneself from the rest of Gopeshwar's inhabitants. Residence in Kund is offered primarily to those who are transferred into Chamoli from without and are situated comparatively higher in the state's bureaucratic hierarchy. The colony itself is segregated and ordered on the basis of the same hierarchical system. The top-ranked employees – Class I, as they are officially termed by the Government of India (GoI) – reside in the centre of the colony, in the lake basin, in three-bedroom apartments. The size of the residences decreases as one moves outward from the basin of Kund to the periphery where the lowest level employees – Class IV – live in single-room, multi-storied habitations. Just as the split into 'above' and 'below' allowed for a segregation between *sarkari* people and commonplace town residents, the status hierarchy of the state machinery itself is quite literally mapped onto the buildings located 'above', be they the officials' homes or workplaces. Reminiscent of the spatial formations of hill stations, Gopeshwar attests to Ludden's claim that the end of imperialism and the onset of national sovereignty has not eliminated 'imperial forms of territoriality', which continue *de facto* (2012, p. 584) (Figure 1.2).

There is just one exception to the centre-periphery assemblage in Kund. This is the seemingly strategic location, on the highest point of Kund's boundary, of a large colonial-style bungalow designated for the Superintendent of Police (SP), the top police official in the district. The backyard of this residence is carved onto a protruding edge overlooking the town below. From here you can look down on the town, level by level, almost till the *maidan*. It would be difficult to identify individuals at that level, but it is easy enough to observe the goings-on of Kund colony and the movements of people up to the petrol pump. In the evenings, the SP would often seat himself just behind the edge of the wall in his backyard so that nobody from below could see him nursing his 'English whisky', watching the activities of the town. The SP was my landlord and I would often be invited over to his bungalow for a chat as he indulged in this hobby, as he described it to me.[7] 'My job never ends', he would sigh dolefully, 'for I have to constantly keep an eye on these useless (*nalayak*) Gopeshwar-*wallahs*'. An argument can be made for the SP's backyard being the material realization of Foucault's (1995) principle of Panopticism. The arrangement of the backyard did impose a visibility on the residents of the state space of Gopeshwar while maintaining the invisibility of the seer. The SP did closely observe the goings on of some particularly 'dangerous people' (*khatarnak log*): the Nepalis who lived in shacks

Figure 1.2: Gopeshwar from above (*upar se*)

just under his bungalow, the young men who would play cricket and then smoke or drink, some old men who were forever gambling, unmarried young women or the particularly 'dolled up' (*bani-thani*) married ones, and, of course, his own policemen and other government officials. Further, it was common knowledge in Kund that the SP might be observing them. Power was, certainly, visible in the shape of the protruding backyard with its low wall from behind which one could be spied upon, and unverifiable in that the SP might be at home watching them, but then again, he might just as well not be. Yet, it did not seem 'to induce in the inmate a state of conscious and permanent visibility that assures the automatic functioning of power', which is what Foucault considers to be the major effect of the Panopticon (1995, p. 201).

In fact, I would argue that in Gopeshwar, there was a very different form of surveillance in operation: a form in which no one individual was the sole seer, but in which everyone without exception (including the SP with his panoptical backyard) was watched by everyone else. The gaze of all upon all was constant and all-encompassing, in that everyone seemed to be acquainted with all the townspeople, as well as bizarrely well informed of each other's daily movements through the town. Novels and travelogues set within small towns in India describe such a form of surveillance in humorous detail (Chatterjee, 1988; Mishra, 1995; Desai, 2006). The fact of the vertical layering of a mountain town such as Gopeshwar aids the observation of individuals moving about, especially on levels below one's own location. In addition, in this tiny town, there are few destinations worth the name. One is either at work/school, or at home, or in the *bazaar*, or taking an evening walk in the public park at the edge of town, or paying obeisance to the lord at Gopinath temple. In a sense, then, there is a surveillance of all by all, or as Foucault puts it in a different context, 'inspection functions ceaselessly' (1995, p. 195).

This aspect of ceaselessly being inspected by the residents of the small town 'suffocated' the senior functionaries of the state. They felt that they were constantly in the public gaze, which stifled them by disallowing that much-required relaxation into the private self. As the young Chief Development Officer (CDO), a member of the highly revered Indian Administrative Service (IAS) grumblingly told me, the only person in the entire district who dared to address him by his first name, since he was 'tired of being CDO-*sahib* twenty-four-seven'. As I observed it in the senior officials stationed at this small Indian town, this exhaustion with being the constant focus of gazes of various sorts did not so much lead to a Foucauldian disciplining of the self, as it became a cause for self-imposed seclusion, a shuttering away of the self, a conscious distancing from the wider social world of the town, which they all religiously practised. It was considered too risky a maneuver to remove the official face of the state that the bureaucrats wore in their daily professional life, and allow the very people they were supposed to rule over, their subjects so to say, to peep into the private self that lay behind the mask. In *Shooting an Elephant* Orwell has compellingly described the pain of the constant presentation of the white man as a *sahib* during the British Raj wherein [h]e becomes a sort of hollow, posing dummy, the conventionalized figure of a sahib ... he wears a mask, and his face grows to fit it' (1950, p. 6).

Quite apart from posing as a 'brown sahib' for the benefit of the citizenry, the more senior bureaucrats found it difficult even to forge genuine friendships with their colleagues and neighbours in Kund. It was simply too difficult for them, working as they did within this highly hierarchical and formalized, if local, state set-up, to relinquish the structure of their official life. A distinction between the public and the private was coherently articulated to me by many of them on numerous occasions. They believed that it was acceptable to have their work – technical and managerial – subjected to public scrutiny, but wished to be able to lead their private lives with some measure of reserve. This reserve they did not think was possible in a small, provincial town such as Gopeshwar, in contradistinction to the modern urban experience of life in Dehradun or Delhi. Simmel refers to the crowdedness of cities as ' … a technique for making and keeping private matters secret, such as earlier could be attained only by means of spatial isolation' (1950, p. 337). It was precisely by means of spatial isolation that the bureaucrats posted in from larger cities attempted to hold on to their private selves. The spatial layout of the town aided this process. Officials living in Kund did not have far to go to their work places, which were either a level or two below their own homes. Further, most of them were provided with official vehicles that would transport them up and down. As they had, again, government-appointed domestic help to look after their household requirements, they rarely, if ever, went into the crowded bazaar area. Life for them remained largely *upar* (above the petrol pump). This isolation, lack of secrecy, and confinement to a small portion of the hill, on which Gopeshwar is set, led to a sense of being incarcerated, stifled, and entrapped. In their own words, life (*zindagi*) as it should ideally be lived is not to be found here; it is elsewhere.

'Life is elsewhere'

In official circles, there is a well-known fast fact about Chamoli, which is that only one of the three Ps can bring you here. The three P's are Promotion, Probation, or Punishment. Most commonly Chamoli was a punishment posting, sometimes a promotion (as it was for the DM who was posted there just before I left, but who told me that he wished he had not been promoted if it entailed living in Gopeshwar) and, often, a probation to assess your guts and your willingness to work. The three Ps are directly related to the level of remoteness of the region. The most junior officials and the ones who are being punished are posted out to far-flung border districts such as Chamoli. The ones next on the seniority/punishment scales are posted to the belt adjoining the farthest outlying districts, and so on in increasing order of seniority and decreasing level of punishment, as one circles closer to the capital. Only the chosen few – the most senior, the most deserving, and the ones with the strongest connections to their political masters – get to remain in Dehradun. A posting to Chamoli is, thus, held in very low esteem by state functionaries.

The Chief Development Officer (CDO) of Chamoli was one such official who considered Chamoli the ultimate punishment posting. More specifically, he described his posting as a 'curse' and as divine retribution for uncharitable thoughts he had once harboured. He loved recounting this story to me: during his training at the IAS Academy, he had come to Chamoli for a trek with his colleagues. On the way up the trail, they had met an old man, who on learning that this IAS officer belonged to the Uttarakhand cadre, had kindly said that it would be nice if he were one day posted to Chamoli.

'At that moment I had silently cursed the old man and thought that I would die if I were posted here in the back of beyond. Lo and behold, I finish my training and guess what my first posting was? My parents scolded me, saying that God was punishing me for having cursed that old man and for having had thoughts of killing myself. I think they are right', he would tell me, only half in jest.

'What is wrong with Chamoli?' though, I would ask. The CDO never failed to be amused by the naivete he saw in this question, coming as it was from someone who had lived her life in metropolises:

'This place is so remote. There is nothing here (*yahan kuch nahin hai*). Everything is lying empty (*har cheez khali pada hua hai*). Nowhere to go, nothing to do. Dehradun is 10 hours away and my work does not allow me to leave my station as often as I would like to. My friends and families are so far away. It is such a dead place … all my colleagues are living it up in their areas. Have you seen the condition of my official residence or the club or the marketplace?'

The lack of entertainment options such as cinemas and shopping malls, and the poor quality of infrastructure, including their own residential quarters in Gopeshwar, were always compared unfavourably with what large towns in the plains offered. Thus, in Dehradun one would live in posher residential areas, have access to educational and health facilities, be able to eat out in restaurants, shop in malls and go to the cinema. The 'emptiness' (*khalipan*) that bureaucrats repeatedly spoke of in reference to Gopeshwar was, first, a very literal and material one. This tangible lack of quality infrastructure contributed to and exacerbated the second sort of emptiness: that of the near-total absence of families.

In my very first conversation with the incredulous District Magistrate (DM) of Chamoli, I had been warned off living in Gopeshwar as it was too 'remote' a place for a young woman of my class background to live in. By way of example, he told me that his own wife and children lived in Dehradun as did the families of all other officials who had been posted into the district. In Gopeshwar, all the senior officials were men. The only wives to be seen were those of recently married officials, who did not have any children yet. Hence, during the time I lived in Kund, only one officer among the more than 30 inhabitants had his wife living with him. However, she too told me that she would 'run home as often as possible, for it is so deadly boring here'. Given that almost all the officials were living alone, half their attention and time were directed to Dehradun or the other plains cities where their families resided. Repeatedly, bureaucrats told me how difficult they found it to 'manage both fronts'.

The apparent incarceration in the mountains seemed to be putting a strain on the families, especially on the marital relations, of all the officials. A senior forest official told me that he was in a real bind because his wife hated it here and his ageing parents would not even survive the strenuous drive up here to 'this nothingness'. With real earnestness, he told me that his wife was threatening to divorce him if he did not get posted out soon. Another forest official told me how Gopeshwar was not a place where one could 'keep a family' (*yahaan family ko nahin rakh sakte hai*). Yet another forest official told me that his wife never visited him in Gopeshwar, because 'when we got married she knew that we would spend most of our lives in jungles. But a jungle in the *pahar* in this remote region is more than she had bargained for'. An SDM (Sub-Divisional Magistrate) of the district told me how his wife could not endure living in Gopeshwar for over 2 days as she had grown up in Delhi and was unused to the 'backwardness of a remote region such as Chamoli'. Another official told me how his parents-in-law were aghast to learn of his posting 'in the *pahar*', and said that had they known of this before they would never have married their daughter to him. Two unmarried officers told me that they were being compelled to go down the path of arranged marriages as they did not want to remain bachelors forever and, naturally, there was no chance of ever meeting 'anyone interesting' up here.

The intersection of gender and class was particularly striking in such discussions of Gopeshwar, especially when compared to colonial hill stations where, Kennedy has argued, 'form followed function: the lives led in the hills replicated the social experiences of the upper middle classes at home' (1996, p. 5). These hill stations were intensely social spaces filled with events such as teas, picnics, balls, fetes, strolls and social calls, and all the intrigues, gossip and romances these social activities led to – a life that the fiction of Rudyard Kipling, Paul Scott, and J. G. Farrell vividly depicts. The creation of a home-like space had allowed for a large population of British women to be in residence in hill stations. Indeed, Edwardes has noted 'a hill station was the only place in India where there were more women than men' (quoted in King, 1976, p. 158). Gopeshwar, in sharp contrast, had almost no women in the state space. Quite unlike the official order issued by the Government of UP that declared the new district capital ready for residence in the 1970s, the families of bureaucrats never deemed Gopeshwar fit for habitation: the hospital in town employed no regular medical staff and offered minimal facilities, the various schools were not of a quality that would appeal to the relatively well-off bureaucrats, the bazaar was adjudged inferior and provincial, there were no cinemas and restaurants. The absence of wives and children greatly contributed to the sense of emptiness that officials referred to as looming over the town.

Women officials, in general, are spared from being posted to Chamoli due to the hardships it entails. The gendering of the state space of Gopeshwar then – the offices and Kund – was distinctly and overwhelmingly male. If women were posted up to Chamoli, they tended to go on long or medical leave. The only woman official I encountered in the district was one I call Ruchi, a young new recruit to the provincial civil services (PCS) who was posted as the sub-divisional Magistrate (SDM) of Joshimath, a *tehsil* of Chamoli that lies along the Tibetan border.[8] She told me that she had been posted there since 'those old men in Dehradun' (the senior officials who had ordered her posting) did not think that she – a young, single woman hailing from the plains – could manage it; she was intent on proving them wrong. Ruchi belongs to the category of the 'other backward classes' (OBC), but she was certain that it was not her supposedly lower caste affiliation that had led to this terrible posting, to the most remote sub-division of remote Chamoli. Rather, she believed it was being a young woman from a large town in the plains – a *maidani* – that had made her, as she repeatedly described it to me, 'a victim'. She described her posting to Chamoli as one filled with such hardships that it had ended up eliminating all her capacity for fear:

'I can battle wild bears and leopards, walk up vertical inclines in the snow to identify dead bodies, travel as the only woman with contingents of louts, deal with all sorts of pressure especially that of the local *goondas* (thugs) … you name it and I can deal with it for I have no fear of anyone or anything left in me. Living here all alone in the middle of nowhere, having to deal with the issues and people that I have to, I am now scared of nothing. I am not happy about this for to remain human, one must fear something … at the very least fear god. But I fear nothing. Perhaps these massive mountains have made me inhuman?'

Ruchi herself ascribed her distaste for her posting to the harshness of life in the high Himalaya, peopled with the stereotypical *pahari* male, even as she emphasized her *maidani* origins and identity. At least half of the 30 or so bureaucrats who lived in Kund hailed from the *pahar*. Strikingly, there was little difference between their narratives about Chamoli/Gopeshwar and those of the *maidani* bureaucrats. The top bureaucrats of the district – the DM, SP, CDO, SDM, two DFOs – were, in fact, *paharis*. Yet, they narrated the remoteness and backwardness of Chamoli in terms almost identical to Ruchi's. Pigg has described how distinctions between civil servants charged with administering *bikas*[9] (development) in Nepal are overcome, so that they are amalgamated into a distinct class which 'shares a life and an outlook with their compatriots of whatever regional origin in the civil service' (1992, p. 498). The section of state agents living in Kund, that I similarly study as a class-unto-itself, evaluated Gopeshwar, and the *pahar* per se, as a backwards step in their lives: this was a place where the style of life, the public amenities (that shape middle-class consumption patterns in contemporary urban India), and codes of behaviour and interactions with others, did not match their aspirations.

Everday work in Chamoli, too, possessed many a trying feature. The season of *yatra* (pilgrimage) to the prominent Hindu temple of Badrinath is an instance. Badrinath temple remains open from May through November. The opening of the portals of the temple in early May was followed by a veritable deluge of pilgrims aboard buses, trucks, cars, and motorbikes; the most pious making the pilgrimage on foot. Near Badrinath stands Hemkund Sahib, a Sikh *gurudwara* (place of worship), which adds heavily to the volume of pilgrims. The *yatra* was a source of pride for local residents, for at this time the magnificence and sacredness of this part of the Himalayas was openly acknowledged by all of India. Amongst the bureaucrats, however, the grumbling about Gopeshwar/Chamoli continued. As it was hard to call Gopeshwar 'remote' and 'dead' at a time when half of India was itching to reach it, the complaints during this period were directed at the sort of work the *yatra* period forced upon the state. The bureaucrats were constantly on 'VIP duty', which involved making painstaking logistical arrangements for senior state agents on pilgrimage – bureaucrats, politicians, judges – and escorting them round Badrinath temple and Hemkund Sahib. Further, at this time, their administrative unit came under the critical scrutiny of the aforementioned VIPs. While local residents took great pride in what they possessively considered 'their' temple, senior bureaucrats were left exhausted by the stresses associated with its location within their area of command.

At the end of the *yatra* season, came an even more demanding period in the lives of the officials in Chamoli: the onset of the Monsoons. In early July when the *yatra* was still on, though not at the frenetic pace of May and June, the heavens would open up. Mayhem would result. Landslides, destruction of houses and fields, trees and boulders falling down, waterfalls springing up in the unlikeliest of places, rivers swelling to alarming proportions, failure of telecommunications and power for days on end, road accidents, failure of milk, vegetable, cooking-gas and newspaper supplies coming up from the plains would become the norm. Chamoli would go, overnight it seemed, from being the cosmic centre of the Hindu universe to being, once again, a remote land that struggled to provide the basic amenities of modern life in India. Headlines such as 'Chamoli returns to the age of primitive man', 'Even in the 21st century no road, no electricity, no water, no food in the Abode of Gods' would scream from newspaper pages.[10] There would be constant talk of the lack of development (*vikasheen*), deprivation (*vanchit*), and backwardness (*pichadapan*) of the region. Officials would be left running from one accident site to another. Chaos would reign supreme, a chaos the senior officials could hardly control, given the limited physical and human resources in their hands and the unpredictability of the rains in this ecologically fragile region. During both the *yatra* season and the Monsoons, senior officials would be pointed out as directly responsible for the events unfolding before their eyes. When things went wrong, as they regularly did, the officials would be blamed for it by name and designation, by the vernacular press and the general public alike. Expectations from senior officials in Gopeshwar were, indeed, great.

Escaping Gopeshwar

A posting in to Gopeshwar was often described as being sent to *kala pani* (lit. black water). After the 1857 uprising, the British had established a penal colony on the Andaman Islands. Convicts bound for incarceration in the Cellular Jail located there had to be transported across the 'black waters', or the Bay of Bengal. British officials assumed that the journey across the sea led to 'caste pollution' and hence functioned in and of itself as a form of punishment. *Kala pani* is now everyday idiom, not in the context of loss of caste or pollution but rather to signify a punitive exile from home or a form of involuntary isolation.[11] Continuing the application of this idiom to Gopeshwar, a posting out from it was described metaphorically by officials as a release from prison. At the time of my departure from the town, when I went round the various offices to make my farewells, nearly all the officials congratulated me on having 'served my time in jail'. At their own farewell parties, the speeches were always loudly congratulatory on the richly deserved release, the escape from the constraints of this 'remote', 'underdeveloped' place. The relief on the faces of the 'escapees' was palpable. In Dehradun, I often met with officials formerly posted in Gopeshwar. Shuddering visibly, they would describe their time there as a dark, depressing, lonely period. Many would thank Lord Badri (Vishnu) for blessing them, not only by allowing them to escape from that station but also by letting them come away in one piece.

The narratives and remembrances of Chamoli that I recount above can be all seen as voiced 'spatial stories' in that they 'carry out a labour that constantly transform[s] places into spaces or spaces into places' (de Certeau, 1988, p. 118). The narratives above were transforming a place – the town of Gopeshwar designed by urban planners – into a space – an empty space from which one must escape. The uniformity of the buildings of Kund colony – constructed in the modernist architectural style characterizing all Public Works Department (PWD) buildings in contemporary India, their shuttered windows and derelict gardens, the silence that pervaded the colony, were all at odds with the hustle-bustle of life below in the Bazaar and the residential colonies there. As a space, in de Certeau's sense of the term, Kund was dead.

So far, I have concentrated on the experiences of residents of Kund. Given the locally elite positioning of this mobile *sarkari* community, it might not be altogether surprising that they dismissed Gopeshwar as a *mofussil* town. Their descriptions of Gopeshwar as a remote, backward place were also, however, shared by many other middle-class residents of the town, especially among the younger generation. The most pressing reasons for this were the poor quality of educational institutions and lack of employment opportunities in Chamoli. Those who could afford it sent their children for schooling to towns in the plains, such as Dehradun and Hardwar. Failing that, they were sent to Srinagar, Nainital or Almora. When these children reached college age, the urgency of seeking ways out of Chamoli increased tenfold. Funds were gathered, relatives and contacts ferreted out, colleges and polytechnics identified, and the children were shipped off to make a life for themselves. The pressure on young men to find educational and/or job opportunities was particularly intense. As someone who had experience and knowledge of the world beyond the *pahar*, my informants in Gopeshwar would frequently consult me on the best way through which their children could move away and establish themselves. Many a *chai*-time conversation, in the government offices where I spent the majority of my time, was discussion of exit strategies for the next generation. When not in government offices, I would spend time with three small NGOs. The NGOs were staffed with residents of Chamoli, all of whom stayed in Gopeshwar. All three organizations employed women and men in their twenties who held, at the least, an undergraduate degree. In these offices too, as well as at workshops and on trips to villages for events such as awareness generation or meetings, the conversation would revolve more often than not around possibilities of leaving Chamoli, either via employment or by enrolling for further studies. In the case of the unmarried women, there was the additional option of their parents finding them a groom who lived in the plains. NGO jobs were often seen as a stepping stone to better-paid and more stable jobs in Dehradun or even in one of the metropolises. While I was living in Gopeshwar, I thought these conversations always included me because I could act as a good '*bhagne-ke-chaare-ka* Consultant' (running-away-options-Consultant), as one inquirer memorably put it. I had noticed, however, that such discussions between the NGO workers continued even when I was sitting on the sidelines or during those long shared-Sumo or bus rides to Dehradun. Before my departure from Dehradun in January 2008, I noted that four of the NGO workers had successfully exited Gopeshwar. On my return to Dehradun in the summer of 2009, I met with them and they reeled off long lists of the similarly successful, and of those who had failed in their attempts to escape. Again, I noted just how quick the turnover had been and how these educated, aspirational young men and women had devised channels through which to, as they would often put it, *bhago* (run away). The ones who remained 'stuck' (*phase hue*) in Gopeshwar were objects of pity. The educated, younger people who worked with the NGOs, therefore, would agree with the *sarkari* elite that one should seek a life elsewhere from Gopeshwar. However, they differed somewhat in their motivations for leaving, which included not only the prosaic desire for better educational and employment opportunities but also a curiosity to savour the life of the 'happening' bit of India in Dehradun and other *maidani* towns. As with the officials hailing from the mountains, so also with this set of *paharis* I did not discern a *pahari* identity that manifested itself in a sense of attachment to the mountains.[12]

The younger generation, middle classes, and officials at the higher levels of the administrative hierarchy were, then, seeking to escape, to overcome the distance they constantly posited through use of the word 'remote'. However, the melancholia of Kund's temporary inhabitants, with their dreams of escaping Gopeshwar, was at odds with the feelings of many who lived *neeche* (down below). These long-term residents of Gopeshwar, or of this region of Uttarakhand, experienced a 'special, sensual and intimate attachment' to the mountains, which allowed them to feel as if they were in their proper place, a feeling that John Gray expresses with the phrase 'being-at-home in the hills' (2000, p. 3). To bring out this feeling more explicitly, I offer a short life history of someone who lived *neeche*: Mr N.

Mr N and I shared a desk in the District Rural Development Agency (DRDA) building in Gopeshwar. At the time I met him, he had been at the same job for 28 years, in this very office in Gopeshwar. Mr N hailed from a small village in Chamoli district. A *pahari pundit* (mountain Brahmin) by caste, his father owned a sizeable piece of cultivable land in their village, which was in the valley. The relative wealth of his family allowed him to attend Garhwal University in the town of Srinagar, where he was awarded a Bachelors of Arts (B.A.). Armed with this degree, Mr N set off to make his life and fortune in India's capital city, New Delhi, in the mid-1970s. In Delhi, his uncle helped him get a job fairly quickly with a private legal practice in Hauz Khaz, an up-market South Delhi enclave. Back home, his family was ecstatic at their son's evident success and promptly arranged his wedding to a suitable young woman of the same caste from a neighbouring village. The young Mr N came back home briefly to get married before returning alone to Delhi and to his accounting job at the law firm.

Six months later, Mr N ran away from Delhi. Every time he would tell me about his running away, he would laugh out aloud. 'I ran away from that madhouse' (*mein woh pagalkhane se bhag gaya*) he would tell me again and again, between loud chuckles, as if he could not believe his good fortune in having done so. Needless to say, Mr N's parents were less than delighted by their son's rash decision to quit his comfortable sinecure in the heart of the country. What made him do so? It seems he found the loneliness of life in the metropolis, so far from his family in the village, unbearable. The crowds and the traffic perplexed him, the rudeness of his colleagues and the abruptness of his superiors upset him. Even his material living conditions were poor, for he shared a small room with two other young men, both recent migrants to the city and both equally bewildered by it. At the time I knew him, Mr N had remained convinced that had he remained in 'the madhouse' (*pagalkhana*) he termed Delhi, he too would have 'gone mad' (*pagal ho jata*). So he decided to leave and return home to the *pahar* and to his outraged family. He knew he ran the risk of being unemployed forever, as secure jobs are very hard to come by in the mountains, but he preferred that fate to the one he was certain awaited him in Delhi. On his return he struggled to find a job for close to 3 years. In the end, however, 'Lord Badri came to my rescue' as he put it – Mr N won that most prized of jobs in the mountains, a *sarkari naukari* or a salaried government job, and in his very own district.

Mr N looked at his job in the DRDA as his reward from god for having the courage of his convictions. It had allowed him to build a life and a home in Gopeshwar close to his natal village and his parents. Mr N was not alone in his devotion to Chamoli. A few other permanent local staff who lived *neeche* in the District office had shunned opportunities of leaving the mountains and going to cities such as Dehradun or Delhi. Many had, like Mr N, returned home after brief, unsuccessful stints in such places. For these returnees from the big cities in the plains, Gopeshwar was the place where life could be lived. In that sense, they were diametrically opposed to the more senior state agents or to the aspirational young NGO workers for whom life was, most emphatically, anywhere but here. The case of Mr N and several of his colleagues in the district office, who could not imagine leaving Gopeshwar, indicates how experiences of place are differentiated across diverse subject positions.

The incessant production of remoteness

Villagers and lower-level development workers in Chamoli often equated their marginalized and underdeveloped condition with its low status ranking as a place, deriving from its 'remoteness'. One of the primary reasons for the failure of development attempts, according to local accounts, was the disengagement of state officials and NGO workers, who were alike interested only in finding ways out of this remote land. The very persons supposed to undertake and supervise the everyday labour keeping the state alive were either absent without leave or, when physically present, fretting over their wretched position and searching for avenues of escape.[13] Their open disgust at their location, which I was witness to, exemplified what residents of Chamoli know only too well: there is a pervasive hegemonic discourse of the remote, backward *pahar* in which the skilled, the rich, and the powerful – *maidani* and *pahari* alike – would never live for longer than they could help. There is, as I mention above, a long history to this discourse. The movement for statehood was publicly fought on the ground that it would overturn precisely this damaging conception of the *pahar*. The cruel irony is that the creation of Uttarakhand has done nothing to attenuate this discourse in Chamoli. In fact, by making the contrast between the *maidan* and the *pahar* even starker within the smaller circumference of the new state it has, I argue, actually accentuated it.

Figures attest to the skewed growth of Uttarakhand – its gross state domestic product (GSDP) grew by 11.6 per cent over 2000 – 2005 due to the surge in the manufacturing and service sectors. This growth has been restricted to the three plains districts of the State, with the remaining 10 hill districts, which house 53 per cent of the State's population, remaining more or less untouched by these two industries (Mamgain, 2008). It was estimated that many people would move to Gopeshwar from the surrounding villages to take advantage of the superior facilities it was to offer – accordingly, a 1995 Government assessment predicted that Gopeshwar's population would rise to 27,897 by 2006 (Government of UP, 1995). The census puts its actual population at a figure that is almost one-third less at 19,883. This, too, is a misleading number as it includes individuals registered as hailing from Gopeshwar but not actually residing there throughout the year. Due to high migration to the plains, especially seasonal migration by men in search of employment, local estimates put the long-term residents of the town at a much lower number. In startling contrast, the population of the towns in the plains of Uttarakhand has increased exponentially ever since the creation of the new state in 2000. While reliable statistics on migration from the hills to the plains after the creation of Uttarakhand are hard to come by, the common perception in Chamoli was that the only real 'effect' of the creation of the supposedly Himalayan state in northern India has been to depopulate the Himalayas it was meant to nurture. An oft-heard aphorism delivered with sadness by the older generation of *paharis* neatly catches this sense – the mountains are ending/finishing (*pahar khatam ho rahen hai*).

Gupta and Ferguson rightly observe, 'spaces have always been hierarchically interconnected instead of naturally disconnected' (1992, p. 8).[14] Gopeshwar/ Chamoli has always been connected to the plains of UP/Uttarakhand, but in an entanglement of power relations that casts the former pair in a particular light. This is a relationship of power that, many *paharis* assert, continues to deny the *pahar* access to the opportunities currently being proffered to the *maidan* of Uttarakhand. Statistics on out-migration or figures of regional economic growth in Uttarakhand do not, I believe, tell the whole story. And neither, for that matter, does the historical literature on the region that has, somewhat romantically, highlighted the *pahari*'s capacity to protest (e.g. Guha, 2001; Pathak, 1997). Rather, one must turn to the everyday practices that, as Lefebvre (1991) would have it, produce space.[15] It is in and through everyday narratives of remoteness and the omnipresent desire amongst prominent inhabitants to seek life elsewhere that Gopeshwar is produced as an empty space. Remoteness manifests itself and is experienced daily through various means: through the sheer emptiness of the state space, the shuttered windows and lonely eveningers inside crumbling houses, spatial stories, grimaces and muttered expletives. The melancholia of Kund's temporary inhabitants and the dreams of escape harboured by the younger generation of *paharis* need to be taken seriously as central to the production and reproduction of Gopeshwar as a certain type of space. Further, the unquestioning acceptance and description of Gopeshwar as 'remote' need to be critically interrogated. In this respect, the comparison with hill stations is salutary. The then-remote Himalayas were seen by the colonial rulers as a space of escape, as places to be actively developed, made habitable and lived within. They were valued for their beauty and climate and their distance from the steaming, thronging plains of India.[16] This image of the mountains allowed for certain hill stations to flourish. Gopeshwar, in contrast, is dismissed as remote and almost undevelopable; for the post-colonial inheritors of the state apparatus it is quite simply a place to be escaped from. In what follows we will consistently return to the theme of remoteness to see its concrete and – in the final case – bloody consequences for the residents of this region.

Endnotes

1 Official website of the District Administration, Chamoli, http://chamoli.nic.in/. Accessed May 20, 2009.

2 Looking down on hill people is a generic feature of hills-plains political cultures as the word hillbilly indicates. For instance, Li (2001) notes that hill people in Indonesia's upland Sulawesi frontier also judge each other by a set of standards derived from, and centered on, the coast. Much like the mountains of Uttarakhand, in Sulawesi too, the farther away in the mountains people live, the more backward they are generally considered to be.

3 The differences were temporarily subsumed under the common category of the *pahar* during the movement for statehood (Jayal, 2000; Kumar, 2000).

4 Mitchell estimates that close to eighty hill-stations existed during the colonial era (1972, p. 87). Not all of these, naturally, served as what she calls the 'official multifunctional hill station' but there were key ones – Simla, Darjeeling, Naini Tal, and Ootacamund – that became centers of colonial power.

5   It is worth pointing out that these escapes to hill-stations were not necessarily convenient. Thus, in the case of the summer capital, Simla, the entire Government of India would travel over 1200 miles from Calcutta, across the length of the Indo-Gangetic plain. Interestingly, Kanwar writes that this move was criticised on many grounds, one of them being 'the remoteness and isolation of the bureaucratic machine from the realities of the plains below for more than half the year' (1990, p. 43).

6   Lal speculates that the employment of the term hill-*station* is linked to the space's associations with notions of retreat, pilgrimage, and prestige or the achievement of a certain station in life. See: Vinay Lal, review of *The Magic Mountains: Hill Stations and the British Raj* by Dane Kennedy, *Socialism* 8.3 (September 1997):123–132, http://www.sscnet.ucla.edu/southasia/History/British/HillStations.html. Accessed July 2, 2014.

7   I lived in a single-room police barrack adjoining the 'servant quarters' in the back garden.

8   A tehsil is an administrative division in India carrying certain fiscal powers, especially control over land records, and encompassing a number of villages and municipalities. Chamoli district contains six tehsils within it.

9   My analysis is similar to Pigg's in that I am studying the social imaginary of a place and the implications such a depiction has for its inhabitants. She is concerned with asking how 'an ideology of modernization becomes assimilated into local culture' (1992, p. 492), whereas I wish to foreground how the seeming location of 'modernity' elsewhere makes people wish to flee from the particular place under study.

10 The 'Abode of Gods' is Uttarakhand's chosen sobriquet for itself. According to Hindu mythology, a large number of Hindu gods live in this region of the Indian Himalaya.

11 Anderson (2003) notes that the convicts did not fully share in the British representation of 'caste' and the 'losing of caste' through travel across the supposedly polluting waters. She convincingly argues that after Independence in 1947, nationalist historiography, popular culture (Hindi films such as *Kala Pani*), and the post-colonial state's representations have had the paradoxical effect of resurrecting the colonial state's discourse of the power of *kala pani*.

12 Pathak has noted precisely this lack of belonging as a reason for the weak anti-Tehri dam movement. He writes, '[i]t must be also understood that outmigration for the last 100 years has made the people of Uttarakhand careless and insensitive about their roots. They can leave their mountain home, land, pasture, forest and culture for just a house in Tarai-Bhabhar and Dun areas or in the plains anywhere' (2005, p. 3639).

13 In the literature of Economics and Political Economy, this phenomenon is often studied as 'absenteeism', which is understood as a singular problem that significantly affects administrative and welfare performance.

14 Similarly, Goswami writes that social spaces 'do not emerge from self-evident geographies, nor do they exist in mutual isolation' (2004, p. 5).

15 Goswami has built on Lefebvre's conception of the state as a spatial framework of power to focus on the production of the 'colonial state space' of India or the processes whereby 'the conception of India as a bounded national space and economy was brought into being historically' (2004, p. 5).

16 Arnold has brought out the role played by Romanticism in the love and admiration that the British often professed for the Himalayas. 'Few Europeans,' he writes, 'were unmoved by the Himalaya' (2005, p. 102).

The Paper State

2

The State Life of Law

Ordinarily, Uttarakhand makes an appearance in India's national English-language press only in relation to issues classified as belonging to the realm of 'nature'. Primary amongst these are calamities such as earthquakes, floods, global warming worries like the melting of the Himalayan glaciers, the damming of rivers, the poaching and trafficking of big cats, discovery of rare herbs, and the occasional paeans to the mesmerising beauty of the holy Himalayas.[1] In the summer of 2006 when I was reconnoitering the State, I was surprised to see Golu, the local folk god of justice, make an appearance in *Outlook* (a weekly English-language magazine), in a story that has stayed with me. Golu is said to be the son of a king from Champawat, the ancient capital of Kumaon. At birth he was spirited away from his parents by wicked stepmothers. After the mandatory period of struggle, Golu's story ends happily with his ascension to the throne. A shrine to Golu is located at the Chitai temple, 8 km from the hill station of Almora. Devotees of Golu attempt to attract his attention through a device which is intriguing as a form of worship, if familiar in other contexts: they petition him on government stamp paper, exactly as they would any state agency. The article describes this phenomenon:

'*Parampujya* (most venerated) Golu, says an appeal, in neat schoolgirl-devnagari script, on non-judicial Uttaranchal stamp paper, help me get through my exams ... or, get me a seat in a hostel ... get my son a job in Bangalore ... heal my father. Below the signature, occasionally, is an address, even a telephone number – just in case he decides to call. The petitioners aren't just from the hills, where Golu is a superstar – his name on trucks and shopfronts, his little icons sold in bazaars, his stories told in folk songs, his spirit invoked at *jagars* (seances)—but also from the plains of Uttar Pradesh (UP) ... Arbiter of land disputes, saviour of the swindled, rescuer of young women thrown out of their homes by nasty in-laws, court of appeal for senior officials protesting unfair transfers. Or even a disgruntled job applicant. Strung up among the petitions and damp with rain is a 13-page 2001 ruling of the UP State Public Service Tribunal, on a complaint filed by a man rejected for the post of solar astronomer. Grievance not tenable, says the ruling. Penned in a margin is the complainant's angry scrawl: Golu, do something'.

Do something

Something ... anything, after all, can be done by the Indian state only if it is written down on paper, if the *sarkari kaghaz* (official documents) are in order. A deep attachment to and fetishisation of state practices in an interaction with a non-state dispenser of justice are quite obvious here (c.f. Das, 2004). In recent years, increasing attention has been paid to the enmeshment of paper or documents with the state within a variety of contexts in South Asia and beyond (Tarlo, 2000; Bear, 2007; Hull, 2012a; Cody, 2013; Raman, 2012; Gupta, 2012). In this chapter, I join this conversation by proposing the concept of the 'paper state'. At the most obvious level, the paper state implies a straightforward description of the overwhelming material culture of the Indian state. As anyone who has ever so much as entered an Indian government office will attest, one is almost interred by the sheer overabundance of paper and files that occupies these spaces. In my offices in Gopeshwar, various blocks in Chamoli district, and the Dehradun secretariat, I was always surrounded by bundles of files tied up neatly in white cotton cloth and placed on and around desks, on ledges, and in cupboards. A few rooms in the Gopeshwar office complex contained nothing other than files, which earned them the title of 'store rooms' or 'file rooms' even if they were not originally designed to function as such. 'Paper state' also, of course, captures the historical antecedents of state formation on the Indian sub-continent, one that was premised upon the 'empiricist metaphysics' (Hull, 2008, p. 505) of colonial British rule and is evident in book and article titles such as 'government of paper' (Hull, 2012a), 'document raj' (Raman, 2012), 'Indian ink' (Ogborn, 2007), and the original 'kaghazi raj' (Moir, 1993). I personally find the term 'paper state' felicitous for it allows me to ethnographically describe the life that laws take on in the eyes of the state. It was in the files and documents that surrounded us in my many offices that NREGA, I was told, had been born and currently lived a quiet *sarkari* (government/state) life. Its fate, it was said, would be to join its many predecessors through burial in one of the file-mounds wrapped up, symbolically enough, in a white cotton shroud.

Sarkari zindagi or state-life

One day I asked the DDO (District Development Officer) how the NREGA was doing in the district. In response he picked out an advertisement placed by his office in the local Hindi newspaper *Aniket* and, drolly, read out:

'The NREGS has been operational in district Chamoli since the 2nd of February 2006. Its primary objective is to provide employment in rural areas for men/women willing to undertake manual labour for 100 days on works that shall create productive communal assets in their own village. So far 57,441 families have been registered under the NREGS and provided with job cards. The registered families contain within them 89,917 labourers. Under the scheme the total amount of money available in the district as a whole is Rs. 1654.92 lakh.[2] By October 2006, we had spent 269.64 lakh rupees and provided 16,411 households with employment'.

Tossing aside the typed-out advertisement (which fulfilled a clause in the statute requiring pro-active disclosure, in service of its aim of introducing transparency), he smiled and said, 'This is what *sarkar* says. God alone knows what the real situation is'. Right through the state establishment, the official picture – statistics and reports – of the performance of the NREGS was referred to as a '*sarkari*' (government/state-like) version of events, which is distinct from the *asli* or real one. It was for this reason that, as I mention at the outset, I had been repeatedly warned off from undertaking fieldwork in government offices. The vast quantity of paper that we were surrounded by was adjudged to be 'nothing, just government paper' (*kuch nahin, kewal sarkari kaghaz*). In India to dub something '*sarkari*' is, generally, to question its reality, to dismiss it as a paper tiger. The attempt here, however, is to take seriously the processes whereby the state life (*sarkari zindagi*) of a developmental law is created, to ask what forms this life takes. I will discuss the Wildlife Protection Act in the final chapter but here and in the three chapters that follow, I closely describe the enactment of NREGA as it was observed, described, materially executed, and, most critically, *officially proclaimed to have been accomplished*. I begin my discussion of the state by moving away from the space of the government office and Uttarakhand. Instead I take you first to central India in order to show how the tentacles of the paper state extend to touch the 'remotest' of places.

Show it to the state

I am in Kalahandi district in the State of Odisha. Nearly 86 per cent of Kalahandi's population lives below the poverty line, making it officially one of India's poorest districts.[3] I have travelled here, 1500 km away from Gopeshwar, impelled by an eagerness to see how my radical development scheme is playing itself out in a different region of India. I am part of an NREGA survey team led by Professor Jean Dreze, who was a chief architect of this law. The team includes students from Delhi University, Dreze's research group at Allahabad University, and some activists. I am assigned to a group that includes two students from Delhi University and two interpreters from a local NGO. Our assignment is surveying five villages of Kalahandi's Narla block. We have a fortnight to do so, which means we can spend about 2 or 3 days in each village. The task is to conduct interviews and group discussions and ask villagers to fill out the questionnaires that have been handed over to us.

Our first destination in Narla is an *adivasi*[4] village called Gigina, where the first jobs are to speak to local officials and to the elected village representatives, and to check their records of the NREGA. The Gram Panchayat office (GPO)[5], a rare *pukka* (permanent) construction in the village, is bursting at the seams with files. A long checklist of the forms and registers that should be housed at the level of the Gram Panchayat (GP) has been provided to us. Unsurprisingly, not even half of the listed documents are present in the GPO. In Chamoli too, when I would go to Block or panchayat offices, I would always be struck by just how many registers the operational guidelines (OG) of the NREGS require these offices to maintain, and doubly struck by the insouciance with which officials treat the absence of these very documents. In Gigina, the concerned officials feign ignorance or spin out complicated excuses to account for the missing documentary forms. They complain of their heavy workload and of the bizarreness of the NREGA's paperwork requirements.

At one point I ask to see a particular register. The *pradhan* (head of the gram panchaya) flatly refuses to show it to me. 'Show me a letter from the government (*sarkari chitthi*)', she snaps at me, 'and only then will I show it to you. This is all *sarkari* property ... cannot just show it to any person who turns up here from Delhi'. I produce a letter that has been issued and signed by the District Magistrate (DM) of Kalahandi, clearly specifying that we have full access to all NREGA records in the district. The *pradhan* hands it over to her son, who has been standing sulkily behind her. He reads it carefully, then nods his head at his mother, who produces the register from a cupboard and slams it down on the table in front of me. This register is supposed to list the names of all the labourers who have worked on the NREGS, mark their attendance and record the amount of wages paid to them. It is devoid of even a single entry. In the checklist in my hand, I write 'Register exists but is empty', and that is that.

Tired of dealing with files, reports, registers, letters, and other such documents being reluctantly provided to us by the irate members of the Gram Panchayat, we decide to make the trek down to another hamlet of Gigina to inspect a tank that has recently been constructed under the NREGA. This hamlet is located at a distance of 3.5 km from where we are. As we slowly walk down the dirt track that connects the two hamlets, I notice the *pradhan's* son zoom past us on his motorcycle. It is almost noon by the time we arrive at our destination. I head, at random, towards one hut. A middle-aged woman emerges at the doorstep dressed in a thin terracotta-brown cotton sari. She studies us for a second and before we have a chance to say anything, retreats back into the hut. Fairly quickly she re-emerges holding a box bearing an enormous lock. She unlocks this, removes a document with great care, and hands it to me. It is her job card. We are all surprised that she already knows that we have come, as everyone in Kalahandi puts it, to 'audit' the NREGA. I am even more surprised by how much she evidently prizes what turns out to be, yet again, an empty official document. I flip through it again to check if I have missed any entry. Blank pages stare back at me. She tells us that she has, nevertheless, done some work on NREGA projects in the village.

The woman, whom I call Vimla, walks us down to the site of the work. It is a gaping and empty hole in the ground posturing as the village tank. A thin sheet of rainwater has collected in it. It glistens angrily in the sun's glare. Next to this 'tank' stands a proud signboard, a product of the Right to Information Act (RTI), proclaiming the amount of money spent on the tank, the labour cost and capital cost components of that amount, the date of commencement of work, and the date of end of work. I am still holding Vimla's shiny new job card. The newness of it is suspicious even if it is kept under lock and key. I ask her when she received it. This morning, is the answer. The scheme was launched on 2 February 2006 with the proviso that job cards would be issued immediately after the registration of families desirous of work, with a maximum period of 15 days between registration and issue of job cards. I met Vimla over 20 months later on 17 October 2007.

It transpires that in anticipation of our 'audit', the *pradhan's* son, the contractor who has supervised the construction of the tank, and the PEO (Panchayat

Executive Officer) – 'those three' (*woh teen*) as the villagers refer to them – have hurriedly got together and issued job cards to all the families of Gigina, knowing as they do that this is the key object that can legally be used against them to show their gross neglect; that can serve as an indicator of wrong-doing (*gadbad*) in the operationalization of the scheme. It remains a mystery how news of our study reached the villages we are surveying, for we had tried to keep their identities secret as far as possible. The entire village has been given their job cards either this morning or the night before. I am not sure if 'those three' have handed out empty job cards because they have not had the time to fill them out, or because they genuinely do not know the significance of the job card in serving as 'an instrument of transparency'.

In my talk with Vimla, I discover that she has been paid less than one-third of what she is legally entitled to, and that too after much begging and pleading with the *pradhan's* son. Enraged by the knowledge that this incredibly poor woman has been cheated of amounts so precious to her, we march back into Gigina and decide to hold a village-level awareness meeting about the NREGA. We move from house to house requesting everyone to assemble in Vimla's backyard. This is a small hamlet of 20 or 22 households, but only about 10 men and women are in the village at present. Bimal, a local activist who is a member of my team, launches into a speech on the scheme and the villager's entitlements. Everyone listens politely but their mild disbelief is evident. Bimal is getting into the nitty-gritty of its implementation now. A couple of people show us their recent acquisitions – the job cards – and ask us what it does, what its point is. Is it just another identity card such as the 'below poverty line' card, does it get them subsidies on jobs like the ration card gets them subsidized rations?

Everyone in the assembled group has been employed on NREGA works under the supervision of the contractor, even if only for a few days. They have all been paid substantially less than the minimum wage rate. Further, the material for the tank has been bought by the contractor and is of very poor quality. Through the underpayment of wages and the purchase of cheap, substandard material, money has been 'eaten' by 'those three'. Between them they control the muster roll, the job cards, and all the funds, which come into the village in the name either of the *pradhan* or of the PEO (Panchayat Executive Officer). After all, in the normal course of events, who is ever going to come to Gigina to verify whether the job cards even exist, let alone whether their entries match the labourers' testimonies?[6] The villagers ask us what they can do to make sure they get paid the right amount of money. The only advice we have is to check what the officials write in the *pukka* (permanent) muster roll against their name and make sure they make the same entry in the job card. Also, the labourers cannot be paid less than the stipulated basic wage of Rs 55, and they must hold on to their own job cards at all times. This is the law (*kanoon*), says Bimal. The mention of *kanoon* provokes no response. Can something be done about the '*chori*' (robbery) that 'those three' have already done, asks a man. I promise to report it to 'higher authorities' even though I am aware that it will not result in any action (as, alas, it did not). The villagers tell me that we will need proof (*saboot*), though. I nod my head in agreement. One young man spies the camera dangling from my bag and suggests that I take a photograph of everyone holding out their blank job cards and 'show it to *sarkar*' (Figure 2.1).

'To whom?' I ask, amused.

'To them in Delhi', answers the bright young man who has already quizzed me on my place of origin.

Figure 2.1: Show it to *Sarkar*

'To the Prime Minister', answers another woman. They solemnly line up for the photograph that will serve as evidence (*saboot*) of the robbery (*chori*) of the poor (*gareeb*) by 'those three' in a small hamlet of Gigina in a region that remains, as a senior consultant on rural development to India's Planning Commission described it to me, the 'poster boy for poverty in India'.

Chatterji and Mehta point out that in order for slum dwellers in Mumbai to make demands of the state as its rights-bearing citizens, they must possess documentary proofs such as rent receipts, ration cards, and electricity bills. 'But over and above this, documentary claims are also ways by which slum dwellers can make themselves visible to the state' (2007, p. 131). In Gigina, the villagers wished to make themselves visible to the state by providing documentary proof of violation of their rights, which we had passionately read out to them minutes before from a government manual that outlines them. In the remaining villages of Narla, the aspect of possessing or holding documents turned out to be even more critical. Unlike the local 'big men/women' of Gigina, the other four villages had not been so efficient in taking the precautionary measure of producing correct government documentation on the NREGS. Many villagers had never seen their job cards, many had not even had them issued, most had been made to pay for them and/or for the photographs that are stuck onto them though the state is meant to provide them free of cost, and very few actually knew that they had the right to keep this valuable *kaghaz* (paper) in their own possession. In village after village we were told that the job cards were kept with the Panchayat Executive Officer or the local contractor or the *pradhan* or an altogether different entity such as, in one village, the temple priest. The mere possession of these flimsy pieces of cheap paper were seen, by many of the villagers of Kalahandi district, as a privilege, as a right that they could not believe the state would bestow on them, especially free of cost.

The village where India ends

I move from one of the poorest villages in India to one of her farthest and highest. I am now back in Chamoli district in Niti village (3450 m above sea level), which is described locally as 'the nation's last village'. The village is situated at the mouth of the similarly named Niti pass that opens into Tibet. Niti village has recently been provided with a *pukka* gravelled road that connects it to the national highways. Constructed by the Public Works Department (PWD) and Chamoli district's Development Department (*Vikas Vibhag*), this road is to be

Figure 2.2: The village where India ends

inaugurated in an elaborate ceremony, planned as a showcase for the work done by the State for the borderlanders. I am accompanying the senior district officials who have driven up here to do the honours of snipping a series of red ribbons on roads and bridges that shall, finally, join Niti to the rest of Chamoli district and, by extension, to the nation state of India.

Entering Niti is entering a world where all colours other than brown and white have been leeched out of the landscape (Figure 2.2). Naked brown mountains tower over the brown houses, thick white snow lies heaped around, patchily exposing the brown. I wander around clicking photographs. A cherubic young boy with shining brown eyes comes up next to me and, drawing my attention in one direction, gestures beyond it saying, '*Cheen!*' (China). 'This is where Hindustan ends', (*Hindustan yahan khatam hota hai*) he goes on to explain kindly. It is 2nd December, the peak of the Himalayan winter. The bitingly icy wind freezes speech and forces me to seek refuge in the Panchayat Bhawan (village office) of Niti, where I am graciously shown to a seat next to the chief guest of the road-to-Niti inaugural event, the Chief Development Officer (CDO) of the district. By my side sits the *pradhan* of the village and the Block

Development Officer (BDO) of Joshimath, the development block under which Niti falls. The CDO is looking a tad beleaguered, for there is a long line of people outside the village office (Panchayat Bhawan) holding *darkhaasts* (petitions), waiting to meet him. 'This is why I hate getting out of my office', he whispers to me in English in a room lit by some flickering candles and an old kerosene lamp. 'There are always these people waiting with their petitions for me at every step ... at least in my office I don't have to meet them. I just tell them to leave the letters with my Secretary'.

'This is your job', I scoldingly whisper back.

'No it's not!' he shoots right back. 'My job is merely to sign on files'. The CDO's grouse, common among his ilk, is that his job consists of nothing other than '*maaroing* signatures' (slamming out signatures) or 'giving *bhashans*' (speeches/lectures) all day long.

With a sigh of resignation, the CDO gets up and moves towards the entrance from where he can receive the petitions. I follow him out, curious to see what the demands are. The residents of Niti, all members of the *Bhotiya* 'tribe'[7], have politely queued up. They are all formally dressed to mark this important occasion. Some of them touch the CDO's feet on approaching him. Embarrassed by what he considers a 'feudal' gesture, the CDO, sharply, orders them not to do so. One by one, they come up to the CDO and mutter out their problems, which are mixed. Some relate to ownership of land, quite a few are requests for electrification and improved access to water facilities, two relate to pensions that have not been received for months, one or two complains generally about 'no development (*vikas*) work' happening in the village, which should be developed given it is the nation's last village. The residents of Niti practice transhumance or, in local parlance, Niti is a 'migratory village' that moves between its winter and summer locations with its flocks of sheep. The assembled crowd has come up from the summer village purely for the purposes of the road inauguration ceremony. An elderly lady tells me, 'This is the first time that I am seeing big officials (*bade adhikari*). Otherwise, where does *sarkar* have the time for us remote villagers?'

The CDO accepts all the petitions, signing some of them off to the BDO dancing attendance upon him and telling him to 'see to them'.[8] He goes on to deliver a short speech congratulating the villagers of Niti on their new acquisition – the road – that stands as proof of *sarkar's* wish to develop its frontier regions. The CDO is pleased to see that the NREGA has reached Niti before the road, for right at the entrance to the Panchayat Bhawan, just outside the room we are huddled into, is a large wall painting outlining the 'main points' of the scheme.

Largely for my benefit, the CDO asks the residents of Niti about the NREGS. Most of them have heard of it, a few have even worked on construction of a permanent embankment on the nearby river. None of them have their job cards with them. Some claim never to have been issued one, and the remaining have left them in their homes in the summer village. I ask them how much they were paid per day on this scheme. We are stunned by their answer, for the figures that emerge are between Rs 16 and 23 on an average for a full day's work. Not only is that, at the least, Rs 50 below the basic daily wage in Uttarakhand (Rs 73) but also the work conditions in Niti, given its high altitude and hard, icy-rocky surface, are exceptionally hard. The CDO looks visibly taken aback and turns to ask the BDO for his record on NREGA work in Niti. By law the Panchayat Bhawan must store a copy of the *pukka* muster roll (MR). Shaken by the sternness of the CDO's order to produce the documentary evidence this very instant, the BDO begins opening cupboards and rifling manically through the dozens of files contained within them, all by the feeble light of a candle. The villagers repeat that they were paid only this amount and that they were so disgusted by it that they are refusing to work on the scheme anymore. The Panchayat Bhawan is now being ransacked by the BDO and his underlings. No documents pertaining to the NREGA are found. The *pradhan* comes up and says, in front of his fellow villagers, 'they are all lying' (*sab jhooth bol rahen hai*) and glares furiously at them. No one says anything. The CDO breaks the silence by saying, 'Let us see what the papers say' (*dekhte hai kaghaz kya kehte hai*). He calls up the BDO's office in Joshimath and tells them to unearth all NREGA records related to Niti and keep them for him so that he can peruse them on our way back to Gopeshwar. The road-to-Niti inaugural party has been effectively ruined. We sip our sickly sweet *chai* in the candlelit room in an uncomfortable silence. Even the appearance of chocolate biscuits, rare and precious treats up here, cannot revive us to our previous buoyancy.

It is after 8 p.m. by the time we navigate the 4-hour drive back to Joshimath, which is still 2 hours away from our homes in the district headquarters of Gopeshwar. I accompany the CDO to the BDO's office where, miraculously, a few muster rolls and some registers of the NREGA work in Niti have been discovered. We pore over them, only to find that most of the rolls are incomplete, though some show that the workers had been paid far below the minimum wages despite putting in more than 9 hours of daily work. Every person assembled in the partially lit office is suddenly aware of the spectre of the law, which flickers beside us in the darkness of the winter night. The CDO, who is the highest in the hierarchy, quietly announces to his subordinates, 'We shall just have to treat these as *kachcha*. The *pukka* muster rolls better be fixed properly as must the job cards'.

Next morning, on our drive back to Gopeshwar, the CDO is defensive about his decision to 'cook the figures' but not apologetic. This is the only way this 'system' functions, he explains to me. 'The system' is manned by 'corrupt' functionaries who must get their 'cuts' somewhere. Further, the system cannot ever actually function by the rulebook. Despite this impossibility of abiding by the 'rule book', his job is to make it appear *as if* the rules have been followed to the letter, he explains to me over a long, revelatory car ride. It is evident that the CDO, like other state functionaries who dismiss '*sarkari*' accounts, knows that what is in state documents is not the truths but rather, in Tarlo's sense of the phrase, only a 'paper truth'. It is, after all, the material production of official facts and figures in job cards, muster rolls, registers, and reports, and the writing of appropriate letters, that attest to the health of the scheme, and by extension, to the performance of the state's functionaries. The malleability of official documents, the naked fixing of the books, is a taken-for-granted facet of the everyday life of the local state. In my final ethnographic fragment, I turn to a brief description of how writing on official paper sometimes happens or, as the verb itself importantly suggests, how things get *registered*.

The register of demands

Spring has arrived in Chamoli, bringing with it blooming jacaranda trees and scores of pilgrims. I am in a village called Maithana, which is located in the valley below Gopeshwar along the startlingly blue and perennially furious river Alaknanda. This is the ninth *gram sabha baithak* (village council meeting) that I have attended in the past week, and their dynamics intrigue me more and more. Village council meetings are annual events when the local state officials go to each village to mediate discussions on the development requirements of the village as a whole. For the purposes of the NREGA, this is the forum for 'the village' to sequentially list the works it would like to implement over the next year under the auspices of this scheme. In the language of the law, this list reflects the 'demand for work' and gets translated into a 'shelf of work'. If the unit for the beneficiaries of the programme is the hetero-normative nuclear family, the 'village' constitutes the collective body that will democratically deliberate upon the public works required by them and, subsequently, list these demands in the official register.

The *baithaks* (meetings) were conducted against the backdrop of what is colloquially referred to as *hulla-gulla* (roughly, shouting-screaming) often descending into *hatha-pai* (roughly, a brawl or boxing-kicking). My office-mates in Gopeshwar had cautioned me against attending the meetings to be held in some of the more *badmash* (rogue) villages. Initially laughing off their advice, I did subsequently have to nimbly skip out of two of the villages where the 'meetings' had turned into full-fledged brawls. The *hulla-gulla* at the meetings was highly informative and, often, rather entertaining, especially when recounted to my office-mates. On my return to my Gopeshwar office, I would be entreated to recount, in minutest detail, what had taken place at each meeting I had attended. Often, I would whip out my notebooks in which I kept 'minutes' of the meetings and would run through what transpired and who said what. My office-mates were well acquainted with most of the key actors and would fill in their backgrounds and their politics for me. In the process of reliving and recounting the discussions, fights, anger, jokes, and sarcasm of the villagers, it became even more evident just how much is at stake in the business of development (*vikas*). The entry of masses of development funds into the villages has created an entirely new rush to control them or to get close to them, in a region where the primary source of income and employment remains the state. It was precisely this urgency to control the development funds as they entered the village that made the village meetings, more often than not, extremely fraught events.

While my office-mates were keen to hear about the particular persons who dominated the meetings and what the *hulla-gulla* was about, I was more intrigued by an object that was the real centre of attention in these assemblies: the register. The register was normally in the possession of the GPVA (the Gram Panchayat Vikas Adhikari or the village-level development official), who would hold onto it tightly, and also make careful entries into it. Now, in the *baithak* I am attending at Maithana, the star billing of this register is again very much in evidence. The meeting is held in the verandah of the girls' school. Five men, including the GPVA, the village headman (*Pradhan*), and a representative from the Block office, sit on the floor with their backs to the wall. I note that Mr M, a local politician and a member of the Panchayat body at the Block level,

Figure 2.3: Village meeting goes on in hall beyond

has ensconced himself right next to the GPVA. Some women come and stand outside, their heads decorously covered for this dominantly all-male event. In the portico recline some *sadhus* (renunciates) who are taking a break from their pilgrimage on foot all the way up to the god Vishnu's abode in Badrinath temple (Figure 2.3). They listen interestedly. I go and seat myself in the inner core of the gathering for once, as I am eager to get closer to the scene of action, and am acquainted with the GPVA of Maithana, a shy yet friendly young man.

As in most village-level meetings, there is a flurry of movement with people coming and going, someone shouting out some detail that makes absolutely no sense to me without context, and schemes under discussion being changed every other minute. There is no narrative structure to this assembly, quite different from the ritualized performances I see in the English-speaking capital cities of Dehradun and New Delhi, or even the more somber Hindi-speaking ones in Gopeshwar. Someone walks in, snatches the register from the GPVA and flips through it. He then asks threateningly why there is no mention of fixing the dirt track that runs alongside his land and upto his house. The GPVA mumbles, 'No scheme (for it) ' (*yojana nahin hai*). The man scowls and stalks off. Another man demands that the GPVA read out what he has written in the register.

The GPVA complies, reading with a slight stutter the 'demands' that the villagers have made for a particular scheme. I have been in the meeting throughout and have never heard these demands voiced. I cannot help but say so. Mr M. shuts me up by saying, 'We decided this at our previous meeting'. The GPVA says, simultaneously, 'We think this is what they need ...' I am not sure who the 'we' in both these accounts are, but I hold my peace. The man who had demanded that the entries in the register be read aloud says, 'I don't trust this man. He has been bought' (*yeh khareeda gaya hai*). He tells the GPVA to stop reading and instructs him to hand over the register to me as he 'trusts' me. I begin reading with some difficulty, given the GPVA's horrible handwriting. Five minutes in, the man who ordered me to read has lost interest and walks off. Relieved, I hand the register back to the GPVA. The talk turns to the NREGA. Mr M. gives a short speech to everyone assembled, including the pilgrims, on the virtues of the scheme. In the same breath he lists the five things urgently needed in the village. A couple of men in the group say, 'no, no...', but not with much force. Mr M. sits next to the GPVA and begins dictating the works that shall be undertaken in Maithana under the NREGA. The first, I note, is the construction of a boundary wall between his farm and the commons. The NREGA is intended for construction work only on public property, and I see that the Mr M is careful to mention only the common land in his dictation. As the GPVA is writing obediently, a man with a large black moustache comes up next to me and whispers into my ear a long story of how these two have 'eaten' lakhs of rupees from the village funds, and there is no *lekha-jokha* (written stuff) to prove it. Two young men come up dressed in identical T-shirts with the American flag on them and, leaning over the register, whisper something in the GPVA's ears which I cannot catch. He nods in agreement. Mr M finishes dictating the five priorities of Maithana when it comes to the NREGA, and then promptly moves onto another scheme. It took all of 10 minutes and not once was the small assembly asked what work they needed that could be done under the NREGA in the village. In less than 10 minutes, the NREGA's destiny in Maithana for the next year was sealed in the register.

Surprising as it might sound, this was one of the better village-level meetings I attended. For one, it actually took place unlike many others that exist 'only on paper' or, more specifically, in the GPVA's register. Many a time I would make a long trek up to a village that was scheduled to hold a *baithak*, at least according to the lists sent to the Gopeshwar office. I would often find that the meeting had already taken place and the proof would be provided to me in the register, recording a list of demands and bearing a series of signatures from the officials concerned. However, when I would speak to the villagers they would be entirely ignorant of any such gathering and would never have been informed that it was scheduled to take place. Sometimes they would tell me that they went to the meeting but were summarily kicked out of it. Women, in particular, seemed to be regularly excluded from them unless they were, either themselves or through kin relations, part of the Panchayat system. In Maithana, on the other hand, the GPVA was present, as was the headperson, and a handful of other villagers kept dropping in. Of course the quorum requirement of the house was not fulfilled, but then it never was. In all, I attended 18 meetings during the 3-week period over which they were slated to be held in the district. Out of these 18, only 8 were actually 'held', in the sense that people were assembled and some pretence at a discussion was made. The remaining were never even convened, yet they exist in the registers with minutes of discussions and all the required signatures neatly penned in. Three out of the eight meetings that were held broke up, with people coming to blows with each other. The remaining five did not follow the prescribed script.

NREGA is, in its popularized discourse, keen to stress its 'demand-driven' nature and prides itself on being a 'people's legislation' that will usher in a profoundly participatory form of transparent and accountable government. I turn to the transparency and accountability clauses of NREGA in the next chapter to show their effects. My intent here is not to provide another critique of 'the new tyranny' of participation (Cooke and Kothari, 2001), but rather to highlight the objects and practices through which the state claims to have conferred participatory development in the specific context of NREGA. The state life of law, I am arguing, is made manifest materially. Here I have touched upon the role of job cards, muster rolls, and registers respectively in the process of giving NREGA a *sarkari zindagi* (state life). In their form and content, these documents abide by state regulations and when appropriately assembled, they attest to the successful enforcement of the law. To understand the operations of developmental law and the state we need to, then, study what Foucault describes as the 'witches' brew' (1991, p. 81) of practices that produce the paper state. A focus on the 'regime of practices' (*ibid.*) does not only give one a more realistic understanding of how the developmental state functions, it also pushes one to move away from overblown conceptualizations of the law's capacity to craft the social and introduce, in and of itself, a new politics.

The law is a spectre

A key distinguishing feature of the NREGA that its supporters repeatedly emphasize is that it is a law and not a (mere) scheme. Being a law, these people believe, makes it permanent, more readily enforceable, and capable of eliminating corruption by making the state 'transparent' and 'accountable'. This is a clear instance of what Riles describes as 'an instrumentalist conception of law', whereby a law becomes an instrument or a tool that will serve as a means to an end (2006a). The end is corruption-free rural employment provision, the means is the NREGA. Numerous studies have pointed out the limitations on the capacity of law, if not its outright impotence, to make radical changes; such studies have complained of how most of the more progressive enactments remain limited to existing only 'on paper'. This book is devoted to moving beyond the 'only on paper' criticism to show, first, why this is a common refrain in India and, secondly, demonstrating the context-specific effects of different legal assemblages. This endeavour does, however, beg the questions of what difference being a 'law' makes to the welfare-oriented programmes, and in what guise law makes its presence felt in the everyday life of the state.

Given the commotion that is made over the NREGA's being a law, in Delhi and within the English-language media and academia alike, I was somewhat surprised to note the marked silence on its legal status in Uttarakhand. The law did, at moments, mark an entrance into time and space but only fleetingly so. NREGA-the-law, in other words, commanded but a spectral presence in Uttarakhand. This ghost-like presence of the NREGA emerges from the following interlinked factors: ambiguities in the body of the legislation itself; a fair level of confidence that nobody would bother to use the legal recourse to take one to court/file serious complaints; and a generalized sense of confusion over a public works or employment-generation programme suddenly turning into a law, when such programmes have historically existed as schemes which are often withdrawn or re-branded.

Most officials and other involved actors knew that this programme was a *kanoon* (law) sanctioning punitive measures against non-compliance. But what these measures were, who was subject to them and under what conditions, remained obscured by a screen of fog. Even senior bureaucrats were confused by the most basic provisions of the NREGA, often turning to me to ask for clarification. One of the most mystifying aspects of the NREGA remains how difficult it is to understand what it means to 'violate the law'. Chapter VI, Section 25 of the statute deals with 'penalty for non-compliance': 'Whoever contravenes the provisions of this Act shall on conviction be liable to a fine which may extend to one thousand rupees' (The Gazette of India, 2005, 10).[9] This clause, weak to begin with, is practically overturned by Section 30, which protects public servants from having any legal action taken against them if they have acted in 'good faith'.[10] In other words, the consequences for violating the NREGA are negligible. If the parent statute is technically toothless, then a move by the Ministry of Rural Development (MoRD) in 2009 has removed the bite even from the operational guidelines. The Ministry has made clear that these guidelines are not binding but are only a template for 'best practice'. This caveat has led to the implementation of the NREGA in what Dreze and Siddhartha describe as a 'dangerous vacuum. One aspect of this vacuum is the absence of clear remedies against infringements of the Act. Curiously the NREGA talks the language of rights but there is virtual silence on available remedies when rights are violated' (2009, p. 7).

In addition, there is no understanding of which agency or person is truly responsible, in the first place, for conferring the rights guaranteed by NREGA. For instance, one cannot pinpoint who, actually, is the guarantor of this rural employment guarantee. Is it the District Magistrate (DM), the CDO, the DDO, the village-level officials, the *pradhan*, or the local Member of Parliament (MP)? I attended a workshop held for training District Magistrates (DMs) drawn from all over India, held in the Lal Bahadur Shastri National Academy for Administration (LBSNAA) in Mussourie in Uttarakhand over 17 – 19 July 2007. At this event, the attending DMs posed precisely this question to the Joint Secretary (JS) NREGA at the Ministry of Rural Development (MoRD).[11] After much prevarication, they responded, 'it is obvious the guarantor is the DM', much to the astonishment of the assembled DMs. Their response was to protest against the unfairness of putting them in such a position (if indeed this position exists; the texts do not confirm it), especially as they have dozens of development schemes to look after. As one of them rather bravely told the JS, they do not even have time to read the operational guidelines, far less to make sure that they are meeting the guarantee for each and every villager who appeals for work. This meeting descended into a face-off between New Delhi, represented by the Ministry officials, and the States, represented by DMs. The DMs repeatedly blamed the Ministry for making the NREGA too complicated and for not providing them with adequate personnel to push the scheme through. The Ministry, on the other hand, blamed the States for not taking the scheme seriously and not working as they ought to. A senior Ministry official ended the increasingly fraught discussion by telling the DMs that they were all 'illiterate' if they could not read the operational guidelines and therefore should be paid NREGA-mandated wages for unskilled workers; at least then some wages would get paid out.

I never once saw the text of the NREGA in any of the offices in Chamoli. For close to a year after its launch, only an English-language copy of the operational guidelines was available in Chamoli, that too only in the Gopeshwar office. Even after a Hindi version was produced and a few copies distributed, almost none of the Block or village-level staff admitted to reading it. In meetings and training sessions, the lack of knowledge of even the most basic provisions of the NREGA was more than evident, much to the disgust of the district-level officials. The NREGA was, in practice, implemented by lower-level bureaucrats on the basis of precedent and through the continual performance of the practices that constitute the everyday life of the state: working on documents of all sorts, following particular processes, convening and attending meetings, and producing the correct statistics and documents within the stipulated time period. Interestingly, even those officials who knew that the NREGA was a law would still talk of a time in the near future when it would vanish. Development plans (*vikas yojana*) of this nature have come and gone with a remarkable frequency. The presumption was that the NREGA, too, would soon follow its predecessors. Technically, the removal of NREGA would involve an extremely complicated process and will have to be undertaken through repeals in the Indian Parliament. Never once was this technicality discussed in Uttarakhand. Despite general awareness that the NREGA was a *kanoon* (law), the presumption continued to be that it would, someday, simply die the natural death of all *sarkari* schemes.

In Block offices and villages, the awareness that the '*rozgar* guarantee' (employment guarantee), or even just 'Guarantee' as it was locally termed, is rooted in a law was quite low. Many a time *pradhans* and GPVAs would be surprised when I would inform them of it. They would then puzzle over what difference it made that this development scheme was a law (*kanoon*). The only question that truly engaged them was whether they could be sent to prison because of it. But the fear of imprisonment was never particularly strong, not only because there was no precedent for such punishment in Uttarakhand but also because it would entail an extremely complicated process implicating a large number of people through the entire chain of command. Senior officials were cognizant of the capacity of the law to frighten and, therefore, utilized it as a rhetorical device in meetings and public gatherings. They would refer to the law (*kanoon*) in order to impress upon their subordinates the need to work harder and to be more careful with this scheme than with others. Being more 'careful' directly translated into a better maintenance of the paperwork. In one sense, then, through the invocation of the spectre of the law, the NREGA answers to the instrumentalism that underpins it. However, this is not in the realist means-end way that so much of development planning assumes. Further, the fear of going to jail should not be overstressed, for it was not consistently present. The legality of the NREGA did disturb those who were aware that it was a *kanoon*. Yet it did so in fleeting moments of fearful wonderings that ruptured the normalcy of the everyday. Otherwise, on an everyday basis, there was little consciousness of the Guarantee being emplaced in legislation. Even when State functionaries did speculate on it, it was soon forgotten, to be replaced with grumblings about the mountain loads of 'paperwork' it required in order to be implemented. The real distinguishing feature of the NREGA, for its primary implementers, was not that it is a law but rather that it brings a new form of work – all enacted through and on paper. In the next chapter, I focus in detail on the new paperwork to show its counter-intuitive results as well as its originary mooring in the desire to render the state transparent.

Endnotes

1   A case in point are the apocalyptic images of flooding and large-scale devastation in June 2013 after a cloudburst and glacial breach near the Kedarnath temple in Chamoli's adjoining district of Rudraprayag. This horrific disaster led to the death of approximately 5,784 people. I would argue that this event made it to national headlines and led to the marshalling of an enormous humanitarian effort largely because the vast majority of the fatalities were pilgrims visiting Kedarnath temple as well as Badrinath temple in Chamoli district.

2   One Lakh = 100,000.

3   The official district portal for Kalahandi on the Government website for the State of Odisha, http://www.kalahandi.nic.in/. Accessed July 2, 2014.

4   Adivasi literally means 'indigenous people' or 'original inhabitants' and is used in place of 'Scheduled Tribes' that is a constitutional classification made by the Indian state even though the two are not coterminous. See: http://www.pucl.org/Topics/Dalit-tribal/2003/adivasi.htm. Accessed January 7, 2014.

5   Gram Panchayat is the village level office in the Panchayati Raj system, which allows for decentralization of administrative power down to the lowest unit of the village (gram).

6   The law mandates routine inspections of the job card. In the ten months I spent in Chamoli, these inspections only ever occurred, to the best of my knowledge and in my experience, 'on paper'.

7   Bhotiyas are classified as a Scheduled Tribe (ST) by the Indian constitution. In Chamoli district according to the 2001 census they constitute 10 per cent of the total population. As Ramble has noted, 'Literally, a Bhotiya ("Bhote") is someone from Bhot. "Bhot" in turn derives from the Tibetan word "Bod" meaning Tibet, via the late Sanskrit "Bhotah" (1997, p. 391). Bhotiyas inhabit regions along the Indo-Tibetan border and, historically, carried out trans-Himalayan trade. Their population in this region has been on a decline ever since the sealing of the border after the 1962 Sino-Indian war, which resulted in the rude termination of all cross-border trade.

8   This 'routine' bureaucratic practice appeared to greatly please the petitioners. Cody has noted the value placed on the seeing of the DM by petitioners in Tamil Nadu. They had hoped that a meeting with the DM would allow for an 'affective claim' to be made of the state 'through eye contact' (2009, p. 368).

9   Rs 1000 = approximately £10.

10 It reads: 'No suit, prosecution or other legal proceedings shall lie against the District Programme Coordinator, Programme Officer or any other person who is, or who is deemed to be, a public servant within the meaning of section 21 of the Indian Penal Code in respect of anything which is in good faith done or intended to be done under this Act or the rules or Schemes made thereunder' (The Gazette of India, 2005, p. 11).

11 The National Workshop on NREGA held at the LBS National Academy of Administration, Mussoorie, Uttarakhand from 17 to 19 July 2007.

3

The Material Production of Transparency

NREGA was widely dismissed as an 'un-implementable' programme by lower-level officials and members of the Panchayat system. As I started travelling to different villages, on my own or as part of a larger entourage, I struggled to find any public asset built under NREGA or to meet any labourers who had worked under the scheme. NREGA was conspicuous by its absence. This lack of visibility of NREGA was perplexing given the socio-economic profile of Chamoli, which was one of my primary reasons for choosing it as my field work site: official statistics claim that 47.5 per cent of its population lives below the poverty line; by all accounts unemployment is the biggest problem. For these reasons, Chamoli figures on the Indian Planning Commission's list of '200 most backward districts' in the country, making it an eligible recipient for the very first round of benefits dispensed under the NREGA. Further, there is a high level of distress out-migration of male employment-seekers to urban centres in the plains, where they typically end up working as menial and/or manual labour. Surely, I had reasoned, villagers would prefer working in their own villages on what the scheme describes as 'productive assets' to seeking similar forms of work in alien and much harsher conditions in the plains? Employing the same logic, NREGA sets up curtailment of distress migration as one of its key objectives.

To my queries on why there seemed to be no work happening under the auspices of the programme, senior officials and development practitioners alike had a ready answer. They highlighted certain defining features of Chamoli: the district has a primarily 'upper' caste,[1] highly literate population[2] with a large number of female-headed households, as men tend to out-migrate to the plains in search for jobs.[3] This sort of a population, they claimed, makes for a very low demand for public works programmes. Further, Chamoli's location in the middle and the upper Himalayas, with 50 per cent of its landmass under snow, makes it a difficult region in which to undertake laborious public works; most unskilled and manual labour tends to be outsourced to immigrant Nepalis who are not legally entitled to work under the NREGA; and the daily wage rate of Rs 73 is too low in a market where private contractors pay anything between Rs 100 and 150 per day for unskilled labour. I contend on two grounds that these were not the factors impeding implementation of NREGA. First, in my own interactions with villagers, they evinced a deep interest in the scheme. There is an almost total lack of employment opportunities in these villages and the reliance on remittances from family members who have out-migrated to the plains and are sending money home, makes for a precarious existence. In this context, NREGS was welcome and one particular item from the permitted list of works – construction of roads – was very much sought after. Secondly, rural employment programmes of a very similar form to the NREGS have been operational in the district since 1980. The district bureaucracy clearly told me they faced no problems in implementing these programmes. What, then, was the difference between these previous employment generation/public works programmes and the shiny new NREGA? In this chapter, I argue that the difference arises directly from the transparency clauses that the law has built into itself. How can an unalloyed public good such as transparency complicate the implementation of a welfare programme? To understand this capacity of a transparency-inducing legislation to impede the very process of governance, we need the context and history of developmental efforts by the Indian state.

The ogre of corruption

Despite the commotion around the NREGA, public works programmes in India can be traced as far back as to the Famine Codes instituted by the colonial British regime in the latter half of the nineteenth century (see Mathur 2013). These Codes were to remain 'the basic doctrine of famine relief until the 1970s' (Brennan, 1984, p. 91). From the late 1970s, the post-colonial Indian state began to launch a series of government programmes focusing on food security and employment generation in rural India. The objective of the NREGA, in fact, is similar to that of the plethora of employment schemes/public works programmes that has preceded it: provision of employment and wages to rural citizens. Further, it swallows up extant schemes, allowing for the establishment of a clear genealogy of rural employment programmes in post-1947 India. Public works programmes in India have traditionally been associated with high levels of corruption or, as the popular euphemism in policy circles goes: 'leakages'. The massive budget that the NREGA would command would surely, the critics claimed, only precipitate corruption in an already faulty delivery system. Thus, Swapan Dasgupta (2005) could write an article in the English-language newspaper, the *Pioneer*, with the title 'Rename NREGA as Corruption Guarantee Scheme' and Surjit Bhalla (2005) in *Business Standard*, one entitled 'Corruption with a human face' (a dig at the UPA's slogan of 'Development with a human face'). Reading the academic, official, and popular literatures on public works programmes in India, it is striking that the dominant theme is 'corruption'.[4] Corruption, it appears, is what explains their failure to develop. Advocates of the NREGA responded to these well-founded allegations of corruption with a nod towards the law. They pointed out the very different legal status enjoyed by this programme and the strong transparency safeguards that have been built into what a prominent proponent describes as a 'new-age legislation' (Dreze, 2009). Laws also, continues this argument, create durable entitlements, which will empower the labourer and allow he/she to challenge the corrupt state. The legality of the NREGA, argue its formulators and interpreters, will make sure that this social security measure will be implemented with the highest level of efficiency. Deviations from the law would be minimal as, naturally, no rational actor wishes to lay him/herself vulnerable to penalties by the state. NREGA, then, is premised first on the idea of *homo oeconomicus* or the economical man, who shall be self-animating and shall wish to appeal rationally to the state for her engagement in productive labour for a fair and equitable wage, but also, secondly, it has in mind its implementers as *homo penalis*.

The operational guidelines (OG) of NREGA state: 'Commitment to transparency and accountability runs throughout the NREGA. This commitment also flows from the Right to Information Act (RTI), 2005' (2008, p. 51). The RTI was passed at the same time as the NREGA in 2005, and is directly aimed at making the Indian state 'transparent' by overturning the terms set up, under the Officials Secret Act of 1923, against disclosure of state information. The NREGA is popularly and in official circles described as the 'sister legislation' to the RTI. The NREGA was passed in the Indian parliament on the heels of RTI, with transparency in NREGA stemming from, in the words of the OG, 'the letter and the spirit of the RTI' (Government of India, 2008, p. 56). The OG repeatedly invokes the RTI and states that, in the implementation of the NREGA, a proactive disclosure of information and public access to key records must be ensured at all levels and at all times. Both these 'sister legislations', foreground the centrality of releasing and exhibiting official documents.

Activists such as Aruna Roy and Nikhil Dey (2005), who strongly lobbied for the NREGA and the RTI, are very cognizant of what they describe as the 'diabolical significance' of documents and files for the destinies of people in India. The RTI campaign, in fact, was premised on the very belief that enabling citizens to inspect hitherto-inaccessible state documents would result in a drastic reduction in corruption and, hence, in the exploitation of people. In her analysis of the RTI, Amita Baviskar makes the important point that, 'the actual implementation of such an Act is only possible thanks to a somewhat peculiar characteristic of the Indian bureaucracy – its passion for paper. Despite innumerable and routine subversions, rational-legal record-keeping about its decision-making process remains the hallmark of Indian government. In a system created by the colonial government for internal transparency and oversight, the paper trail is painstakingly laid out' (2006, p. 18). Baviskar goes on to note that '[i]t is this commitment to documentation that makes it possible for the state to now be legible to its citizens' (*ibid.*).

Thus, the body of the law, as well as the discourse of activists, explicitly articulates a foundational assumption that transparency is materially produced or, in other words, transparent governance emerges from control over and access to state documents and records. There is a belief that official information – in its tangible, material form as a document – will allow anyone to, so to say, speak truth to power. The promissory value of information is evident in the formulation (Hetherington, 2012). Both the NREGA and the RTI are premised on the triple assumption that the prescribed documents are actually being produced by the state bureaucracy, that these pieces of paper are accurate representations of reality, and that subaltern subjects can access and hold on to these papers. My observation of the practices through which the NREGA was endowed with a reality in Uttarakhand leads me to seriously question this entire assortment of assumptions, which underpins the creation of transparent governance via law in contemporary India. It leads me to question, *pace* West and Sanders (2003), the very meaning of transparency. As they write: 'What, after all, is claimed when the operation of power is described as transparent? What is *seen through*, and what, then, is *seen*?' (2003, p. 16). I argue that what we were seeing in the implementation of the NREGA in Chamoli district were vast quantities of paper and *very little else*. I exhibit this claim by following the 'trajectory of work' (Riles, 2006b, p. 80) that needed to be undertaken in order to achieve progress in the implementation of the NREGA.

Implementing a transparency-inducing law

How does the NREGA in its schematized form as the National Rural Employment Guarantee Scheme (NREGS) come to be converted from a law issued from New Delhi into developmental practice in a distant Himalayan borderland district? The NREGS begins when rural households exercise their entitlement to register as workers under the NREGA by making an appeal to the state, normally the *Gram Panchayat* or GP (village council). This appeal, the operational guidelines say, can be either oral or in print. If in print it can be on plain paper with relevant details of the appellant such as name, age, sex, and caste listed, or it can be on a printed form made available by the State government. After the details of such an application are verified by the concerned official, the household should be issued with a document called the job card. When a household is registered and has his/her job card in its possession, he/she can appeal to the state for work. This appeal is to be made by submitting an application in writing either on a blank piece of paper or on a printed proforma which the GP should make available free of cost. The applicant should be given a dated receipt for their application for work. If the applicant is not provided with work within 15 days from the date on this receipt, then an unemployment allowance at approved rates must be provided to them. If work is provided, it should be chosen from the list of permissible works that the NREGA spells out and from the shelf of projects that all villages are supposed to have participated in preparing at the beginning of the year. Further, this shelf of works must have obtained technical and administrative approval from the correct authorities. During the execution of such work, it is imperative to maintain a muster roll. The muster roll is another key document and, like the job card, is required to conform to the format prescribed by the operational guidelines; it must bear its own unique identity number as well as certification by the Programme Officer (PO). Further, '[t]he muster roll will indicate the job card number and name of the worker, days worked. Workers attendance and the wages paid will be shown against each name with the signature/thumb impression of the worker' (Government of India, 2008, p. 30). Crucially, the operational guidelines state that '[n]umbered Muster rolls will be maintained on the work site. No *kachcha* (temporary) muster roll is to be used'. Workers must be paid their wages within a fortnight of the date on which work was undertaken. With the objective of aiding transparency and making villagers 'financially literate' there is now a drive to open bank accounts for all NREGS workers and to transfer all financial transactions to this medium. In Chamoli, while I was there, the village-level development worker (GPVA) or the village headperson would distribute the wages in cash to the workers. In any case, through whatever means the wage payment occurs, it must be entered in the concerned job cards, which must always remain with the households that own them. The same figures and names must appear in the *pukka* (permanent/original) muster roll.

Briefly, this is how the NREGS is intended to be implemented in the village. Each and every process, with only one exception, can take place only after or through an impression made on paper, when an official document has been produced or transacted. The single exception to this documentary rule is the making of an appeal for registration of a household under the NREGS, which, technically, can be made orally. This is because the 'number of households registered' is a 'target' for lower-level government functionaries, which makes it, as an official put it, 'safe' to be conducted in a non-written format. The everyday life of the district and Block officials as well as the village-level workers is spent labouring on producing these documents through which the NREGS was endowed with an official reality. While all development schemes operate on similar bureaucratic principles, the NREGS is distinguished by the sheer volume of paperwork and precision in detailing it requires. This meticulous documentation is, I slowly gathered, intimately tied to the drive for transparency.

The operational guidelines of the NREGS declare that it signals a 'paradigm shift' from previous schemes (Government of India, 2008, pp. 2–3). Government functionaries in Chamoli would agree that the NREGS marks such a paradigm-shift. However, their rendition of the distinction between this scheme and its predecessors is somewhat different from that proclaimed in the authoritative texts of the NREGA. Political declarations accompanying the law dwell on its rights-based character, the legal guarantee it provides, and transparency – accountability – participation linkages. In Chamoli, and in contrast, the primary overarching distinction – one made by every single government functionary I spoke to, right across the board – was the tremendous increase in the 'paperwork' (English word used) that the NREGS brought in its wake. Over the 10 months that I spent with government officials there, it was paperwork that occupied and, in fact, overwhelmed them as they went about their task of implementing the NREGS.

In the section explaining the 'paradigm-shift' effected by the NREGA, the operational guidelines read:

'NREGA has extensive inbuilt transparency safeguards:

a. Documents: Job Cards recording entitlements (in the custody of workers), written application for employment, Muster Rolls, Measurement Books, and Asset Registers

b. Processes: Acceptance of employment application, issue of dated receipts, time bound work allocation and wage payment, Citizen Information Boards at worksites, Vigilance Monitoring Committees, regular block, district and state level inspections and social audits (Government of India, 2008, pp 3–4).

Not only are documents listed as a key tool among the safeguards of the scheme, but also, all the processes described above can only be made visible on paper. Acceptance of an employment application, which is written on paper, is said to have happened through the issue of another document, a dated receipt. Wage payments are said to have been done on time once the money had been withdrawn from the bank and entered in the ledger as being distributed to workers. The muster roll and job card, in addition, are to carry proof of this with the exact amount and date of receipt written down in them. The 'citizens information board' that is to be displayed at every worksite, listing details of the basic costs of each asset created, though not made of paper, is an inscription on a permanent surface that is displayed for all to see and read and, perhaps, to photograph and file away as evidence. Additionally, since nobody really has the time, energy, or money to travel to distant mountain villages and check if the 'citizen's information board' has been erected, it is in receipts for the construction of such boards that evidence of their reality is produced for the state. The vigilance monitoring committees existed once it said so 'on paper' in the form of a certificate listing names of the members and carrying their signatures/thumb impressions; inspections and social audits were said to have taken place only once they were produced as reports 'on paper'. In short, 'transparency' is said to have been accomplished through the production and circulation of the correct documents. Furthermore, in the attempt to make the state system 'transparent', a plethora of new documentary practices have been ushered in by this legislation.

In Chamoli district, the burden of producing and transacting with the prescribed documents within the stipulated time frames meant a lot of pressure on an already frail development bureaucracy. A district is divided into three administrative levels: the village, the Block (which oversees a certain number of villages), and at the top, the district which encompasses both these levels, and which reports further up the hierarchy to the State capital and/or to New Delhi. In order to understand the quantum and form of paperwork involved, we need to dwell further on the specificities of what each level is supposed to undertake. At the level of the village, the *Gram Panchayat Vikas Adhikari* (village council development official, or GPVA) is responsible for administering the NREGS. This involves accepting applications for registration, verifying every applicant household's details, registering such households, issuing job cards, accepting applications for work, issuing dated receipts in return, preparing and maintaining the shelf of works and the annual development plan, creating work estimates, getting estimates technically and administratively sanctioned by the district office, issuing work orders, responding to every applicant for work with written invitations to begin work, maintaining the muster roll, checking the supervising engineer's measuring book (MB), purchasing the materials required for construction (such as cement or grit) and keeping a financial record of such purchases, overseeing the work, making payments within a week or a fortnight after estimating wages due to each worker, and simultaneously making entries in the muster roll and job cards. Each GPVA had at least six to eight village councils or GPs under him, each of which comprised several villages that might be scattered around the mountainside. In addition, the NREGS was but one of the many development schemes that GPVAs had to oversee. Indeed, it was not uncommon for them to have more than a dozen schemes operating simultaneously in each village. What worsened this burden of work was the majority of the scattered Himalayan villages remaining unconnected by roads. Unlike the plains, where one could visit multiple villages in a day in 'the jeep' that Ferguson and Gupta (2005) have identified as the vehicle of state surveillance, in the high mountains of Chamoli it could take hours to climb up to a village located miles away from a road.

Some of the tasks described above are, officially, the responsibility of the Programme Officer (PO) of the NREGS. In Uttarakhand, the Block Development Officer (BDO) or the chief manager at the Block level was the appointed PO; but it was virtually impossible for him to, for instance, write to each household in his Block inviting them to begin work or to issue a dated receipt of application for work. Approximately 60,000 families were registered under the NREGA in Chamoli. They were divided into nine Blocks, which means that on an average, each BDO would be answerable to over 6,500 households. In any case, the processes and documents described above were merely what one had to undertake in the village. There was an altogether different system of reporting at the Block level, which included written reports, photographs, and entries in hosts of registers, particularly the financial ledgers in which every rupee spent was noted down. The Block was supposed to collate all the information from the village level, along with directly overseeing the work in every village. The only way to cope with the sea of documentation required of the NREGS was to induct more personnel who would work solely on this all-important 'flagship scheme' of the ruling coalition of parties in India at the time of my fieldwork. Thus, an NGO was hired to recruit some additional contract-based staff. The new NREGS-specific staff was described as consisting of 'professionals': engineers, Masters in Business Administration (MBA), diploma holders, and computer experts. Despite the presence of these 'professionals', officials continued to complain of the excess of (paper)work, which they claimed was making the scheme 'unimplementable'.

The crisis of un-implementability

During my time in Gopeshwar, a mini-crisis was brewing in the implementation of the NREGA. The district authorities had initially anticipated widespread popularity for the scheme and accordingly, Chamoli's annual plan for the financial year 2006 – 2007 had projected a 'demand for work of NREGS' amounting to Rs 68 crore. Of this total demand, the Ministry of Rural Development (MoRD) in Delhi had released a first instalment of funds amounting to Rs 16 crore; 60 per cent of this money, i.e., about Rs 11 crore, had to be spent before the second instalment could be released. Between February when the NREGS had been launched and November, only Rs 2.6 crore had been spent. This created an intense pressure on the district administration to spend more money as quickly as possible, so that they could at least appeal to the Centre for a second instalment of funds in the same financial year. This failure to disburse the funds that had come into the district at the beginning of the financial year, and on the basis of the annual development plan that Chamoli had prepared and sent up to the Centre, was startling. In meeting after meeting, letter after letter, senior bureaucrats would thunder at their sub-ordinates to spend NREGS funds. The utilization of funds (*paisa kharcha karna*) issued from New Delhi is, after all, the primary objective of development bureaucrats. It is upon utilization of funds that a scheme is believed to be officially implemented. Yet, the district struggled to fulfil this objective. Why was the district development bureaucracy unable to spend the funds it had asked for and received? After all, rural employment programmes of a very similar form to the NREGS had been operational in the district since 1980. Further, there was a lot of political pressure from the national and State capitals to implement this flagship scheme of the Government of India. Young professionals had been hired just to work on the programme; a variety of training workshops were constantly being organized; manuals, letters, and guidelines were being posted into the district; monitoring and evaluation were being undertaken. Surely just paperwork could not make a scheme that was flush with funds unimplementable? As I paid closer attention to the much-bemoaned paperwork, I came to realize that it was not the volume of paperwork but rather the work that *certain transparent-making documents were doing* that was creating a crisis of implementation.

This claim about the upsetting nature of transparent-making documents may be illustrated through a comparison with what was described as the *paramparik bandobast* (traditional arrangement/system) through which rural employment programmes ran in Chamoli till the advent of the NREGS. This system is colloquially referred to as the 'Contractor Raj'. Public works schemes, it was openly acknowledged, were primarily run by contractors. For instance, the *Sampoorna Grameen Rozgar Yojana* (SGRY), which is what the NREGS supplanted, was considered 'easy' to implement as the district faced no problem in exhausting the annual budget allocated to it. The ease of implementation of such schemes was directly related to the paperwork involved. As my office-mates told me, if you gave a million rupees today to the village headperson or GPVA, he/she would produce a receipt for the scheme the very next day – and that was that. The way the Contractor Raj worked was, crudely, this. The village headperson would be given, say, Rs 50,000 to build a road in his/her village. He/she would immediately hand over Rs 30,000 of this amount to whichever contractor was dominant in the region and maintained close links with the local politicians. From that Rs 30,000 this contractor would build a road using substandard material, and by employing easily exploitable migrant labourers from neighbouring Nepal or from the north-Indian states of Uttar Pradesh and Bihar, who would work for below-minimum wages. By these means, the contractor would be able to extract his/her own 'cut' from the amount received. As for the remaining Rs 20,000, it would be divided up between the local government functionaries under what is commonly known as the 'PC system'. PC refers to the percentage that is 'cut' from total amounts and reserved for each official depending on his/her position. Thus, a junior engineer can demand a PC of 7 per cent, a BDO of 10 per cent, and a GPVA of, say, 5 per cent. The general belief in Uttarakhand is that the PC system 'eats up' at least 25 – 30 per cent of total funds available.

In direct recognition of the Contractor Raj, the NREGA makes the employment of contractors in execution of works a legally punishable offence. Criminalizing contractors has been coupled with the introduction of new documents designed to remedy the ease with which books could be fixed hitherto. The required documents under previous schemes consisted merely of a work order, a muster roll, and receipts, all of which could be handled by a contractor and/or his/her allies such as the local government functionary. The nexus between government functionaries and contractors in Uttarakhand is so strong that it becomes difficult to disentangle them. Thus, in many villages, in Chamoli, the village headperson was him/herself the contractor, or the village-level development worker was closely related to the local contractor. Between them, they controlled the documents that attested to the existence of the scheme. The MR was always *kachcha*, i.e., temporary that was made *pukka* (permanent/correct) before being submitted for official inspection. Receipts were easily manufactured and work orders just as easily obtained from the engineer incharge, on payment of the appropriate PC. Thus, *on paper*, these previous schemes were easily implementable. Compare this easily controllable and manipulable system to the documentary logic of the NREGA, in which the muster rolls must be *pukka* and bear their unique registration number, be kept at the worksite, be accessible to any who wish to inspect them, and must correspond precisely, in the details of their entries, to the entries made in the job cards. Finally, this vital document – the job card – is legally supposed to be, at all times, in the possession of the household to which it has been issued. In effect, then, this law has created a stringent system of double accounting: one involving not only a large number of mutually corresponding documents that different state actors are required to produce but also, crucially, a document that centrally attests to the truth of the scheme and resides outside the domain of the state, in the hands of the labourer.

The revolutionary document

In the NREGA's quest for transparency this tiny job card has a central role to play. It is described by the operational guidelines as 'a critical legal document, which also helps to ensure transparency and protect labourers against fraud'

(Government of India, 2008, p. 22). The fundamental purpose of the job card is to allow the labourer to verify what the state claims it has officially paid him/her. Accordingly, this document carries a photograph of the registered household as well as the core details: number of days and hours worked for the NREGS, and wages earned. All monitoring of the NREGS at the level of the village is focused upon scrutiny of job cards. Entries in job cards are read against the official muster rolls to check for any discrepancies in accounts. Hence, it is through an examination of documents, especially of the job card, that the operations of the state are believed to have been made transparent.

Newspaper articles, photographs that I myself have taken during visits to various villages in India, and even a Google search of job cards throws up a familiar image of men and women holding up their job cards to the camera. There is a profundity to these images (see Figure 2.1). In turning towards the camera, job card in hand, labourers are sending out a message to a world that lies beyond the immediacy of the village. The precise content of the message varies: joy at having completed a 100 days of employment in the year, anger at being denied work, bewilderment at the absence of any opportunities, a denunciation of exploitation or of non-payment of wages, and so on. For once, however, the job card bestows a perceived concreteness to the message; concreteness in matter and of a form that the Indian state should be forced to acknowledge. Under previous public works programmes, no such document existed that would allow for an independent verification of government records. The labourers had no way of ascertaining what figures were written on the *pukka* muster roll and, therefore, were unable to protest against being paid less than they were entitled to.

The job card laying bare the workings of the state is, of course, an idealized imaginary. In practice, the job card was subjected to a variety of different manipulations that defeated, to a large extent, the objective of exquisite state transparency (Figure 3.1). In Chamoli, the job card, much like the lists that Hull (2008) describes in Islamabad, became an object to be physically controlled. In the first place, getting a job card issued was itself no mean feat. This is despite the legal stipulation that such issuance be free of cost, and completed within 15 days of household registration. In my experience of households holding a job card, it was achieved after the payment of money and/or much pleading. Even 2 years after the launch of the scheme, I would find villagers who had laboured on NREGS programmes but did not possess a job card and, shockingly, did not know that they even had the right to possess this document, and that too free of

Figure 3.1: Seeking to match job cards with muster rolls in Odisha

cost. Most fascinatingly, in Chamoli, a job card economy had sprung up – they were rented out, sold, bought, borrowed, and stolen. 'Renting out' of job cards was undertaken typically to Nepali immigrants who were desperate for any work, but as foreign citizens were ineligible to participate in the NREGS. The wages paid would be divided up between the Nepali worker and the legitimate holder of the document. Needless to say, the Nepali would get but a fraction of the amount. Similarly, one or two enterprising individuals in villages would 'buy' up lots of job cards and then employ labourers on NREGS works, pay but a fraction of the wages legally due to these labourers and pocket the remaining amounts, thus paying nothing at all to the legal owners of the job cards. In my independent visits to villages, I was struck by the number of 'ghosts' that existed on the muster rolls – people who did not exist, were dead, or had migrated away from the village. These ghosts nevertheless had legitimate job cards issued to their non-persons, thus creating a documentary 'life' for them. In cases of separation or divorce, job cards often became bones of contention – which spouse was entitled to retain this card? There was a high-profile case of a village headman in Chamoli who had stolen all the job cards of his village. Allegations of corruption in the implementation of the NREGS had been made against him by a few villagers. Apparently, he had not only refused to let them work, but had also employed his son-in-law as the contractor. The disappearance of the job cards resulted in the impossibility of substantiating these allegations, for the muster roll and other documents were deemed to be 'in order'. Similarly, there were cases of job cards being burnt, torn, 'lost', and, generally, vanishing. The job card, then, was not just a dry bureaucratic artefact but rather a wily little 'actant' (Latour, 2000) that possessed a remarkable knack for vanishing at (in)opportune moments. The disappearance of job cards allows for the state truth of the NREGS to be derived from the documents that remain behind – the *pukka* MR and assorted registers – all of which are easily fixed as they are, right from the start, in the possession of state functionaries.

It was absolutely commonplace for job cards to not be in 'custody of the worker' as the OG mandates it must be (Government of India, 2008, p. 3). Having said that, this transparent-making document was often described to me as 'making NREGS very difficult', 'adding too much work', 'complicating the system'. The verb forms following from this document referred to its upsetting nature, its capacity to mess up the system that had 'traditionally worked so well' or 'smoothly' under the Contractor Raj. Job cards were charged with affect, being described variously as a 'headache', a 'pain in the neck', 'dastardly', 'ridiculous', and, even, 'like an elephant that has gone mad'. Contractors told me in direct terms that given this bizarre paperwork of NREGS, they preferred to concentrate their energies on the myriad other development schemes that continue to operate in Chamoli under the 'older' strictures, i.e., ones not demanding transparency. The non-participation of actors in the village – be they contractors or political leaders or officials – explains why there was no 'demand for work' being generated in the district, so that in bank accounts all over the district hundreds of thousands of rupees were lying unutilized. The correct marshalling of all the prescribed papers, in order to allow funds to be spent, requires a radical overhaul of extant systems of governance, and further, the crafting of a new one premised on an intricate dance of perfectly synchronized transparent-making documents. To make matters worse, one of these documents is actually supposed to physically reside outside government offices, so that exercising control over it adds to the already complicated (paper) work. It is no wonder, then, that the paperwork of the scheme had made it 'unimplementable' in Chamoli district.

Transparency is a dominant ideal of all development efforts being undertaken in India today. As studies of transparency in other contexts (see West and Sanders, 2003; Ballestero, 2012) point out, the ascendance of transparency, in its discourse, practice and institutionalization, is but a recent occurrence.[5] Assessments of the rise of auditing techniques aimed at introducing transparency and/or accountability vary. For instance, in the case of higher education in the UK, the rise of an audit culture has been critiqued as a technology of neoliberal governmentality (Strathern, 2000). In India, on the other hand, the introduction of a 'social audit' in NREGA and the emphasis on monitoring, transparency, and accountability more generally have been energetically celebrated in the official and activist literature on the RTI and NREGA. These measures have been praised as giving birth to a new form of politics, and for posing a challenge to the regular operations of state power. In contrast to the euphoria of these declarations, new audit ethnographies have begun to show them to be productive of a range of other effects (see Bear and Mathur, 2015).

In this chapter, I have tried to show the singular importance of the material production of official attestations of transparency, what I describe as 'transparent-making documents', in the implementation of NREGA. In its quest to 'make things auditable' (Power, 1999, p. 68), NREGA has converted easily-executed – at least on paper – public works schemes into unimplementable ones *even on paper*. On 17 January 2012, Sonia Gandhi, the president of the Congress party, started off her party's electoral campaign in Uttarakhand by highlighting the corruption of the incumbent Bharatiya Janata Party (BJP) government. In her speech she declared: '[t]he rampant loot and the cheating are still prevailing. Only 10 per cent of the people got the benefits of the Congress-led UPA Governments Mahatma Gandhi NREGA policy. Only 40 per cent of the funds were utilized by the BJP Government'.[6] I have located the under-utilization of NREGA funds – NREGA's 'unimplementability' – in the workings of transparent-making documents, which are aimed, ironically enough, at stemming the 'rampant loot and cheating' to which Gandhi referred.

Endnotes

1 According to the 2001 Census, 9 per cent of Chamoli's population comprises Scheduled Castes, and 10 per cent Scheduled Tribes, with a negligible number belonging to the Other Backward Classes (OBCs).

2 The national adult literacy rate is 74.04 per cent. Chamoli boasts an average of 82.65 per cent with male literacy pitched at 93.40 per cent and female at 72.32 per cent (Census of India, 2011) http://www.census2011.co.in/census/district/575-chamoli.html. Accessed August 7, 2013.

3   The mountains of Uttarakhand are said to run on what is called a 'money order economy', as many families are heavily dependent on remittances coming in through the means of postal orders sent by male members of the family from the plains.

4   Corruption follows the commonplace definition of diversion of state money into private pockets (Lazar, 2008, p. 112).

5   As Hetherington notes, '[t]he idea of transparency as a bureaucratic virtue is not entirely new, but in the 1990s it came to prominence as the central idea in at least two international reform projects, one having to do with governance, the other with economic performance' (2011, p. 3).

6   http://pressbrief.in/index.php/Latest/We-need-to-change-the-Government-not-the-CM-says-Sonia-Gandhi-in-Roorkee.html. Accessed January 1, 2012.

4

The Letter of the State

Bertolt Brecht famously advocated stripping the familiar of its inconspicuousness through estrangement. A typical day in the life of the NREGS cell requires little effort to make it strange. For, even though it consists of familiar practices of the type de Certeau (1988) has described as those that 'produce without capitalising' – reading, writing, talking, filing, attending meetings, drinking *chai* – the repetitive and invariable nature of the work with its extreme reliance on paper lends it, on the first encounter, a somewhat odd hue.

Chamoli district's development apparatus is split into two institutions – the District Rural Development Agency (DRDA), which is funded from New Delhi, i.e., by the Centre; and the *Vikas Vibhag* (Development Department), which is funded by the State of Uttarakhand. Their distinction is rigidly maintained, even physically – the two institutions are housed in separate buildings, though they are both directly controlled by the district's Chief Development Officer (CDO) and, ultimately, by the District Magistrate (DM). Being a Centre-sponsored scheme, the NREGS had a room allotted to it in the DRDA, which was located directly opposite the DM's office.[1] This tiny space contained two tables, five chairs, a map of Uttarakhand on the wall, and a window that opened on to the distracting sight of a bright blue *dhaba* (tea-stall). On the tables and on every available inch of floor space, files were neatly arranged. In March 2007, this cell was allocated a computer, in order that the statistics being generated out of the NREGS could be consigned to permanence through their entry into the virtual world. For the first 2 months after its arrival, this computer was kaput. A new one, eventually, made its way up from Dehradun. As this one was functional, we had to find a 'computer boy' (*computer-wallah ladka*), since nobody in the office knew how to operate this strange device. A rather fraught process ensued, involving an advertisement, applications, shortlists, interviews, and much 'political pressure' being exerted on officials in favour of a particular candidate. Finally, the NREGS cell appointed a 'computer boy'.[2] The computer boy could type but not write letters for, as I explain below, that is an art (*kala*) demanding slow inculcation. There was no internet connection, so the computer was mostly used to play games on and, sometimes, watch DVDs. All the work took place with and on paper.

Government offices in Chamoli were supposed to be open Monday through Saturday, from 10 a.m. to 5 p.m. With all of a novice's enthusiasm, I began by arriving in office 5 minutes before 10 a.m., only to find a lock staring me in the face or, even if the doors had been opened on time, an entirely empty office. I quickly learned that office time *really* began only about 10:30 a.m., by when everyone would trickle into position, so that one could find them seated behind their appointed desks. Morning greetings were always polite but curt, a mere *namaste* to each other. On settling down on to their *kursi* (chair) most of the members of the cell would pull out files left over from the day before, or rummage through some other documents placed on their desks. Around 11 a.m. the post-woman would deliver the mail. This was also the time for the first round of *chai* in the office. Over *chai*, the five permanent members of the NREGS cell – Mr N (Section Officer), Mr P (District Accountant), Mr J (Accountant), Mr B (the Computer boy), Mr D (the peon) – and I would carefully open and read every missive. The letters and reports the postal bag contained were sorted into different piles, worked upon, and then filed. The very urgent ones were largely related to demands for monitoring and transparency from the Centre or to financial aspects of the scheme. These were carefully marked to the relevant office, placed in a file that would establish the history of the issue they raised, and transported to the office by Mr D. For instance, a letter from New Delhi, asking for the latest district figures on the number of women employed under the NREGS in the last quarter, would be forwarded to the CDO. This would be done in the knowledge that the CDO would reply to the cell ordering that a letter be written immediately to all the BDOs, to obtain the relevant figures at the earliest. This letter would be placed on top in a similar file that would establish the history of employment provided to particular categories of the unemployed – women, the Scheduled Castes, Scheduled Tribes – and also be used to demonstrate that the statistic demanded by the Central Ministry was not, at the time of the demand, available in the Gopeshwar office. While an issue such as this one would have been considered a regular procedural matter, there were some other letters that provoked great anxiety. Once, groans of horror greeted a letter from Dehradun informing the district of the arrival of surprise evaluators of the NREGS, and Mr D was entreated to run down to the CDO immediately with this epistolary harbinger of bad news. At other times, certain letters/documents were greeted with relief, especially when they related to the release of funds or to the deployment of new personnel. Financial correspondence was treated with kid gloves, photocopies were made, figures entered into large ledgers, and the documents were carefully filed before being locked up in a cupboard located in the adjoining room. In striking contrast, some of the mail was termed pure 'trash' (*kooda*). The 'trash' included, for one, letters that did not fall under the purview of this programme or this level (*sthar*) of the state; they had made their way to our office accidentally, like lost travellers. Yet other 'trashy' correspondence was of the type that would create annoyance, that should be suppressed (*dabaya jana chahiye*). Such 'trash' was either marked to the relevant office or directly binned.

Approximately half an hour into the arrival and sorting of the post, work would resume in the NREGS cell. This work consisted of Mr P, the Accountant, working on balance sheets and ledgers, collating bills, issuing cheques, and calling up subordinates to cross-verify figures. Mr N and Mr J would also help with numbers of various sorts, particularly with those entered into the all-important monthly progress reports (MPRs), and into the engineer's estimates of works to be undertaken under the NREGS. The majority of their work, however, consisted of writing, reading, and sending letters. Once a letter had been drafted successive times and approved, it would be dictated to the computer boy by one of the three senior members of the cell. Mr D would clear away our teacups, carry files up and down the offices, run other errands for us, and just generally wander around the office compound.[3]

Come 1 p.m. and it was lunch time when everyone, other than the diligent and constantly dieting Mr N, would vanish home or to the canteen in the office compound for a meal. An hour or 90 min later, depending on the pending volume of work, they would straggle back into the office to resume work on the texts they had been dealing with. These post-lunch sessions were markedly more lethargic, verging on the somnolent. During the second *chai* break, which was timed more loosely between 3 and 4 p.m., and lasted for 20 min to half an hour, everyone would perk up again. Over hot *chai* poured out in small glasses, mundane chitchat would ensue about the weather, politics, inflation, or local incidents from bus accidents to feuds, even to the movements of the resident leopard. Often we would wander out onto the roof to see what was happening around the office compound, or just to catch a spot of sun. By 4:30 p.m., everyone would be packing up, and before the clock struck 5 p.m., the NREGS cell would be devoid of a single occupant.

When a meeting was due or being held, or an inspection was scheduled, the pace of work would quicken. *Chai* would be sipped while people frenetically corrected documents; everyone would arrive on time and sometimes even work through lunch. Symmetrically, when there was no big event or deadline in sight, the pace would slacken. The occupants would wander in and out of the room, leave early, or just not return after lunch. In days leading up to a long weekend or to holidays such as Diwali or the New Year, officials would take leave and go to visit their families, or just stay home. When senior bureaucrats such as the CDO and the DDO were away on leave or on official trips, the NREGS cell would be left desolate. A primary motive for its occupants keeping to the ten-to-five regime was the fear that they might, at any time, be summoned by their superiors to explain the contents of a file or to create, or fix, a document. When meetings were held, everyone in the cell (even if they had not been invited to attend) made sure to be present in the office until the event was over. On specific days, such as the BDOs' monthly meeting that I describe subsequently, everyone would arrive at the cell office before 10 a.m. to deal with the BDOs moving in and out of the room, go over their MPRs quickly, scold them for not sending these reports in earlier and, generally, make sure that all the paperwork was in order for the ritual of verification that was to follow.

For more senior officials, the pattern of daily life differed somewhat. The CDO, for instance, would spend his entire day frantically running between meetings, inspections, inaugurations, interactions with 'the public' (*janta*), and other such public events where he would represent *sarkar's* development efforts. In between, he would *niptao* (dispose of) the dozens of files that were perennially to be found stacked on his large desk. He and the DDO were known to stay on in their offices well past 5 p.m. in order to run through their files. Sitting in their durbar-style offices one was struck by the stream of visitors they entertained, each with his or her own request to *sarkar* (always transferred in writing onto paper), and the dexterity with which they would blindly sign files. Their Personal Assistant (PA) or the official concerned would hand the CDO/ DDO a file, softly muttering what it was about, such as 'estimates for check-dams under NREGS', and they would quickly sign in the appropriate place before tossing it into the out tray. Sometimes, if they were slightly unsure of the contents of a proffered file, they would pause in their blitz of *maaroing* (slamming out) signatures and make inquiries. The norm, however, was to trust that the levels of officialdom below had done their job, and the CDO/DDO's signature was mere routine, i.e., the matter required a stamp of approval from the head. Even petitions, however pressing or heart-rending, would be scanned with a practiced eye and marked to the concerned department or official, before the petitioner was quickly dismissed from their presence.

The Block office of Dasholi, where I would often go to spend a day in the week, maintained a rhythm of work similar to the NREGS cell. It was, however, much more loosely structured, with officials walking in and out at different times, normally not arriving before 11 a.m. and vanishing soon afterwards. Block-office life was punctuated by frequent visits, primarily by members of the *Panchayats* (village councils) but also by NGO workers and villagers who came in with complaints or requests. Here, too, the head of the office – the BDO – was almost always to be found in his room, buried in a heap of files and simultaneously entertaining the visitors.

It is no surprise, then, that I was warned off doing ethnographic fieldwork in an Indian government office. What I encountered in my field were unvarying routine and banal, repetitive, pedantic work on documents of various kinds, by men who were practiced in this craft but did not consider it worthy of study. The banality of it all as well as its repetitive nature is, in a way, reminiscent of women's housework. In *The Everyday World as Problematic*, Smith (1987) picks up a study of the daily routine of Mrs T, a working-class housewife. Smith notes that the structuring logic of Mrs T's work was organized in accordance with the wider institutions of bourgeois society, specifically those of her husband's office and her children's schools. Feminist analyses not only bring out the drudgery and neglect of women's labour, they also point out how it is from an analysis of everyday life and work that one can productively and critically encounter the wider structures and power relations of the world. Taking inspiration from this insight, in this chapter we retreat back into the NREGS cell to to ask what the quotidian labour that takes place here can tell us about the state.

Writing and lettering

The primary documentary form that occupied the everyday work of the NREGS cell was the letter. Even when the document under consideration was something else, such as a progress report or a work estimate, it would always be accompanied by a covering letter explaining what the document contained and what action was required from this particular office. Letters had to be deciphered and, crucially, appropriate responses had to be penned – or not penned as the case may be. Writing government letters (*sarkari chitthi*) was not something that just anyone could do. It was an art (*kala*) or skill, to be learned gradually through experience. My own attempts at writing official letters were considered almost entirely useless. It was not merely that I was unfamiliar with the precise vocabulary that would make for a proper letter, but I also lacked, somehow, a finer feel for them. I was not able, as Mr P told me once, to write letters that were 'kadak' (strong) like the *chai* we were drinking. Riles notes, similarly, that in the writing of document by bureaucrats in Fiji 'language had a shape, a rhythm, a feel, not simply a meaning' (2001, p. 80) and where ' [o]ne had to acquire an ear and an eye for the patterns' (81).

Mr P, unlike me, had acquired the art and skill of writing *sarkari chitthis* through long experience, even though his official designation and training was that of an accountant. Having spent close to 30 years in the District Rural Development Agency (DRDA) in Gopeshwar, Mr P claimed to know 'just how to deal with every single official in the district'. So, if he was writing to the 'corrupt BDOs' (*bhrastha* BDOs) he would always brandish a veiled warning of 'enquiries into misdeeds', throw in hints of 'complaints from above', or baldly state that 'the higher officials are cognizant of what you are up to'. In the case of the young, contract-based employees of the NREGS, Mr P was very clear that the authoritative voice of the State had to be used in all communications with them, in order to extract work. Mr P had a reputation for sometimes being too hard on his subordinates and too servile with his own superiors. Often, he would be pulled up by some of the other senior officials for the kinds of letters he would produce. One morning, the Project Economist (PE) of the NREGS barged into our room angrily demanding of Mr P if he 'wanted to kill them all off?' The Project Economist was referring to a sharp letter that Mr P had written to the newly recruited Deputy Programme Officers (DPOs) for the NREGS, telling them that they were not performing to expectations and had better pull up their socks. The DPOs were fresh, young MBA-holders who had been recruited with great difficulty. They did not want to live and work in remote Chamoli district, for salaries that were not commensurate with the value of their degrees, and on work which was not of they type they had been aiming for. The Project Economist had received a barrage of angry letters and phone calls in response to Mr P's letter from these young recruits, who were already disgruntled and on the brink of quitting, and who claimed to be entirely unused to such high-handed behaviour. To salvage the situation, the Project Economist bade Mr P write a more soothing letter that would explain why he had sent off the first, sharp missive. He sat down and dictated this letter to Mr P himself and reviewed its language twice, before departing from our room. After his departure, Mr P grumbled over the way the new recruits were being 'spoiled' (*bigad rahen hai*) and molly-coddled by the senior officials.

In situations of delicacy, then, it was generally understood that the crafting of letters must be left to Mr N, who was considered a past master of the art. He had a remarkable knack for reading the sub-text of all the letters that came into the office, and for quickly penning suitable replies. Mr N., of an equable disposition, would often instruct me on how one maintains relations in *sarkar*: 'government people (*sarkari log*) have big egos and one must know how to manage everyone's egos. The only way to do so is by stifling your own. Working with *sarkar* is all about managing relationships'. Weber (2006) writes of the separation of the bureau (office) from the private domicile of the official (the family) in the modern organization of the civil service, a separation that maps onto the distinction between the official and the private. Kafka found this dichotomization problematic as 'for him, family has at least a family relation to the larger social-political organisation Kafka calls *the office* and which, under the conditions of modernity, displays the features of bureaucracy' (Corngold, 2009, p. 9). Indeed, in *The Castle* Kafka writes of the intertwining of K's life and his office to the point that they begin sometimes to seem as if they have changed places. Mr N and the others in the DRDA certainly did think of the office as a space distinct from their private realm of the family or their natal villages. Yet, they constantly invoked the metaphor of family when referring to the state structure in Chamoli. 'As one has to work hard to maintain relations in one's family, even with one's own husband or wife or children', Mr N paternally explained to me, 'so must we work hard to maintain relations with our *sarkari* family. Neither task is easy, but family is family and must be maintained'. Letters were a central way of maintaining relations. Hence, they had to be carefully drafted, written in the name of the appropriate individual, their form and language moulded to get the work done – but also, they must never lead to a total rupture in the fabric of social relations. Unless, of course, the individual was going to be sacked from the government, it would not do to harm relations with one another in *sarkar*.

Mr J was the third senior member of the cell. He was rather an unknown quantity, since he was also on part-time deputation to another employment-generation programme run by the development office in Chamoli. His loyalties were regarded as being divided between the NREGS and this rival scheme. Further, it was always quite difficult to locate Mr J, for he could be either in our cell or his other office, or, as was most often the case, at the nearby *dhaba*. The most mundane letters, the 'non-political' ones that did not need to be urgently sent off consigned to Mr J's hands. The Project Economist (PE) was left to deal with the very technical letters, especially ones that needed clarification on financial questions. This was not only because his official designation was 'Project Economist' (so that we all referred to him not by his name but as 'the PE'), but also because he was considered a cold, calculating sort of an individual, good with numbers and at allocating budgets, but very little else.[4] Further, the PE considered himself too high up the ladder to be dealing with trivialities and, as he described it, 'the politics of everyday letters'. Trained as an economist, he wished to be left alone in the rarefied realms of numbers and Excel spread sheets. The Project Director (PD), similarly, considered himself too exalted in the pecking order to bother with the minutiae of the NREGS' implementation, and would regularly delegate his official responsibilities with the scheme to the NREGS cell, which meant to Mr N and Mr P. The letters sent in the name of the absolute boss of the NREGS in Chamoli, the Chief Development Officer (CDO), and his 'number two', the District Development Officer (DDO) were also drafted largely by members of the NREGS cell.

In the maintenance of relations, it was important not only to get the tone of the letter right but also to know just how many letters to send, and when. In Chamoli, a running battle was on between the Forest Department (FD) and the Rural Development (RD) department over the NREGA. Afforestation, ordinarily part of the FD's mandate, was on the list of permissible works under the NREGA. On the basis of several meetings held and letters exchanged, it had been decided that the FD would 'provide technical assistance' in NREGS-related afforestation activities. Despite this written agreement, Block officials complained that no assistance was forthcoming, even for small things like the purchase of saplings. This situation led to a series of letters being written by the NREGS cell to the FD on the minutest of matters such as, say, 'can the forest guard please ensure that the saplings planted under the NREGS in X village are not eaten by goats', 'can the forest department please train villagers on how to water their trees', 'can the forest department sell subsidized fertilizers to this particular Block', and so on. In the end, correspondence between the RD department and the FD had to be discontinued because the Divisional Forest Officer (DFO) complained formally to the joint head of the two warring departments – the Forest and Rural Development Commissioner (FRDC) in Dehradun – that this flood of letters constituted 'harassment'. In the NREGS cell, similarly, if we started receiving too many letters from a particular official, it would be angrily commented upon. Sometimes the cell members, too, would use the word 'harassment' to express anger at such excessive letter writing. Frequently, they would be exasperated by the knowledge that the letters would have to be countered by preparing responses of some sort. Mr J had his own way of identifying the volume of a correspondence as excessive, by saying that we were receiving too many 'love letters' (*prem patra*) from such and such official.

Annoyances they might be, but the volume of letters on a topic or a scheme was also an indicator of its importance. By this measure, the NREGS was, by far, the most important (*mahatvapoorna*) development scheme in the district. Adding to the letters attesting to the NREGS's importance was the gigantic budget it demanded, and its commonly believed association with the Gandhi family. The quantity of letters was supplemented by the key fact of who had written the letter to whom. Often discussions in the NREGS cell would centre on whose name a particular letter should be sent in – the DM, CDO, DDO, PD (Project Director), or even the PE. Questions such as 'is the DDO big enough for this topic' or 'isn't this too mundane for the DM?' would be posed and mulled over. It was a well-known fact in the entire district apparatus that my letter of introduction was written by the then Chief Information Commissioner (CIC), a prominent figure, who was believed to harbour political ambitions. Not only did this letter fling doors open for me, it also served to shield me, to a large extent, from potential problems in offices, be it denial of access to files and meetings or sexual harassment. This fact was brought to my notice by the Deputy Programme Officer (DPO) of Dasholi block, who also instructed me to keep a sharp eye not just for the senders and receivers of letters, but also the *kursis* (designations) the letters were copied to. Indeed, deciding whom to include in the 'cc' and whom to exclude would occupy the NREGS cell for periods that might appear inordinately long. The discussions over issues such as whom to 'cc', whether to use the word 'important' (*mahatvapoorna*) or 'very important' (*ati mahatvapoorna*), whether to send the letter by regular post or speed post, whose signature it should bear, and so on, were discussed by everyone present in the room. Each and every letter sent out from Gopeshwar in the name of, say, the CDO had been authored by several people; it was a product of detailed acts of decipherment, writing, discussion, drafting, and re-drafting. Once the copy had been agreed upon, it would be dictated to the computer boy or, as used to happen before his advent, to a secretary on his typewriter. Once printed out and checked over, normally by the PE who sat in his own room just below the NREGS cell, the appropriate signature had to be obtained. This was when Mr D, the peon, would come into action, running between offices with the file carrying the letter to get the concerned official to sign it. Obtaining signatures required legwork, patience, good knowledge of the senior officials' whereabouts, and, crucially, good relations with their Personal Assistants (PAs). PAs had to be convinced that the particular file/letter needed urgent approval, and had to be pleaded with to make sure that such-and-such *sahib* would have a look at it fast. Days and weeks could go by before the concerned *sahib* would have the time to 'slam out' a signature on it; before his PA would even oblige the NREGS cell so far as to make sure that the file was pressed on his notice. So crucial was this act of signing that the performance of senior officials was measured by the speed with which they disposed of files (file *niptana*).

The production of letters as of all other official documents, then, was accomplished by the expenditure of considerable labour. It was vital that this labour be performed, for letters constitute a primary mode whereby the frail world of the local state is held together in the semblance of a functional, communicative unit. Given the thousands of letters that came in and out of the NREGS cell during my time there, it is well-nigh impossible to include them all in my account. What follows below is a rough classification of the letters into types, on the basis of the work they did. One letter could, of course, be doing several types of work all at once.

Introductory letters

I earned my entry into the inner sanctums of the Indian state through the means of an introductory letter. So too did the NREGS. The first official inkling of the NREGS in Uttarakhand was gleaned from its introductory letter to the Chief Minister (CM), written by none other than the Prime Minister (PM) of India from New Delhi on 13 October 2005. Written on his official letterhead, it bore, emblazoned in a rich gold, the national emblem of India – a frieze of the three

Asiatic lions atop the Buddhist Emperor Ashoka's pillar at Sarnath, constructed in the third century BC. Inscribed below in Devanagari script and in glossy gold ink, is the motto that is an integral part of the emblem: *Satyameva Jayate* (Truth Alone Triumphs). Letters in the two official working languages of the Indian state, Hindi and English, had been sent out to all the states on the same day. In the ones sent to Uttarakhand, the Hindi version had been personally signed by the PM, perhaps in recognition of the state's being a Hindi-speaking one. This letter, the first of the many thousands that were subsequently written in order to convert the NREGA doctrine into the NREGS, with 'real' effects in rural India, is a typical instance of the form taken by official letters between senior agents of the state. It is replete with painfully polite forms of address towards the recipient, and its text refers to the grand vision of 'developing our country'. As an interesting specimen of letters exchanged within the upper echelons of the state, it is markedly different from the prosaic, matter-of-fact letters that routinely entered and left the NREGS cell.

The clarificatory letter

One of the most common types of letters received in the NREGS cell as well as sent out within the district was the letter with clarificatory intent. Such letters either made some point concerning the NREGS clearer or requested clarifications on it. The clarifications could be minor, such as 'which agency shall establish priority of works to be undertaken in the village?' or 'can we employ households that have exceeded the guarantee of 100 days of employment on NREGS works?' Even when the answer seemed almost obvious, bureaucrats considered it wise to ask for and receive official clarification from 'above'. The phrase *disha-nirdesh* was almost always to be found in these letters. Peculiar to the 'bureaucratise' I encountered in official letters, it hyphenates two Hindi words: *disha* means direction and *nirdesh* means orders. 'Please show us the correct *disha-nirdesh*', thus, amounted to a request to be ordered in the correct direction. If the letter was written the other way round, i.e., from 'above' to 'below', '*avashyak karyavahi*' was a standard phrase, meaning 'required/necessary action' on the matter under consideration. Or it may seek a clarification on what action had already been undertaken, a query which would involve the phrase '*krit karyavahi*' or 'action taken'. Such a query could be, for example, 'why were so few households provided with employment in this particular Block?' Seeking clarification in writing on minute issues was a daily activity, as regular a feature of office life as the breaks for *chai*. It was through the piecemeal provision of mundane clarifications that erasures of the illegibilities of the authoritative texts were attempted.

The translated letter

The translated letter is similar to the clarificatory letter but differs in providing a programmatic direction. Such letters would break down goals into tasks through the provision of a timeline, a specific – normally quantifiable – goal, and step-by-step instructions on how to accomplish this task. For instance, the operational guidelines of the NREGA have as their goal, involvement of village councils in participatory planning for the scheme. What does that translate into on the ground for the local bureaucracy? Letters written either from New Delhi or Gopeshwar would outline this by instructing (*disha-nirdesh*) the Block- or village-level workers to go to every village within the next week, convene meetings, read the objectives of the NREGA aloud at these meetings, then hold a general discussion to decide on works to be followed, and finally list the desired works in the NREGS register No. XX maintained by the DPO for each village. These entries would be written by the village-level development worker (GPVA) and signed by the *pradhan*, with a counter-signature by the deputy head. The DPO would, subsequently, verify the list himself, returning to the village the week after these activities and checking with the villagers that due process had been followed. By the end of the month in which this *disha-nirdesh* was issued, at the very latest, the CDO was to be presented with news that this order was being carried out, accompanied by a photocopy of the page from the register bearing the list with all the required signatures. One of the primary tasks of the Gopeshwar office was to create and enforce such timelines and tasks. The results of these letters would then be sent back to the Centre, in the form of check marks against the Centre's demands for reports, such as 'have village councils been involved in the planning stage?' or in the form of more tangible evidence, such as letters from the *Kshetra Panchayat* attesting that their village-level members were present at the planning stage.

The procedural letter

All letters are procedural in nature. But there are some which are written solely to exhibit the due observance of procedure. In his beautifully written account of life as a bureaucrat in a princely state under the British Raj in the 1920s, E. M. Forster (1953) mentions an incident in which the Maharajah of the state felt himself to have been 'officially insulted' due to a breach of protocol by the

Agent of the Governor General (AGG) for Central India. A series of letters between the Maharajah and Government of India ensued. The solution to the 'official insult' was arrived at by the penning of another letter, this time by the Political Agent to the Maharajah.

'It is a strange letter', writes Forster, 'for one thing he has omitted to sign it – Freud may have intervened. Beautifully typed, bound with purple ribbon, stamped 'Political Agent in Malwa' around a Lion and Unicorn in blue, it contains such sentences as 'I understood you to say that you had no feeling one way or the other whether Mr Forster should receive *itr* and pan or no, and I so represented it to Colonel Jones, who decided, that as in his opinion there was no room for doubt whether Mr Forster, as a European on Your Highness' staff, should receive *itr* and pan at all, it would be better, as Your Highness has (as I understood) no strong feelings in the matter, it would be better that he should not receive it at least until the question had been settled'. Such a sentence could neither clarify nor conciliate' (1953, p. 96).

Strange letters containing tortuous sentences that can neither clarify nor conciliate were not rare in the NREGS cell either. The point of them, however, much like that of the letter Forster discusses, was merely to have sent a missive. A letter, any letter, will do, as long as it serves as evidence that procedure has been followed. The pre-occupation with visibly proving that due process, to the exclusion of all else, was being followed was, as Riles puts it in another context of bureaucratic practices at a United Nations conference, 'ethnographically instructive' for '... the only internal measure and engine of progress was this formal process – the elaboration of the steps the body should take' (2006, p. 85). In the incident described by Forster, due process dictated that a letter should be written back to the Maharajah with the apparent *intent* of clarification or conciliation but not necessarily, I would argue, with the *content* of either. That is not to say that all official letters are unconcerned with their content or that meaning is unimportant, merely that in certain cases the very fact of having shot off a letter serves on its own, even before the envelope has been torn open, to transmit the desired message. The case of what the letter writer himself dubbed a 'comical letter' (*hasya-patra*) is a case in point.

A member of the NREGS cell asks me to guess what he is doing. 'What?' I ask. 'I am writing a comical letter (*hasya patra*)', he answers. It is a letter to the Ministry of Rural Development (MoRD), New Delhi, requesting the release of the second instalment of funds due in this financial year under the NREGS. It is comical because they are not going to send any proposal with the letter. The funds for the NREGS are sent out from New Delhi to all the districts in a phased manner, in two instalments over the financial year, on the basis of the progress made in disbursement of already-received finances. A proposal should be drafted each time a request is made for more money, to show clearly that demand exists for more works to be undertaken under the scheme. To send a letter without a proposal, then, is an empty gesture. It makes for a funny letter. But then why write and send the letter anyway? The answer is common-sensical. A letter is being written because it is high time it was written. The process of the NREGA requires letters to be written at periodic intervals requesting money, for this is a sign that work is happening. 'It is January now, and if we don't at least send in a letter asking for more money, then they might start wondering what we are up to here in the *pahar*. This way, they won't give us the money for they will write back asking us for a proposal, but that buys us the time to actually draft that blasted proposal', says the experienced letter-writer.

The impotence of such a missive was an open secret. Another example of this is a letter that flew out of an off-hand remark made by the Forest and Rural Development Commissioner (FRDC) of Uttarakhand. The FRDC of Uttarakhand never found the time to visit remote Gopeshwar, but at a meeting in the capital had advised the CDO to direct NREGA funds towards the plantation of fodder for cattle, goats and sheep, as animal husbandry is the 'mainstay of the rural economy in Chamoli'. Not only is this a highly disputable proclamation, and a strange one to make without the regular bureaucratic recourse to statistics, but it is also incompatible with the NREGA, which specifically states that the villagers must themselves, without any external pressure whatsoever, decide the sort of work they need done in their villages. Despite this, the CDO shot off letters to all the BDOs in the district telling them to 'encourage plantation of fodder under the NREGS', and marked a copy to the FRDC in Dehradun. When I queried the CDO on this he shrugged his shoulders and said, 'Orders are orders. Anyway, I have merely written letters and done nothing else', indicating his own knowledge of the impotence of many of these letters. All the BDOs, in their turn, forwarded the CDO's letter to their sub-ordinates in the village – the GPVAs – and told them to undertake the investigation necessary, marking copies with a 'cc' to the CDO and the FRDC. That was the last we heard of this matter.

The photocopied letter/the letter as protective shield

That the process of having written/dispatched a letter be followed is absolutely central to the everyday documentary practices of the state. Each and every level of the state adhered to this practice. The Rural Development department (RD) in Dehradun was often accused by my office-mates as well as by others in Chamoli of functioning merely as a 'photocopying machine'. The RD would photocopy letters sent to them by New Delhi and pass them on to Gopeshwar with instructions to undertake *avashyak karyavahi* (necessary action), or with information on 'action taken' (*krit karyavahi*). The BDOs, similarly, were accused of 'not going into the field' and merely sending letters up and down the district hierarchy. As the CDO once thundered at his assembled BDOs at a particularly conflictual district meeting, 'you forget that you are not professional letter-writers (*chitthikar*), but actually development workers'. The point he was trying to make to his subordinates was that they should go into 'the field', i.e., villages and do 'real' (*asli*) development work instead of (merely) writing letters. Through the writing of a letter or the passing on of instructions to the appropriate level, the artefact attesting to the discharge of one's duty had been created. The chain of command was very clear: the Ministry in New Delhi would write either directly to Chamoli or, on more important matters, to Dehradun. The RD would photocopy the letter and send it up to Gopeshwar accompanied by a covering letter, which would be written in Hindi. Sometimes Dehradun would translate the letter the letter from English to Hindi and sometimes they would leave it to the districts to do so themselves. In the NREGS cell this letter would be translated, sometimes quite literally from English to Hindi, but always in terms of breaking down the order into do-able tasks. This process of translation was a joint product of the energies of everyone in the cell; the resultant text would subsequently be corrected by the Project Economist or the DDO before being approved by the CDO or the DDO. The letter would be then sent to all the nine BDOs of the district. The BDOs were believed to often, in their turn, merely pass on the instructions issued by the district to the village-level development workers (GPVAs). The poor GPVAs, situated at the bottom of the food-chain, felt that all responsibility for the NREGS had descended upon them and wished that they, too, had someone 'below' them to whom they could forward letters. Sending a letter functioned as an abnegation of further responsibility for that chore. Therefore, if the GPVAs had possessed subordinates, then they could have, by forwarding a photocopied letter, displaced responsibility on to that lower tier. As bureaucrats told me on multiple occasions, writing letters and sending them up/down was the best way of *protecting themselves,* since it was read as a performance of their duties. A letter was not just a letter but could function as a protective shield in a system within which each member was keen on making sure that his/her own duty had been seen to be discharged (Herzfeld, 1992). As for the GPVAs, towards the end of my stay in Chamoli, they were to be blessed with the provision of village employment helpers who were placed 'below' or under them in order to assist with the copious amounts of village-level record keeping that the NREGS demanded. Barely had the young village workers taken charge that the GPVAs were to be found forwarding letters to them which they had received from above.

The fantastical letter

Some letters fell into the realm of pure fantasy. Their terms were so fantastical that they could never be executed as ordered. Yet letters went on being exchanged up and down the entire state system – the demands that were being made might have been ridiculous, but the production of letters served to prove that the state was working. A good instance of this type was the series of letters that were written after New Delhi demanded, in November 2006, that bank accounts be opened for the workers registered under the NREGS. Beginning with impossible demands, a fantastical chain of letters continued till August 2007 when I left Chamoli, with negligible results in terms of any actual bank accounts being opened. Some fantastical letters attested to the fundamental inconsistencies in the beautiful plan of the NREGS. They showed clearly how difficult it was to follow a rule even when it was legible and the actors willing to obey it. It was obvious to all that if the paperwork involved in the execution of this plan was ever to be accomplished, then the induction of new staff to carry out this cumbersome chore was a *sine qua non.* At the time I was working in Chamoli, the NREGA stipulated that only 2 per cent of the total amount spent on the scheme could be directed towards administrative expenses such as the recruitment of personnel dedicated to the NREGS. The fact that the scheme did not allow for an adequate recruitment of new personnel into the district bureaucracy was repeatedly discussed as yet another flaw in a statute which looked beautiful when prepared and read in air-conditioned offices in New Delhi. The fundamental inconsistency in this rule of the NREGA comes across well in a letter written on 4 September 2006, in a panic, by the DM of Chamoli to the Secretary, RD, Dehradun.

The letter was related to the salaries of the new workers proposed to be recruited under the NREGS. It stated that, if the district were to go by the orders sent out earlier, then the new appointments would include 39 Junior Engineers (JEs), nine Writers (*Lekhakar*) at the level of the Block; and nine Data Entry Operators (otherwise referred to as computer boys) and 276 Writer Assistants (*Lekha Sahayak*) at the Gram Panchayat (GP) level. Calculated on the basis of their expected salaries, the money required in a month would be Rs 14,31,287.00. A year would require Rs 1,71,75,438.00. At the moment, under the scheme, Rs. 1615.69 lakh was sanctioned. Government of India (GoI) allows only 2 per cent of the total money to be spent on administrative costs, i.e., for the Chamoli district administration it means only Rs 32.31 lakh could be spent on administration, which must cover salaries, stationary, computers, and even document printing costs and other miscellaneous administrative expenditure. If the district administration were to go ahead with the appointment of all the proposed new recruits then they would be able to pay them only for 2 months. According to the NREGS rules in the operational guidelines, Rs 1,71,75,438.00 could be spent only if the district were successful in spending approximately one *arab* (an Indian unit equal to one billion) rupees. Realistically, this was an impossible task. This letter was just one of the many that show how fantastical some state rules are, how fundamentally unimplementable they can be. Tellingly, this letter was ignored, or in the phrase we used to talk about such missives in the office, *deliberately* forgotten.

The forgotten letter

Sometimes the letters were entirely forgotten. Orders, it turns out, are surprisingly forgettable. Even letters sent out by the supposedly all-powerful Prime Minister (PM) can be shelved. In his inaugural address at the National Conference held in the Ministry of Rural Development (MoRD), New Delhi, on 16 – 17 December 2006, the PM had suggested that each NREGS district should prepare an Annual Employment Report of District (AERD) since 'employment generation for the rural poor is the leading focus of policy making in the country'. A format for the proposed AERD was even drawn up. The RD in Dehradun requested Chamoli a few times, through letters, to get to work on the AERD on the basis of the template provided by the GoI. The district was told to hire 'professionals' for this task, using money available from the administrative expenses of the NREGA or the District Rural Development Agency. The report was meant to be prepared by September 2007 and be sent to all the DMs and CDOs of the State. Till the date of this writing, no such report has been prepared for Chamoli. The case of the forgotten letter reminds us of that the quotidian performance of bureaucratic routine must continue lest the scheme meet a premature death, in files which are the graveyards of letters.

Just as all letters are procedural in nature, all letters are also in the precarious position of becoming forgotten letters. The easiest thing to do with these pieces of paper would be to file them away in an obscure place or, even worse, trash them altogether. Often, letters were *deliberately* forgotten. For instance, a particularly active petitioner in a village in Joshimath Block would often send in letters decrying the corruption (*bhrashtachar*) of the *pradhan* and the GPVA in the implementation of the NREGS. The members of the NREGS cell knew this petitioner personally and had decided, for reasons that remained unclear to me, that he should be paid no heed. Accordingly, every time his petitions came in, they would be torn up and binned. One day when the petitioner made his way down from his remote village to Gopeshwar and up to the NREGS cell, everyone feigned ignorance of his painstakingly written letters. One of the members of the NREGS cell even showed him the file entitled 'grievance redressal' and ordered the flummoxed villager to 'show us' (*dikhaon humko*) the so-called letters. After a thorough perusal of the file, and on not finding even a single of his many petitions in it, the villager had to leave chastened. He did continue to send in regular petitions that, tragically, kept meeting the same fate as their predecessors. Laxman Singh Negi, the head of a small NGO called Janadesh (literally, order of the people), had a cannier appreciation of the state's tendency to 'forget' or 'lose' letters whilst simultaneously appreciating the energy they radiated. He therefore decided to wage a 'non-violent agitation' (*andolan*) against Chamoli *sarkar's* shoddy implementation of the NREGS. This *andolan* was waged by sending letters of complaint to every single official in Chamoli from the DM downwards, as well as to officials in Dehradun including, even, the Chief Minister (CM) of the State. The letters listed details of non-payment or non-employment under the NREGS. His *andolan* had surprisingly good results, for these letters did make senior officials uncomfortable; it made them reach for their telephones and ring up the concerned BDO to tell him to do *avashyak karyavahi* (necessary action). Basking in the glow of the success of his *andolan*, Negi told me that he had decided to 'play the same paper-games that *sarkar* plays'. He was, then, deliberately and to good effect, mimicking the Indian state's beloved practice of 'lettering'.

State writing is generally considered uniform, dry, verging on the authoritarian. Yet, it became clear to me over the course of my immersion in Uttarakhand's bureaucracy that however formulaic the writing may be it is never completely constrained within a simple meaning, nor is it mechanically interpreted and implemented. The countless documents that flow through state channels, by virtue of their iterability, open themselves up to multiple interpretations (Das, 2007). Even when mere copies of a checklist are sent by one official to another, there are slight and subtle modifications in the manner in which they are read, understood, and acted upon. The interpretation of writing and the production of more written words on paper are absolutely central to the everyday life of the state in Himalayan India. The excess of writing that is believed to characterize the Indian state results in large part from the fact that rules and laws never quite achieve complete legibility through the issuance of bureaucratic documents. In order to follow the letter of the state, unceasing clarifications, translations, interpretations are required – in writing, and specifically in the form of letters. Letters, I have tried to show, can introduce, translate, clarify, complain, harass, act as protective shields, exhibit the observance of procedure or the fantastical nature of state rules/demands, they can be forgotten, feared, lost, or deliberately thrown away. Considerable time, energy and emotion is invested by middle- and lower-level bureaucrats in to the process of producing letters; a process that requires the hard labour of writing, interpreting, reading, drafting, re-drafting, obtaining signatures and stamps, packaging and posting-out. It is through the quotidian expending of this labour on documents, especially letters, that the paper state comes to be assembled and maintained. Performance of this labour is critical for the state and its project of welfare to remain alive. Officials had to work hard to make sure that even the regular procedural letters internal to the state apparatus were not forgotten. Responses were not simply written down; discussions on implementation aspects or reports on performance were not just produced. Rather these documents had to be made to be produced and circulated, often through the means of other letters, phone calls, or scolding (*daat*) or, as I show in the next chapter, through the strange seductions of *sarkari* affect that is most powerfully felt in meetings.

Endnotes

1 The District Magistrate's office is referred to as the *Collectorate* in Hindi and English. The DM is also known as 'the Collector', deriving from his/her traditional responsibility of collecting revenue as it was instituted under the British colonial state.

2 At the same time, one 'computer boy' was gifted to all the nine Blocks so that they could maintain the NREGS's computerized MIS (monitoring and information system). While the

ten new recruits under the NREGS referred to themselves as 'software professionals', every one else called them 'computer-*wallah ladka*' (computer boy).

3   There was no *kursi* (chair) earmarked for him. When he spent time in the room, he would drag in a rickety blue plastic stool from the adjoining room, and seat himself on that even if there were vacant chairs available.

4   In the district's government hierarchy there was a tacit cut-off point where one lost one's name and just became a sahib. All member of the NREGS cell were addressed by their surnames with the honorific *ji* suffixed. The PE and PD were simply the PE and the PD. From the DDO 'up' everyone was a sahib. Thus, it was DDO-sahib, CDO-sahib, SP-sahib etc.

5

Meeting One Another

Meetings, or face-to-face structured encounters, were integral to the everyday life of the state. These were moments when officials escaped the world of paper to face one another in public. The themes of these meetings (the English word was universally utilized) were just as varied as they were numerous: awareness generation, planning, capacity-building, trainings of officials or training-of-trainers, new personnel induction, monthly inspection, development council, NGO-state encounters, information dissemination to the media, and so on. The emphasis placed on 'transparency' and 'accountability' in the NREGA substantially added to the already enormous volume of meetings that all state development schemes bring in their wake. Meetings were held at every administrative level – village, Block, district, State (Uttarakhand), and Centre (New Delhi) – and comprised all sorts of actors, state and non-state alike. Some meetings were impromptu gatherings to thresh out responses to emergency situations such as surprise audits or predatory wild animals, but mostly they were planned and co-ordinated events with specific agendas and expected inputs from the invited participants.

Figure 5.1: Heading up to the meeting room © Sarnath Banerjee

In what is to follow, I concentrate on two types of meetings – the Block Development Officer (BDO) meetings and the Block Development Council meetings (BDCs). The BDO meetings are held in Gopeshwar, their dates poignantly marking the monthly calendar as the days when different layers of the district's development bureaucracy came together. The primary participants in these meetings are the trinity that commanded the district development bureaucracy – the Chief Development Officer (CDO), District Development Officer (DDO), and Project Director (PD) – and the heads of the nine Blocks, the BDOs of the district. The Block Development Council meetings (BDCs), by contrast, are held once every 3 months. They comprise the elected political representatives of the Block in question and the Block-level development bureaucracy, as well as some representatives from the District. The BDO meetings and the BDCs are deserving of special attention as the bureacrats themselves described them as the most critical events. Institutional rules command their regular occurrence as well as the archiving of their outcomes in official minutes and, in the case of the BDCs, publication of their discussions in the local newspapers.

The stated purpose of both these types of meetings is 'audit' of *sarkari vikas* (state-led development). Important works on audit society (Power, 1999) and audit culture (Strathern, 2000) have pointed out the contemporary obsession with auditing and linked it to neo-liberal techniques of governance. In this chapter, I build upon this literature by taking meetings seriously as ethnographic objects, not just as rational – legal ways of getting things done. The operational guidelines (OG) of NREGA give strict and chronological instructions on how the programme is to be audited. Operationally, though, audit was a much more diffuse practice than that imagined in the guidelines, with meetings constituting a constant instantiation. The BDCs and the BDO meetings were events in which wings of the state were made publicly accountable for their work, when aspects of the NREGS were brought into visibility through the revelation of statistics and the enactment of stipulated procedures. However, I argue that these meetings were not empty or instrumental rituals, and further, that we cannot capture their essence by thinking of them as mere facets of neoliberal governmentality. Rather, these moments during which the local state briefly assembles itself together are suffused in what I term 'sarkari affect'. Meetings constitute a key means through which a member of the state learns how to act and behave like one who is associated with Bharat *sarkar*. Moving away, once again, from perspectives that highlight the role of rationality, violence, discipline, or governmentality in the upkeep of the state, I argue that it is through participation in these frequent public theatres and the concomitant generation of *sarkari* affect that the state reproduces itself.

The practice of meetings is built into the very architecture of state buildings in Uttarakhand. In Chamoli, all of them have a designated meeting room separate from the regular office spaces. In Gopeshwar, the District Magistrate's office contained a big conference hall, which was used only for the most important gatherings, or when the number of participants could not be assembled in other meeting rooms. This conference hall was imposingly large, and adorned with a map of Uttarakhand and with portraits of Gandhi, Nehru, the present Chief Minister of the State, and, somewhat puzzlingly, the Bengali freedom fighter Subhash Chandra Bose.[1] For important events, the room was further ornamented with flower arrangements – rose bouquets and, once, festive marigold garlands. Thick blinds that were perpetually drawn, coupled with its high ceiling, lent the hall a cold, cavernous look, one that heightened the unease most officials confessed to experiencing when entering it for what they knew would be an act of high-level scrutinization. The BDO meetings were held in the smaller and more intimate setting of the meeting room of the Development Office (*Vikas Bhawan*). The meeting room in *Vikas Bhawan* was located a level above the CDO's office. It contained a rectangular conference table, with additional seating available on chairs placed along the walls. At the head of the table, three swivel chairs were set up on which would be seated the CDO, DDO, and the PD; the most senior official – the CDO – being always seated centrally, with his two deputies flanking him. The BDOs would cluster nervously around, attempting to stay as far away from the head of the table as they possibly could. Other staff, such as those from the NREGS cell in the Gopeshwar office and representatives from line departments, would be seated either along the wall or around the conference table at a slight distance from the BDOs.

The Block office of Dasholi, like most of the other eight block offices, possessed a slightly more theatrical meeting room, which provided an apt stage for the BDCs. This room had a large dais at one end, on which only the convenor of the meeting, the chief guest, and the single most important personage present, would be placed. Often, there would be a jostling for the privilege of sitting up on the dais with the luminaries, with demands for extra chairs and expression of outright anger at not being offered a seat *upar* (above). *Neeche* (below), chairs were arranged classroom-style in neat lines, with the audience directly facing the rostrum. The one step up onto the platform would differentiate the interrogator from the interrogated, even though which party occupied what space varied depending on the form of the particular gathering. Thus, in regular meetings, such as the monthly Block-level *sameekshan* (assessment) meeting, those sitting on the dais interrogated and volubly commanded the one's sitting below. In BDCs, however, the equation was reversed with the 'people's representatives' – the elected local body (*Panchayat*) office holders – seated below, hassling those 'above' for details/clarifications and demanding better performance from the government-appointed officials – the local bureaucrats – who were positioned on the dais. The staging of the meetings might occur in different theatres, so to say, but both of them constituted state 'rituals of verification' (Power, 1999).

The *tamasha* of the BDCs

In my Gopeshwar office, the BDCs were termed *tamashas* (raucous gatherings). Every time I would return from a BDC my office-mates would sit me down and make me read out the 'minutes', as they called my field notes. The script of the BDCs was quite simple. Elected local political representatives assembled four times in a year in the Block office to quiz *sarkar's* developmental efforts. The meeting was chaired by the BDO who would begin with a small introductory speech, which would include the progress achieved by the Block, recount new schemes and measures being introduced to develop the region, and end with profuse thanks to the assembled audience for their assistance in *sarkar's* work. Immediately, discussion of different schemes would spring up, with the audience asking the bureaucrats positioned on the dais for details of money spent and specific aspects of different development programs. The discussion was almost always about why things were not working as they ought to, why *sarkar* was so lazy/incompetent/corrupt and why more funds were not coming into the villages. There was always an attempt to maintain a structure in this question-and-order session, but it was hard to impose with multiple people speaking at the same time, different schemes being discussed simultaneously, loud protests and open expressions of anger the whole time. It was not uncommon for expletives to be hurled, with a serious altercation breaking out on one occasion when an inebriated village headman stabbed a political rival from the adjoining village. All through the session, people would walk in and out, tea would be drunk, even *beedis* (locally rolled cigarettes) smoked and food eaten. Groups would form in corners of the hall and begin discussing altogether different issues.

Below are the minutes I kept of a BDC held in Gairsain block in early 2007. It was not a particularly eventful BDC, but this snippet might provide a flavour of BDCs in general.

Gairsain 30/02/07, block office

A crowd of about 30 people are assembled in the large meeting hall. About eight of them are women, who sit clustered together in one corner at the back of the room. People are walking in and out. The young Junior Engineers (JEs) and the DPO (Deputy Programme Officer) stand out sartorially. They are dressed in denim jeans with bright sweaters and/or denim jackets and are wearing (fake) branded sneakers. It's freezing cold, a wind rips in from the open door and the broken windows.

11.20 a.m. The BDC begins with the BDO standing up on the dais and shouting, 'we are beginning now'. At his side is seated the *Kshetra Panchayat Pramukh* (KPP), the head of the Block *Panchayat*. The District Engineer from the Gopeshwar office is seated to his right. Two senior ADOs (Additional Development Officers) are also on the dais, seated near the BDO. The BDO welcomes everyone to Gairsain and thanks them for making the trip up here in this cold weather and in the face of the 'terror of the human-eating big cat' (*bagh ka aatank*) that is haunting the town and its adjoining villages. He follows this with a long speech on how hard the Block officials and the KPP have been working in order to 'bring development in to Gairsain' (*vikas ko Gairsain mein lane ke liye*). He thanks the KPP for all the assistance he has been providing *sarkar* in this endeavour. The KPP nods graciously. The BDO asks the KPP for his permission to begin the BDC. With an imperial wave of the hand, the KPP signifies his assent.

The BDO sits down, rummages through some papers, stands up again and announces, loudly, '*Rozgar Guarantee*' (Employment Guarantee).[2] He reads out the budget still available for the Block for this financial year, a staggering Rs 13 crore. 'To spend this money, we have hired a Deputy Program Officer (DPO) and some junior engineers (JE). I invite them to introduce themselves and tell us what work they are doing for us'.

The DPO goes up first. His introduction consists of his qualifications (a MBA from an institute in the town of Allahabad in UP) and the work he is doing which is 'helping BDO-sahib'. Five JEs trail up behind him. They introduce themselves and read out the list of estimates of NREGS works that they have prepared in different villages. They read haltingly and slowly; it's all mostly inaudible. In any case, nobody is really listening for they are all conversing amongst themselves.

Once the introductions are done, the KPP gets up and launches into speech: 'It is a matter of pride for Chamoli that the NREGA is being implemented here. We have been facing big difficulties in the implementation of this plan (*yojana*) as we did not have enough manpower. The new recruits are, therefore, very welcome. I welcome them all to our Gairsain and hope that employment (*rozgar*) and development (*vikas*) will follow them in. Note this government order (GO) [*he waves a document in the air*] says that 50 per cent of the work is to be done by the *Gram Panchayat* (village council), 25 per cent by the Block and 25 per cent by the *Zila Panchayat* (District Council). Therefore, all three must work in harmony (*taal-mel se kam kare*)'.

At this point there are sniggers and shouts of laughter from the assembled crowd. It is evident that they don't believe such harmony is possible.

The KPP ignores the jeering and continues: 'Are there any problems with the Guarantee?' He sits down.

The laughter only gets louder. A *pradhan* gets up and says, 'You have painted the wall of my *panchayat bhawan* (*council* office) but what is this *Rozgar* Guarantee, after all?'

The BDO stands up to respond: 'It is a scheme by which villagers can ask *sarkar* for work. There is no dearth of money in this scheme. So make more demands. The more the demand, the more the money. The more the money the better it is for Gairsain'.

At this point another *pradhan* says, '*Sarkari paisa* (government money) might be there but because it is *sarkari paisa*, nobody wants to work. How do I make them work?'

This question provokes a deluge of similar questions/comments from the other assembled *pradhans*. The subjects of their complaints range from the 'lazy villagers' who don't want to work but just want *sarkari paisa muft mein* (government money for free), through the corrupt village-level development workers (GPVAs) who don't give them money, through problems with the low-standard material coming in, to the circles they have to run around (*chakkar maaro*) the Block begging to have money released. The BDO and the KPP attempt to field these queries simultaneously. The discussion gets simply too entangled for note-taking. For about 20 min this goes on. The DPO sidles up to me to complain that all his hair has fallen out due to the stress caused by this *haraami* Guarantee (bastard NREGS). The JEs have slipped out and can be sighted smoking in the adjoining garden. Abruptly, the BDO terminates discussions on the NREGS by loudly announcing the name of another development scheme. The mention of this scheme, related to housing for families falling below the poverty line, leads to an immediate shifting of gears, and the assembly begins a whole host of new inquiries into and complaints against the scheme. The NREGS has, thus, been wound up for this quarter in Gairsain block.

I walk out of the BDC with the DPO and three of the new junior engineers. We get some *chai* and I begin asking them about their experience of the district and the NREGS. All four express their disappointment with their remote locations. Two of the four originally hail from the plains and are finding it extremely difficult to adjust to life in the distant mountains. The other two, though they do come from different areas of Uttarakhand, are as desperate as the plainsmen to get jobs in a big city in the plains. In reference to the NREGA, they complain about the masses of paperwork and the 'lazy *paharis*' who have no interest in working. I try to keep the conversation on the NREGA but they are keener to discuss how one can run away from the remote mountains, and what my life is like in Delhi and in the UK. Three months later, when I return to Gairsain for another BDC, I note that two of the four have quit their jobs. By this time, the DPO is beside himself with frustration at having failed to manage a similar escape, and feverishly discusses options for exiting this remote land. The BDC is dismissed as a '*tamasha*' that needs to be periodically undertaken for the benefit of the local newspapers, the people of the Block, and Gopeshwar. 'It's just about making a noise…noise that signifies *sarkar* is doing something', the DPO says to me.

The unbearable silence of the BDOs

The BDCs were all about creating noise and making yourself heard; the BDO meetings were their polar opposite, punctuated by long uncomfortable silences in which the BDOs did their utmost not to be spotted or asked to speak. The BDO meetings had a date fixed for them – the 24th of each month. If the 24th was a Sunday, it would be shifted to the 25th. The planned nature of these meetings was not limited to their date but also extended to the documents underpinning the meetings – the 'upwardly oriented' (Mosse, 2005, p. 11) monthly progress report (MPR). It was expected that the BDO would send in his progress report by the 22nd of each month to the NREGS cell. Very rarely was this request fulfilled. The norm was the nine BDOs of the district rushing into the NREGS cell an hour or so before the meeting, to thrust the hastily made *kachcha* (raw) progress reports into the hands of the three senior functionaries of the NREGS cell. Between themselves, they would glance quickly through the one on financial performance for 'even if the others are *farzee* (fake) *toh chalta hai* (it will work) but not if there is any *gadbad* (mismatch or wrongdoing) with the money'. If there were serious *gadbad* with the reports, they would be hastily 'fixed' by one of the members of the cell. Once verified by the NREGS cell for not possessing glaring problems, the semi-pukka progress reports would be taken into the meeting hall for the monthly evaluation.

The BDO meetings were chaired by the CDO, but the job of running it was left to the DDO. Typically, the meetings would begin as soon as the CDO had walked into the room. The CDO was always the last one to enter as everyone else made sure, somehow, to be in position before he had made his way up the one flight of stairs that separated his large office from the meeting hall. With little ceremony other than a barely perceptible nod of the head and a quick *namaste*, the CDO would request the DDO to begin at once. The DDO would do so by immediately announcing the name of a scheme and then, apparently at random, naming a Block. The BDO of this Block would stand up and state the statistics on the scheme. Through the ritual of running through every scheme and obtaining figures on its performance from every BDO (on the parameters previously identified), the district meetings became a forum for extracting basic information on development works in the outlying mountain villages from lower-level functionaries. The precise statistics or the information required of each programme varied. So when the name of *Rozgar Guarantee* (NREGS) would be called out, the two key figures the BDO publicly announced were 'number of households employment has been provided to' and 'money spent'.

I reproduce here some of my notes from a meeting held in 2007:

11:00 a.m.

The room is empty save for a cleaner who is lackadaisically dusting the table. The meeting is meant to begin at 11 a.m. I make the mistake of actually turning up on time, much to the cleaner's surprise.

11.20 a.m.

A few men enter. Slowly the room fills up. The nine BDOs seat themselves by the table, close to its head. The heads of the line departments settle down rather nervously on chairs alongside the wall. The Project Director, who heads the District Rural Development Agency (DRDA) enters with the DDO, who is supposed to be incharge of *Vikas Bhawan* (Development Office). They seat themselves at the head of the table, leaving the central chair vacant. Directly in front of that chair – the CDO's throne so to say – is a chipped glass doing duty as a vase, a straggly rose dangling despondently out of it.

The meeting begins with the DDO checking to see whether all the BDOs are present. His manner of taking roll call is to reel off a list of the names of the nine Blocks that form part of Chamoli: Dasholi, Deval, Ghat, Joshimath, Karnaprayag, Pokhri and so on. In the midst of this roll call, the Chief Development Officer (CDO) walks in. Everyone leaps to their feet. The CDO sits down on his *kursi*, respectfully left vacant for him. He enquires after the agenda of the meeting, which the DDO hurriedly whispers to him. The CDO takes over the reins of the meeting.

'Rozgar Guarantee',[3] announces the DDO loudly.

CDO to the BDOs: 'What is the problem with making projects?'

Silence

The CDO glares at his assembled BDOs and then proceeds to explain the procedure whereby projects under the NREGA can be started: 'You need to solicit *prarthana patras* (letters of request) from the villagers on the basis of prioritized work. It is important to begin work now. When the elections come around, as they will soon, it will be impossible to get any work done'.

Continued silence

The DDO begins naming Blocks and asking if they have met targets. The target in this case was work begun in a certain number of villages. Names of all the nine Blocks are called out. As a block name is called out, the concerned BDO leaps to his feet and answers with a number, which might or might not be equal to the target that the DDO would, in response, bark out. In most cases, the achievements were significantly lower than the targets, which prompted the CDO to again intervene with that seemingly un-answerable question, 'Why is work not happening in villages? I don't understand what the problem is. There is no dearth of money in *Rozgar* Guarantee'.

Again, silence

The awkward silence in the room is broken only by the snort of disgust uttered by the PD. The DDO and the CDO openly exchange glances of despair mingled with disgust. The situation is salvaged somewhat by the entry of the *Nazir* (personal assistant) bearing a tray with three cups of tea. He goes to the CDO first and serves him his tea, taking care to place a coaster underneath his cup. The DDO is next, followed by the PD. The CDO takes a sip of his tea, signalling that it is all right for the other two to begin as well.

The DDO moves onto the next issue on the agenda under NREGS – wall paintings on *panchayat bhawans*[4] (Village office buildings).

DDO: 'Wall paintings advertising the NREGA must be done at the earliest. Government of India (*Bharat Sarkar*) will not release the second installment of funds unless we get 100 per cent *Panchayat Bhawans* painted'.

Again, there is no response from the assembled BDOs

The DDO, unsurprised by this lack of response, moves on to specific issues under the NREGS, dealt with Block by Block. The first one in the line of fire is Joshimath Block.

CDO to BDO of Joshimath who has promptly jumped to his feet for the interrogation: 'Why are your Junior Engineers (JEs) not performing? Why are you not able to use them? No project designs are ever sent up to me for sanctioning. They never put in any new projects, I never see any files from your Block, what is happening?'

Silence is the BDO's only answer.

CDO (getting cross now): 'Stop their salaries if they are not working. Do you know how poorly it reflects on us if we are unable to get work out of them? We are paying them from the scheme's money, after all'.

The BDO nods his head in mute agreement and sits down hurriedly before more issues can be discussed with regard to his Block.

And so it went on, with BDO after BDO getting up to state his monthly progress in facts and figures. Almost always the trinity at the head of the table would express their disappointment at the figures read out by the BDOs – for all the schemes, but especially for the Guarantee. The BDOs had hardly ever met the targets set for them by the district – for money spent, man-days created, people employed, structures constructed – and the rare claim of having met a target was treated with incredulity. It was noteworthy that the self-selection mechanism that the NREGA boasts of was never in evidence at these events. Senior officials 'knew' (as they put it) that their subordinates could only work to a target, be it number of works opened in a village, money spent, or bank accounts opened. Indeed, it was entirely through the metric of having met the target or, at least, having come close to it that the NREGA worked. Juniors and colleagues were pressed – scolded and, more rarely, cajoled – to present better results the next time round. Meetings, thus, not only made performance visible but also served as moments when betterment – in the form of improved statistics – could be pushed for. The NREGS brought in vast amounts of money to the district; failure to spend this money on finding employment for the large population of the rural unemployed would be the failure of everyone in that meeting hall, but especially that of the CDO who was the one answerable to the tiers of government above him.[5] Hence, the non-expenditure of the funds made him particularly anxious. If his subordinates stated any reasons for the non-performance of the NREGS, they would be ignored or, more commonly, shouted down. Unemployment continues the biggest grievance in the mountain districts of Uttarakhand, especially in the middle and upper Himalayan belt where employment opportunities remain minimal. Yet, BDOs found it extremely hard to implement the NREGS in Chamoli, for the reasons listed in the previous chapter. The reasons for the unimplementability of the NREGA – its staggering volume of paperwork and the work that certain transparent-making documents were doing – could not be officially acknowledged. The former was deemed unacceptable because new recruits were constantly being hired to do the paperwork; the latter could not be discussed as it would imply acknowledgment of the 'real system' through which development schemes are implemented. On a few occasions, officials did hesitantly refer to the lack of demand for work by the villagers, but this was immediately shot down by the higher officials as an impossible scenario. Just as there could be no public, minuted discussion of the unsettling characteristics of the NREGA; similarly, there was no space to contemplate the suggestion that there was no keen citizenry wishing to work under this flagship legislation. This public disavowal was doubly interesting for, in private, officials would endlessly complain about the lazy, alcoholic, *pahari* men who had no interest in putting in hard labour but only in getting *sarkari paisa* for free (*muft mein*). I noticed these public dismissals right from the beginning of my study.

CDO to BDO of X block in response to the very low expenditure noted in his MPR under the NREGS: 'Why are you not spending the money? Why is all that money just lying there rotting in your account? Why is no work happening in your Block?'

BDO (*very softly*): 'There is no demand, sir'.

CDO (*immensely irritated*): 'What do you mean there is no demand? I refuse to believe that!'

DDO (*shouting*): 'You are wasting *sarkar's* time!'

CDO: 'Begin work in ten villages at the very least within a week. If you do not do so then I will hold you personally responsible for this failure'.

The CDO, DDO and PD repeatedly exhorted their subordinates to make 'the people' (*janta*) understand the scheme. The DDO and the PD made it clear that the lack of demand for work was the direct result of the sloth of their subordinates, who were not taking the initiative to 'create the demand'. The CDO assumed that the way forward was re-clarification of the procedure by educating the BDOs on the rules of the scheme. He kept focusing on the procedure whereby 'the people' could be made to understand how beneficial the scheme was for them in this time of low-employment opportunities, the concrete and sequential measures government functionaries had to take to operationalize the program, all of which would culminate in the success of this initiative. A couple of days after this particular meeting, a district-level workshop was held as part of the capacity-building initiative required under the NREGS. At this event, the CDO invited anyone from the NREGS staff to stand up and 'openly and fearlessly' tell him why they were not able to implement the scheme. Taking heart from this rather unfamiliarly pleasant language, a few BDOs stood up to complain of infighting in their Block offices, of flagrant insubordination, of officials perennially absent from their workstations, of signatures withheld due to spite or anger, of files that other officials were 'sitting on', of the lies that officials made up on *kaghaz*, of inspections not undertaken but written up as reports, of personality clashes and village-level politics, and of the disinterest shown in the NREGS by elected members of local government bodies due to the slim possibilities of 'eating money' from the scheme. I was fascinated by these highly personalized accounts of the mundane politics of offices in the district. The CDO, DDO, and the PD, however, exchanged exasperated glances that clearly signified their disdain for these 'politics' (the English word was used).

CDO (*dismissively*): 'I am not interested in these politics. You have to sort them out yourself. Don't eat up my head with them. Can you not see that I have more important things to think about rather than try to make peace between you and your *pradhans*? You are all grown men, not children so please stop squabbling and get back to work on this scheme of national importance and stop wasting my and *sarkar's* precious time. Further, here in the district I just want to hear of the technical problems faced by all of you'.

In the meetings, the 'politics' that was shot down referred to challenges, contestations, disputes, and ill feelings at the local official level. Localized power struggles and the messiness of the everyday functioning of local bureaucracies – 'politics' – that did not adhere to Weber's ideal rational, modern bureaucracy were not, officially, to be considered serious factors impeding the implementation of a complex central plan of 'national importance'. In contrast, discussions of 'technical' problems – shortages of staff, lack of stationary and other material tools, lack of clarity on precise procedures – were fit for the office and for the attention of superior officers. The CDO, like other senior development bureaucrats in Dehradun, was of the opinion that the NREGA was a well-designed scheme, which was facing problems in implementation due to lack of manpower, the lazy *paharis* who were not interested in working for their keep, the difficult terrain and poor connectivity of the mountains (especially of the remote regions), the low capacity of middle- and lower-level functionaries, and rampant corruption. If all these factors could just somehow be rectified, the NREGA would work exactly as envisioned by the planners in New Delhi. The CDO's view of the NREGA was quite different from that of the levels below him, though of course nobody ever dared contradict CDO *sahib* openly. It is worth noting that the opinions of officials located higher up the state hierarchy, who hail from the elite civil services, map almost seamlessly onto those held by development experts, journalists, and activists holding similar class positions and locations in urban India.

'On paper' doublethink

A central feature of the BDO meetings, I noted, was the indication by senior officials that they are well aware of the falsifications in lower-level reporting, or what was constantly discussed as *'farzee'* (fake) reporting or papers or statistics. Subordinates were threatened with amorphously dire consequences if they did not work properly or if they continued to put forth *farzee* reports, the conviction of whose falsity derived from the figures therein being intuitively or logically suspect. I was stunned at the regularity with which figures or reports were adjudged *farzee* or false/fake. If the number of self-help groups created or number of households provided with employment in the NREGS had increased from its previous figure, then the allegation of *farzee* reporting was levelled at the BDO. If too much money appeared to have been spent in too short a time then, again, it would be considered a case of *farzee* reporting. When statistics contradicted each other or balance sheets did not tally up as they ought to, this was seen as an indicator of the fundamental falsity of the entire report/documents that the BDO was presenting to the district. But even when the reports did not appear illogical or hold any element of surprise, subordinate officials were sternly instructed to present only *asli* (real) results rather than continue producing their wonted fake/constructed reports.

I was initially surprised to hear senior officials tell their juniors that they didn't want to hear what was there 'on paper' (*kaghaz pe*) for they knew just how *farzee* that all was, they wanted to know what the *vastavik* (realistic) and *asli* (real) *soochna* (news/report) was from their area. In BDCs, similarly, the elected representatives would rail against *sarkari* functionaries for restricting all their work only to their meticulously maintained papers. An objective of all meetings, it soon became evident, was to verbalize the senior officials' knowledge of the fundamentally *farzee* nature of all state reporting. In the meetings, it would be impossible to precisely locate and identify fraud, for all the evidence lay in the documents prepared by BDOs themselves. What occurred was a more generalized warning against continuing with fraudulent practices, and ominous signals that higher-up officials were cognizant, and intolerant, of the murky practices that go on in the dark recesses of the lower wings of the state. Furthermore, even while officials were threatened for doing *farzee* work, they were also told to 'fix' the papers or reports, ordered to make sure what was 'on paper' was fine. In general parlance, to say that something is only 'on paper' is to signify, as Derrida (2005) notes, its virtual presence or ineffectiveness. Thus for activists to say an anti-dowry law or the NREGA remains 'on paper', constitutes a major critique of the enactment process and, by extension, of the state's inability to enforce its writ. Government functionaries used the 'on paper' (*kaghaz pe*) phrase simultaneously in both of its twin senses. Their saying that something was on paper implied its ineffectiveness *but also*, at the very same moment, its effectiveness. Senior officials would scold their juniors for maintaining progress only on paper while simultaneously ordering them to look after the paperwork properly for, after all, what really counted was what was on paper. Thus, the field officers were berated for not visiting their villages and seeing for themselves what was happening. If officials would protest that they did visit villages, they would be told that there was no point in their conducting an inspection or an audit unless they afterwards produced a written and signed report testifying to the same.

At the very same time that development was being made visible as a reality through the material production of a slew of documents, there was an acknowledgment by bureaucrats that this was so only on paper; but, then, 'on paper' was almost all that counted. This somewhat confusing use of the 'on paper' phrase can be best understood through the Orwellian term doublethink: 'To know and not to know, to be conscious of complete truthfulness while telling carefully constructed lies, to hold simultaneously two opinions which cancelled out, knowing them to be contradictory and believing in both of them ...' (1949, p. 35) is what doublethink consists of. The 'on paper' logic consisted of just such a piece of doublethink whereby a speaker could hold on to two contradictory meanings without inducing a state of cognitive dissonance in themself. This was probably the most complicated piece of the everyday grammar of bureaucratic life that I encountered; and made sense of it only after months of immersion in *sarkari* life, during which I had internalized the fundamentals of its functioning. After all, as Orwell has noted, '[e]ven to understand the word 'doublethink' involved the use of doublethink' (*ibid*).

BDO meetings, then, were a practice aimed at allowing the district's development apparatus to monitor itself and rail against what is 'on paper' even as it simultaneously made sure that the papers were in order. In addition to ensuring the proper maintenance of material testaments to development, meetings allowed the creation of the effect of a coherent system through their self-description of working-as-one on the NREGA. Strathern writes that through audit 'organizations have learned how to describe themselves' (2006, p. 189). This self-description must be convincing, in the sense that they have 'to persuade others that it is 'themselves' they are describing' (*ibid*, emphases removed). Indeed, 'the system' that agents of the state refer to so often was, during these events, turning a scrutinizing gaze inwards in a public assembly.

The outcomes of the BDO meetings and BDCs alike were consigned to reports that were sent up the state hierarchy, were relayed to local newspapers and NGOs, and were discussed amongst the district bureaucracy. Did meetings end or even curtail *farzee* reporting? Did they lead to the production of better results? There is almost no way to provide an answer to these questions empirically; it lies outside the knowledge generated by this system. What the meetings did achieve, though, is the creation of the effect of a unified system working towards a common objective – of implementing a development scheme by the rulebook.

There is a danger, however, in studying meetings purely as institutionalized practices, deriving from neo-liberal techniques of governance, that attempt to set up systems of self-accounting: it might lead to viewing meetings, reductively, as empty rituals performed for the benefit of the state. Yurchak (2006) has explored a set of heavily ritualized practices and texts under a very different system – that of late socialism in the Soviet Union. He gives the instance of the Komsomol meetings, which consisted of participation by young people in a strictly scripted procedure with little attention paid to their literal meanings (15 – 16). 'Can', he asks, 'these acts be described as pure masquerade and dissimulation, practiced in public for the gaze of the state and collective surveillance?' (16). Similarly, a question I pose here is, what did it mean for the functionaries of the state to participate in the rituals of verification I describe above? Did the repetition of form, the facticity of having to pay public obeisance to the authoritative discourse of 'development' and having to abide by the regulations present in the authoritative texts of the NREGA, the temporally fixed quality of the meetings and, in fact, of their outcomes as well, mean that the participants in these rituals merely came onto the stage of the conference room to perform their *sarkari* roles and leave, their task accomplished? Initially, this is what I took these meetings to consist of – empty rituals (in the regular sense of the word), in which agents of the state participated because they had to. However, as time went on and different meetings revealed themselves to me as variegated events, though they shared a hegemonic form and were performed under the terms of an authoritative discourse, I began to notice other facets to them.

Becoming *sarkari*

An important aspect of meetings, one that was openly taught to the novices, was how to become and behave like a member of *sarkar* (state). At a training programme for Junior Engineers (JEs), for instance, a senior engineer launched into a long, elaborate speech on how the young graduates and initiates into the NREGS and *sarkar*, must conduct themselves differentially with 'the people' (*janta*), with the peoples' representatives (*jan-pratinidhi*), and with state officials. This speech included semi-humorous instances of his own faux-pas as a young and gauche engineer in awe of powerful officials, such as being tongue-tied in meetings, not standing up when such-and-such a dignitary entered the room, turning up in casual attire for important state events, not knowing whom to address as a *sahib* and whom as a peer, and so on. At the end of this particular meeting, a sprightly young Junior Engineer turned to me and remarked that this was a training programme in 'becoming *sarkari*' (*sarkari banna*) rather than on the NREGS. This was much more useful to him, he claimed, for '*engineer to koeen bhi ban jaye lekin sarkari banana zaida mushkil hai*' (anyone can become an engineer, but it is more difficult to become *sarkari*).

The aspect of becoming and being *sarkari* (state-like/official) was stressed in all BDO meetings. Emphasis was placed on knowing where to sit, when to stand up, when to speak, what to say, and how to deliver the speech. Thus, one was to stand up and answer questions from the DM when in the larger conference hall. In the BDO's meeting, it was not necessary for the BDOs assembled around the conference table to stand, though the more lowly line department officials, seated on the chairs along the walls, mostly jumped to their feet when any query was directly addressed to them by the trinity at the head of the table. Further, when a question on, say, the performance of the NREGS was posed, the BDOs knew what figures to reel out, and in what particular order. Were they to miss a statistic or not respond at all, or profess ignorance of the issue in question, it would be considered a fundamental failure on their part. To not perform as a *sarkari adhikari* (state official) ought to – an aspect that was consistently stressed as being of the utmost importance in meetings – was a malfunction of the most condemnable sort. 'Being *sarkari*' is not a skill one automatically acquires by virtue of obtaining employment in the hallowed interiors of the Indian state's gargantuan bureaucracy. Rather, it needs to be learned and publicly performed, be it through the capacity to pen letters, to scold subordinates, to handle politicians, or, in this case, to perform amongst one's colleagues as one who is cognizant of the system within which all are working and living. Thus, to read the monotonous recitation of figures, head-nodding, or even the silences as empty acts, would not do justice to what it means to become and perform being *sarkari*.

Correct performance aside, the mere attendance of officials at meetings was, in and of itself, an act signifying their compliance with the state. When certain

BDOs, for instance, absented themselves from successive meetings without permission or legitimate reasons, their absence was publicly discussed as insubordination. There was particular worry expressed about remote Blocks, or those spaces that were far away from Gopeshwar. As the tabled documents were regularly believed to be *farzee* and district officials rarely visited the more remote areas of the district, it was important for the Block representative – the BDO – to be present at the district headquarters. His physical presence in Gopeshwar and his correct performance in the meetings, alongside the production of the appropriate pieces of paper, allowed the district authorities to claim that the remote Blocks were not being left ungoverned. Monthly meetings, therefore, had to be attended by all the BDOs. On the 24th of each month they had to make their way from their distant Block offices up to *mukhyalaya* (headquarters), as this was what was required from an actor occupying their position in the hierarchy of the state, for a public demonstration to his peers and superiors alike that he was, indeed, doing his job. He must arrive on time, be dressed semi-formally (some men wore suits and ties), seat himself on the spot allocated to him, produce the requisite statistics, and comply duly and publicly with the orders that were being issued to him from above.

The affect of *sarkar*

Bureaucracies are all too often studied, implicitly or explicitly, as rationalized institutional practice. An enduring association with disenchanted Weberian iron cages of modernity has distracted attention away from following through their specific histories and variable effects (Bear and Mathur, 2015). Mazarella makes the point that in *Discipline and Punish* Foucault, too, posits a sharp contrast between the middle of the eighteenth century and the beginning of the nineteenth century when 'the normative forms of European sovereignty shifted from spectacular theatricality to rationalized, affect-evacuated technicism' (2009, p. 295). More recent work has turned to study the affective life of states (Aretxaga, 2003; Stoler, 2009; Reeves, 2011) and has focused on the role of affect within bureaucracy (Bear, 2007; Navaro-Yashin, 2012), which has served as a welcome corrective to an excessive focus on rationality. My own ethnography presents bureaucratic practices and the spaces within which they are undertaken as shot through with affect. Whether it is the reading and interpretation of the official guidelines of a law or the writing of letters or the holding of meetings, there is, I have tried to show, an affective charge to these practices. 'The labile terrain of affect is not', as Mazzarella correctly observes, 'in fact external to bureaucratic process' (2009, p. 298).

A meditation on affect helps us understand how the bureaucratic apparatus of the state persists. If we are to approach the state as a set of relational practices, then a question that must be asked is how or what allows these practices to repeatedly perform themselves? One way of understanding this staying-alive of the state bureaucracy is to locate it squarely within the violence that underpins this structure (Graeber, 2012). The bureaucracies I worked in are, after all, underpinned by what Althusser terms a Repressive State Apparatus (RSA), a tangible coercive apparatus, which allows for hierarchical dominance to be practised.[6] To be part of this apparatus means that laws and orders emanating from Dehradun and Delhi must be followed in Gopeshwar – or, more specifically, must be shown, through the production of material proof, to have been followed. Everyday energies in Chamoli were undeniably concentrated on producing material evidence of adherence to what had been commanded from higher up in the hierarchy. Yet, violence cannot fully account for the compliance of functionaries with the state's rules and procedures. It does not explain their eagerness to learn how to properly fit in and become *sarkari*, or why banal practices and pieces of paper, and the bodies of certain officials, provoked a variety of emotions ranging from anxiety, anger, awe, hilarity, and sadness to pride.

Ferguson and Gupta's study of the spatialization of states or the production of 'spatial and scalar hierarchies' (2005, p. 119) might offer another way of thinking of the working of government. There is a key self-depiction of the centralized Indian state in documentary products such as the operational guidelines of the NREGS with its neat organizational diagrams and flow charts, and in the language of letters and meetings, which constantly invokes and identifies the levels 'above' and 'below' spatially – Delhi is above while Dehradun is below – as well as levels of 'senior' and 'junior' officials. The state, in such an image, is a vertical hierarchy with each level encompassing the one below. The village is enfolded into the Block, the Block into the district, the district into the provincial state and so on up to New Delhi, which is the repository of all power; it is the throne from which all of India is ruled. It is similarly so with officials – the 'higher up' an official is, the further up his/her office and organizational location is. The DM, thus, is the most *ucha adhikari* (high official) in the district while, say, the sweeper is a mere *neecha karamchari* (lowly worker). In meetings, grumbling by any of the staff grumbled about the non-performance/inefficiencies of those 'below them' would be met with incredulity. For instance, the CDO claimed never to understand quite why BDOs were unable to control their JEs and DPOs, who were located well 'below' them in the hierarchy. He and his two deputies would often remind the BDOs that if they were unable to extract work from their sub-ordinates then they had failed in their job, and were not fit to be called BDO-*sahib*. The location 'above' was demonstrable not only in the acronyms and official rank accompanied with the attached, ever-present *sahib* suffix, but also more materially in office space, access to government vehicles for official purposes, the power of writing annual confidential reports on performance or control over release of salaries, and, quite crucially, the chair (*kursi*) which one occupied in meetings.

Yet, both an exclusive focus on violence and on state spatialization leave out something that is vital to the state: the charge that infuses the everyday and allows it to be accomplished without incessantly questioning why one is doing what one is doing. Fear of reprimand or of breaking the law, or even of being suspended, as well as a cultivated awe for state hierarchy were all present but only ephemerally so. What was much more powerful was a difficult-to-articulate affordance at play, one that is perhaps best expressed through the word *sarkari*. As discussed previously, this word carries pejorative connotations of being, somehow, jaded and/or fake. But, as I describe in this chapter, it carries a different – aspirational and deeply desirable – meaning for agents of the state. For new recruits to the bureaucracy as well as its more seasoned players, it is imperative to learn and inhabit *sarkariness*. Being a *sarkari* official means that you are associated with the state, get space within government buildings, touch and work with official documents, encounter and attend meetings with other *sarkari* people. There is an affective charge to all of these practices, encounters, and moments. In the previous chapter on letters I show how these apparently dry artefacts were laden with affect, right from the point of their writing to their posting-out and in the anticipation of responses. In this chapter, I dwell on the affect induced by different rooms, how some meetings were carnivalesque and some deeply sombre, and how officials responded to and acted within them. Mazzarella makes the point that 'any social project that is not imposed through force alone must be affective in order to be effective' (2009, p. 299). Precisely so, I propose that it is not violence or a spatialized state imaginary that allows for the everyday life of the state to persist, but rather, the powerful affect of *sarkar*.

Sarkari affect can be sensed acutely in meetings, when there is an inter-subjective, embodied, physical gathering of agents associated with the state apparatus. A particular meeting in Gopeshwar brought this home to me. After the *Bharatiya Janta* Party's (BJP's) election victory in Uttarakhand in February 2007, the newly appointed Chief Minister made it a point to visit the remote *pahari* districts of his State. During his visit to Chamoli he held a *janta ki durbar* (a people's durbar), at which supplicants arrived, waited patiently, then queued up neatly to present the CM with their demands or to air their grievances by means of petitions. The durbar was held in lawns of the district guesthouse in Gopeshwar. The CM sat flanked by his aide-de-camp and the DM and other senior district officials, to whom he handed over the petitions. In the days leading up to the CM's arrival there was a frenzy of preparation, with support staff being pulled in from all the Blocks. In the NREGS cell, we were frantically ensuring that all the files were up-to-date, and that documents containing statistics on the performance of the scheme were to hand. This was a big moment for Chamoli district and for its official headquarters it was, in my experience, the most intense period of work, filled with trepidation and happy anticipation. The previous CM had never managed to fly down in his personal helicopter to Chamoli, a fact that was pointed out to me repeatedly by residents of the district. This CM's arrival, the holding of the durbar, and his staying overnight in Gopeshwar were heralded by the DM as a visit by *sarkar* to this border district. The durbar that he held was described in glowing terms as the presence of a benign ruler in a remote land, *sarkar* making itself manifest.

The DM might have seen the state in the visit of his political master, but within the district he himself is considered *sarkar*. When DM *sahib* sets off for villages in his white Ambassador car, bearing his nameplate and a flashing blue light, to inspect NREGA constructions, he is considered an embodiment of *sarkar*. When he accepts petitions or hands them over to his local staff with a quick scribble of 'please see' on them – or even just a signature carrying his initials – then *sarkar* is seen to be doing something. When a village-level development worker makes a trip to Gopeshwar, to the district headquarters, and participates tremulously in an assessment meeting presided over by a stern DM in a large conference hall, he is engaged in an affective, anxiogenic encounter with *sarkar* wherein he strains to perform as a *sarkari* official. Bureaucratic practices such as meetings and the production of documents have to be enacted daily lest the state vanishes. To keep *sarkar* and its projects alive is constant work-in-progress requiring a labour that is affective, repetitive, and concerned with producing documentary testaments of its enactment. In the case under consideration, the process began with the identification of a little village as the future headquarters of a new district in 1960. The plans made then, modelled on colonial hill stations, set out the physical structure that would house the local state in this region. Slowly, bit by bit, Gopeshwar the mountain town was built up. Now officials are posted in and out. Development schemes are introduced and withdrawn. Documents are written, circulated, exhibited, filed, archived, lost, and burnt. Meetings are held and inspections are undertaken, with minutes and reports duly produced and filed. In the process, 'the State' and 'Development' are continually assembled in the Indian Himalaya.

Endnotes

1　For the first quarter of my fieldwork in Chamoli, the Congress party was in power in the State legislature. During this period, glossy lithographs of Indira and Rajiv Gandhi were prominently displayed as well. When, in February 2007, the *Bharatiya Janata Party* (BJP) displaced the Congress party in the State elections, these were swiftly removed in a move that was described to me by a local newspaper reporter as reflective of the 'change in the political environment' of the State.

2　Due to its prominence and its huge budget, the NREGS was almost always the first scheme to be discussed in BDCs and BDO meetings alike.

3　The National Rural Employment Guarantee Act (NREGA) was referred to as *Rozgar* (Employment) Guarantee in everyday parlance.

4　A *Panchayat* is the most localized institution of self-governance in India. It refers to the village-level elected body comprising the *Pradhan* (the village head man) and his/her committee. By the 73rd Amendment to the Indian Constitution in 1992, *Panchayats* have been endowed with significant powers, especially such as apply to the utilization of development funds.

5　For the financial year 2008–2009 the district received Rs. 1022.26 lakh just for the NREGS {1 lakh = 100,000}.

6　Althusser additionally demarcates an Ideological state apparatus (ISA), which functions more by ideology. He does, crucially, make it clear that in everyday life both the RSA and the ISA function by repression and ideology, there is 'very subtle explicit or tacit combination' of the two (2006, p. 93).

Paper Tiger?

Round II: Leopard vs forest officials

Forest officials try to capture a leopard, which strayed into Laxminagar in Amrut Dham locality of Panchavati, in Nashik on Wednesday. *Express*

6

The Reign of Terror of the Big Cat

It was an ordinary morning in late November in the NREGS cell. I was struggling to decipher the contents of a file while the other four members of the office busily worked on documents of all sorts. The cold had frozen all conversation. All of a sudden, a man burst into the room to announce dramatically: 'The *bagh* (leopard) has returned!' My office-mates gasped aloud in horror. Our informant rapidly recited his story: a woman had been climbing to the top of the mountain on which Gopeshwar is located to collect some grass for her goat. Out of the blue a *bagh* leapt upon her, horribly lacerating her face. Screaming in agony and terror, she fell down the steep slope. Her screams attracted the attention of other people nearby, who started making a noise, scaring the *bagh* so that, in a trice, he had vanished into the bushes. Mercifully, this attack had not proven fatal but the bad news, I was told solemnly, was that the *bagh* had returned to haunt the little town of Gopeshwar again. Everyone in the district office came out of their rooms to talk about the 'return of the *bagh*' in hushed and horrified tones.

Years before that November morning, I had read what I had then merely considered thrilling bed-time stories – the *Man-eaters of Kumaon* and the *Man-eating Leopard of Rudraprayag*[1] penned by the hunter-turned-conservationist Jim Corbett. Corbett's books were set in the early part of the twentieth century, which had led to my assumption that incidents of man-eating leopards and tigers were not (surely could not be?) really frequent in this region anymore. On the drive up to Gopeshwar, I had passed the shrine erected on the very spot where Corbett had killed the famous man-eating leopard of Rudraprayag (Figure 6.1). Despite this prominent landmark erected in proximity to Chamoli, at no point during my initial research on the district had anyone told me about the *bagh*, nor had I found any written references to what I was now learning was an endemic feature of life in this district. I was, therefore, confounded by all this *bagh*-talk. As I had an interview scheduled with a senior official in the district, I could not stay for long but hurried over to his office. When I arrived in his room, two other

Figure 6.1: Shrine at the very place the man-eating leopard of
Rudraprayag was hunted down by Corbett

top officials of the district were already there, and all three deep in conversation
on the 'return of the *bagh*'. The trio informed me of the regular appearance
of man-eating leopards in Gopeshwar and its outlying regions.[2] Given the
unprovoked nature of the attack, the bureaucrats were certain that, yet again,
we had a maneater in our midst. 'So what will you do to tackle the man-eater?'
I asked. One of them replied matter-of-factly, 'There is nothing we can do about
the *bagh* at the moment – hunt him down or even capture him. We will have to
wait before he has killed a few people'. The *bagh* did, as it turned out, 'kill a few
people' before any action was taken against him by the state. For over 2 months,
the *bagh* haunted the town of Gopeshwar and its surrounding villages, attacking
and killing humans and livestock and unleashing what was popularly described
as 'a reign of terror'.[3] Perplexingly, and much to the fury of its citizens, the local
state appeared incapable of stemming this terror. For town residents, this period
in which the big cat appeared to assume sovereignty over us all was yet another
example of the perennial failure of the Indian state. The Indian state is nothing
but a paper tiger (*kaghaz ka bagh*), they proclaimed loudly.

The Hindi word *bagh* refers, as I mentioned at the outset, to both leopards and tigers. The phrase, 'paper tiger', poignantly captured the chilling irony of the moment. There is the literal sense in which paper – the substance that the Indian state is eternally consumed by – and the *bagh* (tiger/leopard) – the animal that was haunting the town – were both magnified during this period. At the more metaphorical and general level, 'paper tiger', indicating that which appears powerful but is in practice entirely ineffectual, is an oft-used descriptor for the Indian state. In this concluding chapter, I explore why this phrase appears so apt. I do so by asking why the state seemed incapable of immediately killing or capturing the big cat and protecting human lives. Why did we all have to wait for over 2 months for the end of the terror of the big cat? Why were human lives sacrificed, or so it seemed, at the altar of the maneater's caprice as *sarkar* cowered in fear of the *bagh*? My answer to this set of mystifying questions moves away from the familiar accounts of domination, subjugation, discipline, violence, and indifference of the state and/or bureaucracy. Instead, my analysis of the reign of terror of the big cat has led me to identify and focus on certain temporal processes and associated material practices that were taking place within the state's bureaucratic apparatus during this period. I propose that we need to radically rethink the *waiting* that is so strongly associated with the Indian bureaucratic state. In this chapter, I argue that the wait in question (for the reign of the big cat to end) emerged from a complex concatenation of different forms of social time, material practices, and legal assemblages.

Bureaucratic times

There is a conspicuous absence in anthropology of detailed ethnographic work on time in bureaucracy. Complex timescapes are evident in novels such as Kafka's *The Trial*, which are able to move away from the homogeneity of linear time. Ever since Weber's influential account of bureaucracy as a product of an increasingly disenchanted modernity, bureaucracies have been *de facto* understood to have institutionalized linear time be it through law (Greenhouse, 1989) or through planning, which is concerned with 'the transition over time from current states to desired ones' (Abram and Weszkalnys, 2011, p. 4). When time is discussed with reference to modern bureaucracy and the state, it is often under the theme of waiting. As Jefrrey points out, '[d]uring the 20th century the increasing regimentation and bureaucratization of time in the West, combined with the growing reach of the state into people's everyday lives, created multiple settings – such as traffic jams, offices, and clinics – in which people were compelled to wait' (2008, p. 954). The capacity to make its subjects wait is seen as a technique of the exhibition of power by the modern state. 'Waiting', Bourdieu writes, 'implies submission' (2000, p. 228). Drawing out the link between time and power, he makes the point that 'waiting is one of the privileged ways of experiencing the effects of power' (ibid).[4] The social value of a person can be gauged by how much time they have to 'give', with important people always being busy and the time of 'subproletarians' being worthless. As Corbridge observes from his work in India, '[w]aiting is something that poorer people do' (2004, p. 184). Auyero similarly notes that in Argentina '[s]hanty residents are always waiting for something to happen' (2012, p. 4). His study of the poor's 'grueling pilgrimages through state bureaucracies' leads him to argue that these are 'temporal processes in and through which political subordination is reproduced' (2). 'Poor people learn that they have to remain temporarily neglected, unattended to, or postponed', thus becoming, in his words, 'patients of the state'. 'In recurrently being forced to accommodate and yield to the state's dictates, the urban poor thereby receive a subtle, and usually not explicit, daily lesson in political subordination' (9). *Contra* Auyero, I argue that waiting for the big cat's reign of terror to end in Gopeshwar did not make its residents patients of the state. Rather, as I show below, they became the state's strongest and most articulate critics. Another influential work on waiting describes it as 'a de-realisation of the present' (Cranpanzano, 1985). 'Waiting means to be oriented in time in a special way. It is directed towards the future – not an expansive future, however, but a constructed one that closes in on the present … Its only meaning lies in the future – in the arrival or non-arrival of the object of waiting' (1985, p. 44). An anxious waiting, for a future in which the big cat had gone away or been killed, was very much in evidence in Gopeshwar but, again, this was not the only affect generated by waiting. Anger, fear, dark humour, politicized commentaries on the value of life and on the structural inequities embedded in the space of the Himalayas, along with, even, a grudging respect for the big cat were all voiced. Not only were the affective experiences and political subjectification induced by waiting multiple and contradictory; I also argue below that if the state made its subjects wait before it allowed the big cat to be killed, it was not in order to demonstrate its power, or to mould submissive citizens, or because (as was the common refrain in Gopeshwar) it is 'uncaring'.

The second mode through which the question of time is commonly addressed in analyses of modern bureaucracy is, broadly, by reference to the future. The future is frequently invoked by recourse to the concept of risk, which as Reith notes has assumed 'a central explanatory role in the indeterminate world of late modernity' (2004, p. 384). Risk, she writes, 'is defined by and through temporality: the notion of 'risk' expresses not something that *has* happened or *is* happening, but something that *might* happen' (386). Reith points out that risk is not 'an objective feature of post-industrial society', rather 'it is a measure of calculation' (385), it can 'be defined largely through its attempt to calculate and so manage the uncertainties of the future' (386). The work of Lakoff (2006) has examined the specific manifestations of this temporal orientation by focusing on 'preparedness' and the method of 'imaginative enactment' through which bureaucracies are tutored in the present in how to react to a potentially catastrophic event in the future. Adams et al. (2009) have observed that a peculiarity of the current moment is the regime of 'anticipation' within which we live, and the affective states and politics of temporality that it gives rise to. My analysis draws on this work to think through how conservationist regimes, that seek to manage the specific risk of the extinction of big cats in the future, effect the responses of the bureaucracy to the threat of a man-eating leopard. Future projections of big-cat populations are constantly being made, on the basis of the historical decline in these figures. A long-term risk-aversion strategy aimed at saving the big cat is clearly reflected in the wildlife protection laws, programmes, and agencies that abound in present-day India. I show, however, that this was not the only risk analysis at work in the bureaucracy: there was also the more immediate and localized risk of losing more human lives if the big cat were not killed. This more immediate risk, and how best to avert it, consumed senior bureaucrats in Gopeshwar. Both these orientations to risk – the future of big cats as species, and the present of the human residents of a marginal Himalayan town located on the Indian borderland – were operating simultaneously, leading to severe contradictions within the district bureaucracy. The literature on risk and anticipation notes, importantly, a contemporary orientation to time that looks to the future, as well as the affects, techniques and politics such a way of being in time produces, and the forms of expertise and modes of calculation it calls upon. While I draw upon these themes, I further argue that the particular case I present here did not evince only a singular temporal orientation, and that too only oriented towards the future. Rather, there were various bureaucratic temporalities at play that looked to the past, the present, the immediate, near future, and a long-term future.

I identify five forms of time that were in operation during the reign of terror of the big cat (cf. Ssorin-Chaikov, 2006). The first four of these were evidenced within the state bureaucracy, hence my focus on thinking through the complexity of 'bureaucratic times'. First and foremost, there is the social discipline of everyday time within the setting of a government office in India (Thrift and May, 2001). The everyday life of the state, I have argued thus far, is constituted through the enactment of routine bureaucratic practices centred upon the production, consumption and circulation of documents and the convening of meetings. In contrast to the regularized rhythm of quotidian bureaucratic life, a sense of urgency – a palpable immediacy, caused by the risk to human lives – enveloped senior officials as they attempted to govern the big cat. Thirdly, there was a concern with what Guyer (2007) calls the 'near future'[5], which instead of being 'relatively evacuated' as she puts it, was being constantly contemplated by asking 'what-if?' What if, in the near future, the town residents were to revolt against the state? What if, in the near future, the big cat was to become even bolder and enter the district office? What if more than one maneater started operating in this small town? What if we eventually fail to hunt down the big cat? In contemplating what might happen if the big cat was not dealt with, there were also nostalgic representations of a past in which state officials were allowed to immediately and independently deal with wild animals. Finally, there were representations of a long-term temporality which sought to avert the risk of the extinction of big cats, and this temporality made its presence felt in the district bureaucracy via the entry of national law that covers (and protects) wildlife in contemporary India. Constituting an absolute other to bureaucratic time were the unpredictable timings of the movement and activities of the *bagh* himself. These remained radically unpredictable and unknowable. It was precisely the unpredictability of what the *bagh* would do next, where and when he would appear, how long he would stay for, when he might return or when he would be hunted down, that led to widespread terror.

'Saving' big cats

The global move towards conservationism, combined with the particular history and symbolism of big cats on the sub-continent, has led to the construction of a strong legal regime in contemporary India directed towards the preservation of big cats.[6] Conservationism is premised on the identification of a present that contains a specified population of big cats. It builds upon this worrying present to project a long-term platform of action for the future. The future for conservationist time is one in which the endangerment of big cats is omnipresent and, hence, all policies are geared towards 'saving the big cat'. In addition to conservationist impulses, nationalist pride also figures in the protection of India's official national animal and its representative in the international animal kingdom, the royal Bengal tiger. In 1969, a Wildlife Board was set up by the Government of India to completely ban the export of tiger and leopard skins. In 1970, a total ban on tiger shooting was imposed by legislation and in 1972, the Wildlife (Protection) Act was introduced into India. In April 1973, a scheme to protect the tiger – 'Project Tiger' – was launched with a budget of 40 million rupees, making it the world's largest conservation project at the time (Rangarajan, 1996). Ever since, efforts to preserve big cats have only increased, spurred also by the global project of 'saving the big cat' (see the Tiger Task Force, 2005; Jhala et al., 2008). The World Bank is just one such powerful international organization that has joined this noble cause. It plans to keep a close watch on the population of tigers and leopards in the world, as the table below, taken from a recent report, makes clear. This report – entitled, tellingly enough, *A Future for Wild Tigers* – congratulates India on her response to what is described as a big cat 'crisis'. The report notes that in India 'planned allocation for tiger protection will soon be increased to about $150 million over 5 years. This is equivalent to approximately $20,000 annually per living tiger or about $8 per hectare and amounts to a three- to fourfold increase in the available budget' (2008, p. 15).

Criticisms of specific aspects of India's wildlife conservationist regime have surfaced, with Saberwal, Rangarajan, and Kothari (2001), for instance, exhibiting the connections between the colonial practice of *shikar* (hunting) and the nationalist project of conservation, and their very similar location in elite aesthetics and practices. In a study of man-eating tigers in the Sundarbans in West Bengal, Jalais brings out the stark distinction between what she terms the 'cosmopolitan tiger' and the 'Sundarbans tiger'. The cosmopolitan tiger for her is one that personifies, '... the very universalism of a Western particular – that of 'wildlife' and its need to be protected' (2008, p. 25). Guha cautions against the form of national park management at work in much of the Third World, which emerges from a 'distinctively North Atlantic brand of environmentalism' (2005, p. 151). Such an approach argues for vast regions of 'wilderness' to be carved out and emptied of all human habitation and activity. To uncritically adopt this approach, argues Guha, amounts to something akin to a form of 'green imperialism'. The adoption of precisely this logic of demarcated spaces is what led to the description of the Gopeshwar *bagh* as an animal that was 'escaping' from its own territory. The tiny town of Gopeshwar is surrounded on all sides by PA (protected areas). Close to the town limits, on the west, is the Kedarnath musk deer sanctuary that was established in 1972 to protect the endangered musk deer, and which occupies 967 sq. km. To the north of Gopeshwar, covering almost half of the entire district, is the Nanda Devi Biosphere Reserve (NDBR). What happens when a *bagh* with man-eating predilections 'escapes' from his own PA-land into human habitations? Quite simply, he unleashes a reign of sheer terror.

The reign of terror

Gopeshwar, never the liveliest of places, became a veritable ghost town over the 2½ months that the *bagh* haunted it. Moving out of the home was kept to a bare minimum. When travel was absolutely unavoidable, one would hastily scurry between destinations in large groups, never alone. Shops shut well before sunset. Doors were bolted firmly all day and people were wary of so much as stepping out onto the porch. Children, in particular, were strongly guarded by their families. No school or college allowed any physical activity that involved movement outside the classroom. Evening promenades were entirely discontinued by one and all. Pet dogs were not allowed outdoors. Women, who were in any case rarely seen alone on the streets, now virtually disappeared from the public sphere. Orders were given for lights to be installed everywhere. A special request was sent to the State capital of Dehradun for uninterrupted power supply to the town (unhappily, this demand was not complied with, leaving us plunged in darkness many a night). Policemen and forest guards, again in large groups, frequently monitored the roads. These monitoring groups held large torches of fire or beamed flashlights around. The Government Girls Inter College (GGIC), which has the misfortune of being located in Kund colony, was shut down for over a month once it became clear that the *bagh*, too, was living in the same colony. All large foliage growing in Kund was lopped off in order to lessen the hiding spaces for this new resident. This did not prevent a woman from falling down the hill and sustaining multiple fractures when she thought she had caught sight of the *bagh*. In the neighbouring village of Roli-Gwad, a woman actually lost her life when she mistook a dog for the *bagh* and fell off a tree. Terror, over these cold winter months, was so palpable that even the sound of a leaf falling was enough to make one's blood run cold with fright.

When the *bagh* first arrived, and as it became increasingly obvious it was a maneater, the state made its presence 'official' by means of public announcements. A man was hired to walk around town with a huge *dhol* (drum-like musical instrument) slung round his neck on a white cloth. For the first fortnight or so he would go to public spaces (such as the office square or round a cluster of houses) and, beating the *dhol* to draw attention to himself, would in a loud yet clear voice recite details of the *bagh's* recent activities from the document he held in his hands, listing the places and times at which the animal had been sighted or had attacked a human. Once the sun had set there was not a soul to be seen anywhere. Along with the darkness and emptiness of roads and other spaces came an eerie silence. This silence was broken only by a piercing siren, a banshee's wail, at dawn. The siren, which would rudely jolt us all out of sleep at 4:00 a.m., was designed to frighten the *bagh* away from the town precincts. In addition, it daily awakened us anew to his presence – that was only reinforced by the constant *bagh*-talk in hushed tones, the accounts in the newspapers, gossip, jokes, and the increasing anger against the state for not doing anything to counter the terror of the *bagh*.

The *bagh* became a larger-than-life presence in our lives in the town over these months. He was not just feared, but also anthropomorphized – to the point that he became a co-resident, one that we could joke about and get angry at. From our daily conversations about the *bagh,* it appeared as if there was just one *bagh*, and that too a male one, with 'him' always being used to refer to the animal even after it became clear, on the basis of an analysis of pug marks, that the *bagh* in question was a female, i.e., it was a *baghin* (leopardess).[7] Over the course of 2006 alone, there had been three distinct man-eating leopards that had 'visited' the region and killed humans. All the *bagh*-stories that were related to me, however, referred to him monotheistically, as if there was just one single *bagh* that was ruling over us at all times, which explains the reference to the 'return of the *bagh*'.

The Gopeshwar *bagh* was most generally considered to be 'cunning' (*chatur*) and entirely 'unreliable' (*bharosa nahin kar sakte hai*). His cunning in locating, stalking, and obtaining human prey despite the precautions they took was incredulously discussed. Furthermore, his ability to just turn up anywhere at any time (*kahin bhi kabhi bhi*) made him entirely unreliable. It was thus, for instance, that he one day turned up outside the district development office where I was working, at precisely 5 p.m. There were loud giggles, mixed with fear, in the office over the cunning *bagh* who knew very well that the office shuts at 5 p.m. In general, the unreliable *bagh* could be seen in the full light of the day (*din-dahade*), insouciantly walking around government offices, sunning himself on ledges in full sight of the busy bazaar, taking naps in the town's only public park, leaving his pug marks in the unlikeliest places – such as at the entrance to the village temple. The cunning, unreliable *bagh* was also described, in English, as being 'gender-biased', for his attacks were largely directed at women. As a category, women are more vulnerable to attacks by wild animals in the mountains as they are the ones who gather and fetch water, fuel and fodder for their households. This aspect was acknowledged; but it was simultaneously said that the *bagh* liked women's blood, and that he knew women are weaker than men, which made him 'gender-biased'. The *bagh*, then, was stereotypically gendered as male and his victims as female. This cunning and unrealiable, gender-biased *bagh* was also described by residents of Gopeshwar, especially by children, as shaking hands, smiling, winking, leering, thinking, soliloquizing, sun-bathing, and visiting his neighbours in Kund colony where he was believed to have taken up residence along with senior state officials. Further, this complicated creature liked the taste of certain bloods in the same way as we like certain teas, grimaced when he licked some petrol by the petrol pump, was capable of prophesy – as evidenced by the pre-emptive moves he made – and even worshiped the Hindu god Shiva, as his circumambulation of the town's Shiva temple proved.

One night the *bagh* decided to spend some time in the District Magistrate's bungalow. This 'visit' was reported on the front pages of all the local newspapers the next day and became the subject of much hilarity for the longest time. From pug marks it was clear that the *bagh* walked around the District Magistrate's garden, took a nap near a rose bush, and then made off in the morning before being spotted by anyone, including the various security guards stationed permanently in the compound. The local newspaper headlines the next day ran, '*Bagh* visits District Magistrate (DM), but catches him sleeping'. This incident proved to everyone in Gopeshwar that the *bagh*, too, was fully aware of how incapable agents of the state were and how, therefore, one need not fear them. The *bagh* could (mis)behave as he wished for, as usual, *sarkar*, as represented in the person of the DM, the highest-ranked state official in the district, was sleeping, as were his guards.

The sleeping state

Was the state really just sleeping through the reign of the Gopeshwar-*wallah bagh*? I follow the state's activities through an analysis of files and via participation in the official meetings that were hurriedly convened during the reign of the big cat, as well as through my general attendance at the main district office. A set of two thick files named 'Attacks by Wild Animals in the District' are maintained in room no. 14 in the District Magistrate's office in Gopeshwar. They are classified by the district bureaucracy as constituting 'sensitive' state matter and are, hence, kept under lock and key in a large steel *almirah*. Tracing the process whereby documents related to the *bagh* were produced, circulated, and filed, as well as following the impact of these very documents on future events, brings out the local state's tussle with the *bagh* that commonly terrorize this region. These two files contain a variety of documents – lists, faxes, telegrams, memos of phone conversations, hunting licenses, medical certificates, government orders (GOs) issued by the government of India (GoI), i.e., from New Delhi, Department orders (DOs) coming from the provincial state's various departments in Dehradun, a copy of the Wildlife Act, Excel sheets of budgets, newspaper cuttings, copies of state-issued appeals, photographs, and, most abundantly, letters, letters, and more letters. From this rich hoard of documents of various sorts, I trace out the process of the government of the big cat, starting with his official declaration as a maneater.

Chapter 3 of the Indian Wildlife Preservation Act, 1972 (WPA), which deals with the hunting of wild animals, begins with the statement: 'No person shall hunt any wild animal specified in Schedule, I, II, III and IV except as provided below'. The leopard or panther (*panthera pardus*) along with the tiger (*panthera tigris*) are listed in the category of mammals under Schedule I of the Act.[8] Hunting them is absolutely prohibited barring certain cases, with the one concerning us here falling under the purview of Section 11(1)(a) of the WPA, whereby:

'The Chief Wildlife Warden may, if he is satisfied that any wild animal specified in Sch. 1 has become dangerous to human life or is so disabled or diseased as to be beyond recovery, by order in writing and stating the reasons therefor, permit any person to hunt such animal or cause animal to be hunted;' (Government of India, 1972).

Declaring the *bagh* a maneater (*narbhakshee/adam-khor*) was done through the invocation of this Section 11(1)(a) of the WPA. The Chief Wildlife Warden (CWW) of Uttarakhand is stationed in Dehradun. To get him to order *in writing* that the *bagh* must be hunted down turned out to be no mean feat, one that required gallons of suasive government ink to be spilled, with a flurry of letters and telegrams being sent back and forth before the written declaration was won. Basically, the process of obtaining a hunting license for a *bagh* consists of convincing the Chief Wildlife Warden that the *bagh* in question had actually become 'dangerous to human life'. In the case of the Gopeshwar *bagh* this was achieved by the local state making a case against the *bagh* and in favour of humans. This case was argued, as everything else in the Indian state is, on paper through official documents.

Even after the *bagh* had attacked at least three other humans after the first incident with the woman in Kund, the local state had to struggle to obtain its declaration as a maneater. So the *bagh* kept appearing, even during daytime, in and around Gopeshwar. He carried off a cow and a dog, mauled three humans and killed two before they could make a serious case against him. The first of the victims was a 7-year-old girl in December; then a 12-year-old boy. This boy – Vishal – was killed in dramatic fashion. He was walking home from school on the afternoon of the 18 December when, suddenly, the *bagh* pounced on him from the bushes and carried him off. As this attack occurred in the daytime, it was witnessed by people in the vicinity who began to create a huge din, hoping to make the *bagh* drop his victim. They succeeded, the *bagh* abandoned his prey and ran off to a nearby cave to seek shelter. Unfortunately, by this point, Vishal was already dead. The horrified crowd surrounded the cave in an attempt to trap the *bagh*, and senior officials of the district – the SP (Superintendent of Police) who heads the police force and the DFO (Divisonal Forest Officer) who heads the forest department – were summoned to the site, with their departmental forces, to nab the *bagh*. Despite their presence, the *bagh* managed to wriggle out of the cave and escape unharmed.

The events of 18 December led to a great upsurge of anger mixed with fear in Gopeshwar. The DM shot off an emergency telegram to the Chief Wildlife Warden describing the event and beseeching him to declare the *bagh* a maneater. He had been sending regular updates to the Chief Wildlife Warden on the doings of the *bagh* ever since the animal's 'return' to Gopeshwar and his very first attack, on the woman in Kund colony. The DM and the DFO followed up their written requests to Dehradun with phone calls explaining the enormity of the situation and consistently underlining how *akroshit* (furious) the *janta* (people) were. On 19 December 2006, the Chief Wildlife Warden sent a letter to the DFO, with a copy to the DM, recounting the above incident and quoting the DFO's and the DM's letters back to them. He ended by writing:

'Keeping in mind the information provided by you and the DM as well as the anger of the villagers and with the objective of protecting their lives, under Government Order number 111(6)/14-3-107-72 dated 01-02-1973 and the WPA 1972 and 1991, on the basis of Section 11 (1) (a), I give you the power to catch this particular leopard using a cage, failing which you may destroy him'.

The caution with which the letter proceeds is noteworthy. The Chief Wildlife Warden is squarely telling the DFO and the DM that he is transferring this power to destroy (*nashta karna*) the *bagh* on the basis of their own claims that he is dangerous (*khatarnak*), that the villagers are *akroshit* (furious), and that the *bagh* may cause further damage to the population. Further, it is only if they fail to catch the *bagh* through the means of a cage that they are allowed to kill him. The DM was relieved to 'win' this hunting license, a document for which he had to, as he said, 'always fight a lot'.

The government of big cats

District officials held up the hunting permit as a prize they had won after a long wait and a fight with the Chief Wildlife Warden. The length of the wait was evident, in that it took two deaths, at least half a dozen attacks, numerous official documents, and 5 weeks to 'win' the hunting license that would allow the local state to legally kill the *bagh*. The fight was more than evident in the files, which contained a variety of documents prepared by the district furnishing proof that the *bagh* in question was, undeniably, a confirmed maneater, and asking the Chief Wildlife Warden, therefore, please to let them catch or kill him. The proof collected included daily updates, newspaper cuttings, copies of angry letters written by villagers/victims/'prominent persons', some rather gruesome photographs of victims, lists of deaths and injuries, medical certificates testifying that the human deaths have certainly been caused by big cats, and reports sent in to the district headquarter from villages and lower-level administrative staff.

The variety of what I term 'suasive documents' produced by the district administration to convince its superiors of the facticity of its claims, and of the enormity of the problem, is quite staggering. The rhetoric of these various documents invokes images of the masses as simultaneously terrified, angry and helpless, while the documents continue to follow the rather dry, accepted form and stylistics of the letter-based exchanges that constitute a central mode of communication between state functionaries. To give an instance, the District

Forest Officer (DFO) wrote a letter to the Chief Wildlife Warden in July 2006 requesting him to declare a *bagh* that had been attacking humans in Gopeshwar a maneater. He began the letter with a detailed and vivid recreation of a bizarre attack by the *bagh* on a group of four women walking at sunset in the middle of the town. This text narrates, step-by-step, the perambulations of the women as they weave their way through Gopeshwar, up to the point they were, all of a sudden, attacked by The *Bagh*. The letter goes on to dwell on the injuries sustained, the tears shed, and the anger caused by this alarmingly impertinent *bagh*. The forester adjudges this *bagh* to be 'very dangerous' (*atyanta khatarnak*) as he is exhibiting 'Aberrant Behaviour' (English term used in a letter otherwise entirely in the Hindi language). The letter ends with a formal request:

'This sort of behaviour is increasing the possibility of destruction of life in the near future due to which it is imperative to immediately discipline the concerned *bagh*. In order to regulate the concerned *bagh* and seeing the failure of the present efforts to do so, I request you to utilize Section 11 of the Wildlife Protection Act of 1972 on a priority basis and give me the permission to do the required work at my level to get him killed'.

Letters consistently deployed verbs such as 'regulate', 'govern', 'discipline', 'control', or 'curb' with reference to what the state should be doing to the *bagh*. Furthermore, these letters consistently aimed to characterize the *bagh* as extremely dangerous to human lives and thus to the upkeep of 'law and order'. It was easier to obtain a death warrant for an aberrant, cunning *bagh* that was behaving like, as one letter put it, 'a real desperado'. Speedier responses on claims of man-eating were received in cases of 'high profile' leopards, such as the ones that made the mistake of entering the district headquarters, which was the largest town of the district and also the place where all the agents of the state resided. Burton writes of the 'evil reputation' of the Sundarbans as the territory of man-eating tigers in India (1933, p. 143). In Chamoli district, the town of Gopeshwar and the development Blocks of Karnaprayag and Gairsain possess a similarly evil reputation due to the high incidence of man-eating leopards in these regions. Of the two blocks, Gairsain experienced multiple attacks by not one, but two and sometimes even three, man-eating leopards that would haunt the region simultaneously. Despite the gravity of the situation there, local administrators told me how much more difficult they found it to obtain hunting permits for leopards in their areas of command than in the town of Gopeshwar, which is the district headquarters. The maneaters that haunted the more remote parts of Chamoli district were able to extend their reigns of terror over much longer periods, thanks to the lack of officials to do the paperwork and produce the suasive documents. When deaths and attacks happen in remote villages that are not very close to the road and do not possess good communication links with the Block's headquarters located in the towns of Gairsain and Karnaprayag, it is easy for them to go officially unrecorded and, hence, unrecognized by the state.

Setting aside the lack of officials to shoulder the labour of regulating the big cat there existed another striking element in the government of maneaters: in accounts of deaths caused by the *bagh*, calculations of the value of life of different humans would often crop up. The death of 'a few' women in 'remote' villages of Gairsain did not seem to worry the local state quite as much as the attack by the *bagh* in broad daylight on a woman living in their own residential colony.

I was repeatedly told by well-wishers that I should be very careful with this *bagh*, for he 'does not know who you are'. Similarly, senior officials would tell me that *even they* had to be constantly alert for the *bagh* would not 'know who they are'. In response to my query on the relationship between their individual identity and the *bagh* attacking them, one said: 'I am the Block Development Officer (BDO) of Gairsain. The foolish (*bewaqoof*) *bagh* does not know that'. Similarly, the DM told me that the *bagh* had come over to his official residence and, much to the mirth of the local residents, spent the night in his rose garden only because 'the *bagh* does not know who I am'. If the entry of the *bagh* in Kund colony in Gopeshwar was incongruous, it was even more bizarre that he could think of attacking one of the many sahibs who lived there (DM-sahib, BDO-sahib, SDM-sahib) or other such 'eminent citizens' of the town. For a *bagh* to be haunting villages in remote Gairsain block did not appear, to participants in most general conversations, as anomalous as a *bagh* having the cheek to saunter around Gopeshwar, the seat of state power in the district, and to attack humans close to the district offices.

Stoler has distinguished various types of 'the unwritten' (2009, p. 3). An unwritten in the documents on the man-eating big cats was what the senior district officials had uttered to me on the very first day of the *bagh's* appearance. Everyone in the district office knew that getting a written death warrant for the big cat would take a lot of convincing, by means of a barrage of suasive documents, combined with the loss of a few human lives. Tracing the career of the documents in the wild animals files, this truly emerges as the unwritten code, for it was only after attacks on, and even deaths of 'a few' people that the declaration was won. In my interview with the then-CWW, he listed the reasons for his cautious approach to the declaration of a maneater. He was of the opinion that often a 'stray encounter' between a *bagh* and humans was, in panic, described as a case of a maneater. He believed it wise to 'wait for a history' of the same *bagh's* activities to come to light before taking an irrevocable step that would be a 'rash decision'. Therefore, he often recommended the capture of the *bagh* in a cage by laying a trap or by stunning the animal with a tranquilizer gun before 'jumping to the conclusion' that this 'poor *bagh*' (*bichara bagh*) was, indeed, a maneater. Fresh from the novel and hair-raising experience of living under the terrifying shadow of the Gopeshwar-*wallah bagh* for over 2 months, I could not help but comment that his sympathies seemed to be lying more with what he had just called a 'poor' *bagh* and less with the humans it was maiming, who would certainly not describe the beast as he did. His response was, naturally, to deny such a charge by gently telling me 'in government one must follow the law', which was succeeded by reading aloud certain clauses from conservation laws, and listing the many 'innocent' *bagh* which had been presumed maneaters and mistakenly killed in the past.[9] The killing of the 'innocent' *bagh* was a big worry for the Forest Department (FD) but specifically for him as he was responsible for 'each and every *bagh* in the State', and was answerable to his bosses in New Delhi for every permit that was issued from his office. It 'just does not look good' (*achha nahin lagata hai*) if we kill too many *bagh*, the CWW told me worriedly. In Gopeshwar, too, bureaucrats referred to how 'bad it looks' (*kharab lagata hai*) to kill too many *bagh*. And, indeed, there was immense pressure on these forest and wildlife officials from within the state bureaucracy to protect big cats, stemming from the laws and conservationist pressures I mentioned above. Each and every hunting permit that was issued would result in an addition to the list of leopards killed in India – a list like those included in the World Bank report. Thus, it was only after incontrovertible evidence had accumulated in documentary form that these officials felt they could safely sign off a hunting permit.

To return to Gopeshwar, the 'winning' of the prized permit allowed the local district officials to send out an appeal to professional hunters. Given the remote location of Gopeshwar, in a borderland district in Himalayan India, it proved very hard to find trained hunters. Local forest officials did not possess the basic equipment with which they could hunt down the *bagh* themselves, such as cages, tranquilizer guns, guns, and other sorts of ammunition. The hunting permit had been won on 19 December but the *shikaris* (hunters) arrived in town only by 4 January 2007. By this time, the *bagh* had killed another young woman, taking its tally thus far to three humans.[10] The *shikaris* made a grand entry into Gopeshwar in an open white jeep, clutching big guns, dressed in camouflage with sunglasses and safari hats. On the very day of their arrival they publicly declared, much to our collective delight, that the *bagh* now had only 3 days, at the most, to live. For the next 3 days the entire town waited with bated breath. The local newspapers would daily carry photographs of the *shikaris* at work, scouring the mountainside dressed in their hunting gear and wielding impressively large guns. Senior officials grumbled that this lot 'looked too Bollywood-ish' to actually be the real thing, but locals seemed to be somewhat comforted by their presence. For over 2 weeks the *shikaris* attempted to shoot the *bagh*, but they were unsuccessful in their venture and had to leave the district with their tails between their legs, or as it was described in Hindi, like wet cats (*bheegi billi*).

Ineffectual as the *shikaris* were, the spectacle of their attempts to hunt eased the pressure on the local state to exhibit action. For the very first time since the 'return of the *bagh*' on that fateful November morning, senior officials were not being berated for doing nothing or not caring. Before the arrival of the *shikaris*, there were constant comparisons being made between present-day officials who were incapable of handling the *bagh* and the men-of-state of the past who would have immediately gone out and hunted the beast down. Hussain (2012) has made the point that the hunting of man-eating big cats in India was central to the colonial British welfare-oriented programme of governance. The colonial state saw the 'hunting of man-eating tigers in the foothills and plains as an effort to prevent fierce and unpredictable nature intervening in their day-to-day governance practices in Indian society' (2012, p. 2). He notes that so important did the British consider it to be able to impose order, 'civilize' the wild nature of India and exhibit their capacity to protect the natives, that in hunting man-eating big cats they suspended the fair-hunting codes that were otherwise essential to their identity as sportsmen. The hunt has, more generally, been studied as central to the culture of imperialism (Mackenzie, 1988; Rangarajan, 2005). *Shikar* in British India '...constituted propaganda: it showed emperor, king, or lord exhibiting power' (Mackenzie, 1988, p. 10). In Gopeshwar, for a brief tantalizing moment, an exhibition of state power was presented in the form of the hired professional *shikaris*. Pandian (2001) reads stories on the 'terror of man-eating big cats in India' as colonial accounts that recover the figure of the Oriental despot to characterize both the big cat and the rulers who preceded them in India. The terror is dispelled only through 'the masculine intervention of the white hunter' (2001, p. 87). Yet it was precisely such a masculinist intervention, such a forceful display of authority from the state, which the residents of Gopeshwar were seeking. The confusion and fright, which marked the officials' response to the *bagh's* terror, were met with popular disdain and anger. Orwell's story *Shooting an Elephant* beautifully captures this pressure on state officials to behave and act as a *sahib* ought to when it comes to an incident such as an animal that has 'gone rogue'. In Gopeshwar, oral histories on man-eating big cats nostalgically recount the time of the British Raj and the early years of Independent India, when officials or the local royalty would immediately and personally take it upon themselves to protect their subjects by killing the beast. Today, in contrast, the people encounter officials who struggle for ages to 'win' a flimsy piece of paper that would allow them to commence looking for a hunter.

'Anything might happen'

While bureaucrats were preoccupied with enacting the routine procedures of the state, what a disgruntled colonial officer in Orwell's *Burmese Days* (1948, p. 21) describes as consisting merely of 'paper-chewing and chit-passing', the anger of the Gopeshwar residents at *sarkar* was nearing boiling point. On 21 December, at the peak of the terror created by the *bagh*, a procession (*jaloos*) of over a hundred people, under the banner of the district residents' forum, came to meet the DM in order to give him a *gyapan* (letter of appeal) addressed to the Chief Minister. It made its way to this meeting amidst the beating of drums and with cries of 'Uttarakhand *Shasan Hai Hai*' (Shame on Uttarakhand Administration) and 'District Magistrate *Murdabad*' (death to the DM). The subject line of the *gyapan* read, in bold: 'The terror of the man-eating leopard in Gopeshwar, district Chamoli'. It described the spread of this reign of terror in different districts of this Himalayan region, a subject that is regularly covered by local newspapers. 'Yet, the central government, Uttarakhand State government and district administration do not regard it gravely. The state has today put the worth of a leopard greater than the worth of humans. Is there no value left to humans in Indian democracy today?' (cf. Jalais, 2005). The letter goes on to list a series of recent attacks by the *bagh*, stressing the manner in which in broad daylight (*din dahade*) the increasingly fearless *bagh* was barging into houses and grabbing children or attacking women: 'After the experiencing of these incredible incidents, too, our *sarkar* remains mute'. The tone of this letter was intended to highlight the urgency of the situation. Its demands were directed at increasing the speed with which decisions were made. Accordingly, it sought an immediate amendment to the WPA, with the aim of empowering local officials to instantly kill what they knew to be a man-eating big cat. The letter demanded that compensation for injury or death should paid in good time, especially for the killing of livestock, which was a very common problem. Finally, it demanded that anyone who killed a maneater should be considered not a criminal but a 'brave' (*bahadur*) person.[11]

Around the time, the procession came to petition the DM, the Gopeshwar-*wallah bagh* was being sighted almost every single day and indulging in all sort of 'activities', creating an atmosphere of terror so intense that you could almost see it hanging over us like a cloud in the cold, silent, empty mountain town.[12] During this period the DM, as the head of the district administration, was under tremendous amounts of pressure and expressed to me in private more than once that he was worried 'anything might happen' (*kuch bhi ho sakta hai*) in the town. The procession that had come to petition him had clearly articulated their fury with *sarkar* for 'doing nothing' and for valuing the *bagh* more than humans. Immediately after the procession, the DM hurriedly called an emergency meeting with all the concerned officers and the forest department. In a letter written to various senior bureaucrats in Dehradun after the emergency meeting, he set out detailed recommendations to better the situation. These included provisioning the Forest Department with adequate equipment such as tranquilizer guns and light cages, speeding up the process for handling suspected maneaters or for handling emergencies by transferring the power to declare a maneater from the CWW to the concerned forest official, provisioning a budget from which to award *shikaris* and to compensate victims. Enclosed with this letter was a copy of the *gyapan* he had just received. The high level of fear and helplessness that was being experienced within the state apparatus comes across clearly in this particular letter, where the DM writes of the increase in the attacks on humans by *bagh* in Chamoli and describes the procession that came to meet him:

'On speaking to them I felt that inside the people there is a tremendous amount of anger bubbling due to these incidents and in the near future we cannot overrule the possibility of a violent movement, which could lead to the development of grave dangers for the forest department and the district administration.'

Through this exhaustive letter, the DM performed a show of unity; all the departments of the district were seen to be working in concert to eradicate the *bagh ka aatank* (terror of the leopard). Back in the multiple offices in Gopeshwar, the reality of the situation could not have been more different. The schisms between and within the three primary wings of the local state – the district administrator's office, the forest department, and the police – came out in plain sight during this period. The myth of the state as a singular unit was sharply dispelled, as the struggle about jurisdiction over, and regulation of, the *bagh* went back and forth. As a television reporter grumbled to me, the *bagh* had 'become a volleyball ... you go to one office and they say this *bagh* is not mine, go to that office. When you go to that office, they say this *bagh* is not mine, go to yet another office'. The *bagh* did, indeed, become a metaphorical volleyball being bounced between offices, as different parts of the local state apparatus attempted to carefully carve out their own responsibility to exclude *bagh*-handling, even while informing the others of what their job was. Over the months of November, December, and January, it became hard to keep up with the rapid-fire letter-based communication that went on *within* different wings of the district administration alone. While officials were passing the *bagh* around like a volleyball, the residents of Gopeshwar were accusing *sarkar* as a monolithic unity of 'doing nothing' other than indulging in their routine paper games. At a press conference, for instance, held in the DM's office on 23 December, the increasingly hapless state was subjected to much public ridicule for its utter incapacity to regulate the *bagh* and was denounced by one and all for being a '*kaghazi bagh*' (paper tiger).

The emptiness of the state's pretensions of being in control or genuinely caring about its citizens was evident, not just in the long delays accompanying the declaration and capture/death of the *bagh*, but also in the process through which official figures were generated and compensation paid to victims. The practice of maintaining statistics of attacks on humans by wild animals goes back to the British Raj. Thus, the Garhwal Gazetteer, which covers this part of present-day Uttarakhand notes: 'From a return of inquests held in Garhwal between 1850 and 1863, the number of deaths from the attacks of wild animals was recorded at 276 during that period, and Rs. 13,784 were paid as rewards for the destruction of 91 tigers, 1,300 leopards and 2,602 bears. Taking the decade 1870 – 1879, the returns show that 211 persons (123 males) were killed by wild animals and Rs 9,317 were paid as rewards for destroying 62 tigers, 905 leopards and 1,740 bears' (Atkinson, 2002 [1881], p. 15). Crucially, the Gazetteer admits, '[t]his return is avowedly imperfect, as it only includes the deaths reported to the authorities and the animals killed for which rewards have been claimed' (16). In fact, Boomgaard has surmised that so strong were the misgivings of the British government that 'they discontinued the annual publication on killings – though not the data gathering – in 1927, owing to the unreliability of the data' (2001, p. 63). Underreporting and generation of watered-down statistics for these incidences continues unabated till today, as does the practice of not publishing annual figures on fatalities.

The construction of dubious statistics on deaths and injuries caused by *bagh* in Chamoli is intimately linked to the convoluted and tortuous process of petitioning the state for compensation. Compensation for injury to self or property by the *bagh*, or for the death of a family member, was to be issued on the production of – but of course – the correct documents. Awarding and receiving compensation is, again, not a straightforward case of submitting an application and receiving the established amount within a fixed time frame. First of all there is a complicated process that must be followed in order to prove eligible to receive the compensation. Further, to my observation this process kept changing for no conceivable reason, and the changes in procedure were poorly advertised. Having followed due process is not enough for, yet again, the unwrittens creep in. One must couch the request letter/petition to the state (*prarthana patra*) in a language of appeal, need and rights, a delicate balance to be achieved by one who is proficient in these paper exchanges with the state. The vast majority of petitioners are, of course, not trained for this task, which leads not only to failed documentary interactions with the state but also high levels of panic, anxiety and despair in the very process of these interactions.

It is not as if, once a petition has been written and submitted to the correct officer in the appropriate department, the job is done. One must *maaro chakkar* (go round and round) the offices to make sure that the document is not buried in some file and thus forever forgotten or, even worse, lost altogether. Follow-up letters must be penned to serve as material reminders of the original issue, a key tactic of the Indian state's paper games. In the rare event that the compensation was released, the pitiable amounts add to the sense of human lives being inferior. The death of anyone below the age of 18 years, for instance, was to be compensated with Rs 50,000 to the victim's family. Compare this to the $ 20,000 that every single tiger in India is currently being allocated on an annual basis by the state.

With Rs 50,000, said one grieving father, you can barely buy two horses. 'Is the life of my dead seven-year-old daughter worth only two horses to *sarkar*? How does one make *sarkar* understand what the value of my daughter's life *really* was? What do they care anyway for they value the life of a *bagh* more than a humans', he said as he ran around offices begging for the release even of this pittance.

The end of the terror

On 28 January 2007 the reign of terror of the big cat came to an end, with local hero Lakhpat Singh Rawat successfully hunting him down. Residents of Gopeshwar and the nearby villages were jubilant. Bureaucrats heaved a sigh of relief and feted Mr Rawat with accolades and awards for his bravery. Proof of the death of the maneater was published in the form of photographs that we all happily showed to each other (Figure 6.2).[13] Newspapers ran front-page articles proclaiming 'The end of the terror: the man-eating leopard has been killed' (*Atank ka ant: mara gaya adamkhor bagh*). At first glance, the case of the man-eating leopard of Gopeshwar would attest to the systematic production of indifference within the large, haphazard bureaucratic apparatus that underpins the Indian state (Herzfeld, 1992). If not reading it as an illustration of bureaucratic indifference or as the realization of a Weberian nightmare of the iron cage of modernity, one might

Figure 6.2: The hunter posing with a slain leopard and state representatives

choose to focus on the wait involved in events related to the *bagh*, be it his shooting or the eventual payment of compensation to his victims. Following Bourdieu (2000), this wait might be read as an assertion of state power. A Foucauldian lens, on the other hand, would lead one to consider the act of making subjects wait indefinitely as an exercise aimed at disciplining them into becoming patients of the state, *pace* Auyero (2012). However, the ethnography that I have presented here allows us to draw out a different interpretation, both of what delays or waiting can lead to – a searing critique of the state in this case[14] – and of why this seemingly bizarre wait occurred in the first place.

The ethnography presented above presents a scenario where a variety of forms of social time and associated material practices were at play simultaneously, with the bureaucratic apparatus of the state struggling to reconcile them. In the first place we have the long-term strategy of averting the risk of the extinction of big cats that emerges from the global save the tiger project. This powerful global and national-level conservationist agenda has coalesced in the framing of a legal regime that stipulates extreme precaution before a big cat can be legally killed by the state in contemporary India. These legislations are interpreted and translated through the everyday social discipline of office life or by the enactment of slow and tedious documentary practices of various branches of the Indian state bureaucracy before the vital Section 11(1)(a) of the WPA can be enforced. Thus, we had the Forest Department, the Police Department, and the District Magistrate's office within the district, and various departments in Dehradun, all involved in exchanging letters and making phone calls before the permit could be won. The slow pace of the bureaucratic practices when set against the urgency of dealing with the menace of a hungry big cat furnishes another (and particularly chilling) example of the ubiquitous 'clash between technocratic and lived time' (Abram and Weszkalnys, 2011, p. 14). Once the document was won, time was spent on the practical considerations of finding hunters and/or of procuring the required material such as guns. Further complications were brought on by the disadvantageous location of Gopeshwar on India's remote Himalayan borderland. Gopeshwar is far away literally, in terms of physical distance from the State capital, as well as metaphorically in terms of figuring as a meaningful space in the national and regional imaginary. In the context of this failure of the state to act swiftly, a particular representation of time emerged. In this representation, the past was the subject of nostalgic reminiscence by citizens of the town – a past in which the state acted immediately to protect its populace. Bureaucrats were faced with residents who, using this past for comparison, loudly proclaimed them ineffectual and uncaring. Even as these bureaucrats waged a documentary war within the labyrinthine and hierarchical Indian state structure, they fretted over what unpredictable events might occur in the near future. The fear of a violent insurrection against the state by an increasingly terrified and furious citizenry was constantly contemplated and discussed. Then there were the rhythms and movements of the hungry big cat itself, which were feared by everyone precisely because he remained entirely outside the realm of predictability. The reign of terror of the big cat led to a variety of affects among the town residents, ranging from extreme fear to anger, even to the generation of nervous laughter; at the same time they formulated compelling critiques of the very peculiar functioning of the Indian state. A close focus on this episode ultimately allows us to move away from straightforward accounts of state failure or bureaucratic indifference to, I suggest, radically reimagine bureaucracy as animated; as a space in which life unfolds within and at the intersection of varying orientations, disciplines, and affects of social time and material practices.

Endnotes

1   Rudraprayag is the district adjoining Chamoli. Until 1997 it was part of Chamoli district.

2   Throughout this chapter, I refer to human-eating big cats as maneaters as this is how they are referred to popularly and in the literature.

3   Historically, this is also the phrase through which events involving man-eating tigers have been written about in colonial accounts (e.g., Corbett, 2007; see Pandian, 2001).

4   This understanding of waiting is particularly salient in studies of the state and bureaucracy. Thus, Schwarz notes that 'waiting is patterned by the distribution of power in a social system' (1974, p. 843) and that '[p]owerful clients are relatively immune from waiting' (848). A study of welfare waiting rooms in the US in the 1980s, however, dismissed the claim that all these spaces were 'dismal' or that waiting constituted a 'degradation ritual' of bureaucracy. Instead, it found marked difference between waiting rooms with some, indeed, being 'most unpleasant' and some 'blandly functional and even pleasant' (Goodsell, 1984, p. 476).

5   Guyer describes the 'near future' thus: '... the process of implicating oneself in the ongoing life of the social and material world that used to be encompassed under an expansively inclusive concept of "reasoning"' (2007, p. 409).

6   For an excellent history of big cats on the Indian sub-continent see Rangarajan (2005).

7   I adopt this gendering and refer all through this paper to the *bagh* as a male in order to remain as faithful as I can to the manner in which this event unfolded.

8   While the Indian state places the leopard and the tiger in the same category, in the IUCN's 'red list' that classifies species by the level of their imperilment, the tiger, along with the snow leopard, figure as 'endangered species', i.e., they face a very high risk of extinction in the near

future. The leopard, on the other hand, is 'near threatened', i.e., it may be considered threatened in the near future (http://www.iucnredlist.org/). Accessed July 2, 2014.

9   There were cases of leopards being shot, only for their post-mortem to reveal that this particular individual was not a man-eater and, therefore, *not* the one for which the hunting permit had been issued. It is impossible, in practice, for a hunter to be sure that the *bagh* he spots is indeed the correct one; it is not as if there is any opportunity to inspect the animal before going for the kill. The death of an 'innocent *bagh*' by an accredited hunter and on the basis of a state-issued license is not really covered by the law. The fuzziness of the law allowed for such (unfortunate) incidences to be 'papered over'.

10 This was the official tally of deaths by the *bagh* thus far. Unofficially, i.e., unvalidated by governmental measures the death count was by now between six and nine.

11 The minimum sentence for the killing of a big cat in India, according to the Wildlife Protection Act of 1972, is three years in prison and a fine of Rs 10,000 and the maximum sentence is seven years in prison. The fine amount goes up with subsequent offences and is also dependent upon where the killing occurs. See http://www.wpsi-india.org/tiger/poaching_crisis.php. Accessed January 2, 2012.

12 The phrase through which this period was described was: '*Gopeshwar mein bagh laga hua hai*' or, roughly, 'there is a leopard stuck to Gopeshwar'.

13 Rawat has emerged as the 'native' heir to Jim Corbett, having become a *shikari* after sedulous study of the habits of his prey. Much like Corbett, Rawat too refuses to accept any honorarium from the government for his successful tracking down of man-eaters in Uttarakhand. A school teacher by profession, he took to hunting down maneaters after three students of his were killed by a *bagh*.

14 In a similar vein, Jeffrey shows how the experience of limbo amongst unemployed educated youth in northern India 'seemed to act as a seed-bed for the generation of somewhat novel youth cultures and political protests' (2011, p. 187).

Conclusion: The State as a Paper Tiger

Let me end this book with the question that I have been asked from the day I began research for it: How is the NREGA doing? Is it performing well or not? At the heart of *Paper Tiger* lies my struggle to answer this question without a measure of reserve; with a sense of adequateness. This struggle is not a shortcoming of this work but, rather, its contribution.

I spent over a year in Uttarakhand tracking the NREGA. I was to emerge from this period with a higher level of incomprehension of its success/failure than I had at the beginning of my fieldwork. In striking contrast, I visited Odisha for less than a month and emerged from that trip with clear 'findings'. The objective of the Odisha trip was succinctly explained by Jean Dreze; we were there to find out *'kitnee chori hooen'* (how much theft happened) in the implementation of the NREGS in the state. Research teams fanned out in different Blocks of a total of three districts in the State. Results were swiftly arrived at after a fortnight of intensive surveying. In Kalahandi's Narla Block, where my group undertook an intensive survey, 48 per cent of the labourers' statements that we recorded did not match the official muster roll. In the rare cases that we were able to locate the job cards, 24.2 per cent of their entries did not match the muster roll, and 12.5 per cent of the names entered in the muster rolls were fake. Gathering together questionnaires for all the Blocks in three districts, and after a daylong brainstorming session with the entire team, Dreze derived concrete results on the performance of the NREGA. They were made public in a meeting with the press and the government at the District Magistrate's office in Boulangir district where he announced that only 60 per cent of the entries in the muster rolls that we sampled had been confirmed by the labourers. He went on to say, 'I am not implying that 40 per cent *chori* happened. It could be more or less. Funds are, in any case, being definitely siphoned off'. The figure of 40 per cent irregularities was a clear outcome of this exercise. The implication of this figure was that an equal, if not greater, amount of money was being 'leaked' or 'diverted', as the popular verbs related to corruption go, away from the planned funds outflow of the NREGS.

The structured nature of the Odisha exercise with its clear aim and methodology did not leave space for the 'epistemic anxieties' (Stoler, 2009) that my long and slow fieldwork in musty offices had left in its trail. The Odisha experience was geared towards the provision of tangible results on the NREGS, of the sort that development consultants, policy analysts and many academics with a positivist bent of mind are adept at producing. The assumption at the base of the Odisha trip was that by finding out the quantity of money that was being 'eaten up' and how this (corrupt) practice occurs, we could arrive at a fairly real assessment of the functioning of the scheme and also suggest ways of fixing the system. Thus, the conclusion of the Odisha audit did not just stop at producing a cold, hard fact of 40 per cent irregularities but further, in the press release written by Dreze, it went on to damn the state for making 'the entire record-keeping system virtually unverifiable. This is due to faulty design of job cards, widespread 'adjustments' in the records (e.g. to accommodate workers without job cards), non-transparent work measurement, and related problems'. Note how the performance of Odisha as a state under the NREGS was largely gauged by a scrutiny of documents, particularly the job card and muster rolls. Moreover, the story of the NREGS in Odisha was narrated as a tale of corrupt officials, poor record keeping, and a faulty design of documents, which was leading to a 'lack of transparency and accountability'. The recommendations on improving the performance of the NREGS, especially to stop theft, included re-designing and replacement of all the job cards in the State by 1 April 2008, and ensuring the transparency of muster rolls so that no 'adjustments' to them could be made.

Broadly similar exercises of audit did periodically take place in Uttarakhand, too, particularly through the practice of assorted meetings such as the monthly Block evaluation meetings. In the audits that I participated in (which were undertaken by state monitors or senior officials coming from 'outside'), no effort was made to speak to the labourers. The assessment was always based upon the documents, particularly upon matching the muster roll against the job card details. Internal district or State evaluations were almost always accompanied, even as they were taking place and during scrutiny of the documents, by talk of *farzee* (fake) reporting. There was an open acknowledgement in these forums that what was being produced was just a *sarkari* rendition, that it was so only *on paper*. The 'on-paper' doublethink aside, my own field location never allowed me to extricate myself from the everydayness of bureaucratic life and stand outside the material (documentary) production of performance. I never, in other words, occupied the position of a development expert. Instead, as an ethnographer of bureaucracy I was immersed in a seemingly humdrum world where, on a daily basis, we were all involved in overcoming illegibilities and making the NREGS real. What separates my Odisha and Uttarakhand experiences, then, are differences in objective, methodology, and, most centrally, the types of expert knowledge the two were aimed at producing. As Li (2007) has pointed out, it is extremely difficult to occupy simultaneously the position of an ethnographer and a development expert. In Odisha, in my guise as a development-*wallah* and as part of a large group of experienced and energetic activists, I was able to arrive at a figure and a definitive narrative on NREGA's performance. In Uttarakhand, the situation could not be more different; it was axiomatically ambiguous. In the Himalayas even during those moments when the official (paper) truths were being put together by the primary implementers of the law, they were discussed as being merely the state's version, as sort-of-non-truths. It is this dubiety of precisely those objects and statistics that are meant to constitute evidence of practice that disables me from making a firm pronouncement on NREGAs performance. Muster rolls, job cards, balance sheets, monthly progress reports, oral recitations in meetings, and other such forms of evidentiary practice are adjudged, by the very people who work on creating them, to be *sarkari*. By definition, *sarkari* documents and statistics possess a complicated relationship with the real (*asli*), and might be – but then again, might not be – *farzee*. Given this state of affairs, how does one authoritatively proclaim performance, particularly through the dualisms of success/failure or by a reliance on statistics? The difficulty of finding a narrative on the performance of development becomes even more acute when one rejects the comfort of turning to 'corruption' (or what I prefer to identify as the practice of 'eating' government money) as the metric through which success/failure can be tabulated (Mathur forthcoming).

To further think through the implications of the knowledge my ethnography of bureaucracy has produced, let us return to where it all started. We are back in Chamoli district in the village of Pipalkoti with the federation of bamboo-basket weavers. A few days before I left Gopeshwar, I went to say goodbye to those weavers whom I had befriended almost a year ago. Two of them – S and K – run a small roadside shop, stocked with fruits, biscuits, soft drinks, cigarettes, bottles of mineral water and bamboo baskets. The shop is kept open only during the *yatra* (pilgrimage) season as it caters primarily to the large number of pilgrims and tourists who travel through Pipalkoti on their way up to Badrinath temple and Hemkund Sahib. As a souvenir I bought a few of the baskets they had put up on display. Admiring their fine craftsmanship, I asked them about the Uttarakhand Bamboo Board and the work that the federation was doing for them. The question met with cynicism. Apparently, soon after the 'high-profile' evaluation that I had attended the previous Autumn, the federation had entirely collapsed. In any case it had ever really existed only 'on paper', the two informed me. I was taken aback to hear this, not least because right down the road from where we stood, a big showroom has been erected, exhibiting beautiful baskets and other artefacts woven out of the fine *ringal* bamboo that grows in Chamoli (Figure 1). Outside the showroom – the Bamboo House as it is called – a map, in English, sets out the plan for present and future development of bamboo-weaving as a livelihood activity in this village.

Sensing my surprise, S. said, with mild irritation: 'You have been working with *sarkar* for so long and have still not understood that all this development work is only for *sarkar*? The Bamboo Board is only for *sarkar*, not for us poor'.

Figure 1: Inside the bamboo house

(*Tum itne dinon se sarkar kai saath kam kar rahin ho aur abhi bhi nahin samajh payee ki yeh sab vikas karya kewal sarkar kai liye hai? Bamboo board kewal sarkar kai liye hai, hum gareeb ke liye nahin*)

Nodding his assent, K added: 'This is the real thing. Don't forget to write this'.

(*Asli baat to yahin hai. Yeh likhna mat bhoolna*)

S and K were, that day, voicing a commonplace criticism of the developmental Indian state. The argument goes that the state undertakes developmental work purely for show – for itself rather than those it claims to be developing – and is thus only concerned with showing progress on paper and, sometimes, through visual and material propaganda such as the Bamboo House. In one way, my work supports this position. For I have demonstrated that it is through the production of variegated documents and through the convening and staging of meetings that the accomplishment of development by the state is said to be 'done'. At an individual level all the labour that is expended is in order to demonstrate that one's work within the network of the state has been performed. Letters translate the NREGA but they also act as evidence of bureaucratic action; they protect the letter-writers. The *lekhakar* (writer) in the District Magistrate's (DM) office proudly described his work to me thus: 'I write letters to save DM sahib's *naukari* (job)'. It is the same with meetings: they might or might not have improved the implementation of the NREGS, but they very certainly did allow the local state to say that they have audited themselves, that the rules laid out for them from 'above' have been followed. The clear distinction made between the 'state-life' and the 'real life' of the NREGS is an indicator that development work is, in one sense and as S and K put it, undertaken by the state for itself. In the NREGS cell, too, despite the perennial grumbling about the copious paperwork of the scheme, there was an acknowledgement that, as Mr P used to often say, 'the Guarantee (NREGA) is our dear friend' (*guarantee hamari pyari dost hai*) – it was due to this and the other assorted development programmes that Mr P and his colleagues had attained a permanent government job.

The allegations of the 'papereality' (Dery, 1998) of a lot of *sarkari vikas* (state-led development) are not unfounded. Thus muster rolls don't match job cards, and labourer's testimonies don't match either the muster rolls or what is written on their own job cards. If we are to take the voice and memory of the labourer as that which constitutes the truth, then these *sarkari* documents are, all too often, *farzee* (fake). It is for this reason that every so often, development 'scams' are exposed. In these revelations of the developmental Indian state, official records are shown to have absolutely no correspondence to real life, such as in the many cases of ghost job cards, fake muster rolls, or pensions and compensations paid to people who don't exist or who claim to have not received them. Similarly, the papers show federations, self-help groups, co-operatives, or other such associations on which government funds have been spent although, in reality, they do not exist and sometimes never have. In the case of the maneater, the state desperately attempted to produce reams of documents that would attest to the *asli*, which was a situation of abject terror and indisputable knowledge that the big cat was posing a deadly threat to all humans. The state struggled on and on to do so in a manner which would convince superiors and enable the gathering of resources to slay the big cat. During the reign of the *bagh* as well as at those frequent moments when NREGA scams are unearthed, it can appear as if the 'paper tiger' that the Indian state is, can continue to function within its world of paper with no regard for anything else, such as grinding rural poverty or a dangerous wild animal.

A central argument of this work, however, is that the *sarkari* and the site of the development programme, be it a village or an urban slum, are *not* hermetically sealed off from each other. I agree that *sarkari kaghaz* does not map onto the *asli* with the degree of precision required by these times of total auditing or assumed as the legacy of a long history of representational politics and materiality. However, instead of dismissing this lack of correspondence as emerging from the idiocy, venality, or under-evolved status of a post-colonial bureaucratic state, I have argued that we need to understand the intimate, complex, and context-dependent entanglement of the *sarkari* and the real. It is precisely in the grasping of this entanglement that the space for a radically new understanding of the developmental Indian state opens up. In my own contribution to this project of ethnographic elucidation, I have tried to show the levels through which the paper state reaches out to, and is touched by, the world beyond. It is a banality to say that citizens, particularly the poor, are dependent upon states. But perhaps what *Paper Tiger* might have brought to the table is a clearer sense of what things this dependence on *sarkar* hinges on and what it means to live in the Indian Himalaya with its attendant remoteness, paucity of employment, and ever-lurking fear of attacks by wild animals. Furthermore, what happens in *sarkari daftars* is affected in almost surreal ways by what happens in times and spaces far removed. Let us begin with the reign of terror of the big cat. The Mughal and colonial state voluptuously practiced *shikar* (the hunt). The astronomical numbers of big cats killed during the Mughal reign and the colonial period and, in fact, upto the banning of big cat hunting in 1969 are almost directly correlated to the current imperilment of big cats in the sub-continent. Presently a 'love' for big cats is professed by all sorts of people ranging from the middle classes in urban India to the likes of Vladimir Putin and Leonardo di Caprio. The impact of this history and of the on-going global 'save the big cat' movement was felt in our little office in Gopeshwar as the officials struggled to win a written death warrant for the charismatic leopard. Let us turn to the NREGA. Elsewhere I have traced the genealogy of this shiny new legislation back to the Famine Codes institutionalized by the British colonial state in the nineteenth century (Mathur, 2013). The design of the NREGA, I have argued, reflects the steady spread of a neoliberal political rationality that posits the market as the central organizing principle of life. The emphasis on a critical scrutiny of every state action – which is definitive of the NREGA's newness – is linked to the increasingly widespread crisis of trust in public institutions and the state. The WPA and NREGA, once invoked, critically shape the space of bureaucratic action.

Laws, in their turn, encounter history and lived reality in surprising ways. I have no doubt that the big-cat lovers of the world don't want little children in the Indian Himalaya to be gobbled up by a leopard with impunity. The gradation of value of lives in the Indian Himalaya that was constantly done – *sarkar* cares five times more for the life of one big cat than one human; *sarkar* thinks the value of my seven-year-old daughter's life is the same as that of two horses – were, however, very real outcomes of the legal apparatus that wishes to protect big cats. Conservationist activism and the wide coverage given by the international and national media to big cats in India, have only added to the pressure officials in Uttarakhand feel to avoid, in any way possible, being responsible for the sensational death of another of these charismatic species. In the case of the NREGA, I have shown the difficulties faced in implementing it, to the extent that, on encountering the longstanding system whereby employment-generation and public works programmes have operated in the Indian Himalaya, it was declared 'unimplementable'. These difficulties arose not just from the volume of the paperwork, as officials claimed, but rather the canny work that certain transparent-making documents were doing. If there really were no correspondence between the paper and the *asli*, then these complications would never have arisen. I have shown the work that a tiny ID – the job card – is capable of doing and the manner in which it could challenge the power of the muscular 'Contractor Raj'. Not only does the upsetting nature of the job card demonstrate the complex interplay between *sarkari kaghaz, daftar,* and the *asli* (paper, office, and the real) but it also shows how small modifications in plans or laws can have major effects.

I have argued that it is not in the tribute paid to transparency, accountability, participation, rights – a global development-speak – that the revolutionary potential of the NREGA lies but in its clever documentary requirements. While the documents under the NREGA are products of the ideology of transparency they do not, I hasten to add, render the state and its functioning transparent. Rather, they build up another order of state-created reality that can materially attest to the transparency of the government of India. This intensification of material proof of effective government in India holds uncanny echoes with the past. In 1852 John Stuart Mill claimed that the most important reason for the satisfactory working of government in the Indian territories was that: '[t]he whole Government of India is carried on in writing...so that there is no single act done in India, the whole of the reasons for which are not placed on record' (quoted in Moir, 1995, p. 185; see Raman, 2012). The *Kaghazi Raj* of the colonial period has morphed into what I study in the present as the paper state. This contemporary iteration of a form of rule that is underpinned by bureaucrats, documents, and files is being given a new lease of life by the demands for transparency and accountability. These ideals of government might appear strikingly of-the-moment. However, I have argued that in India, transparency of the form demanded by the RTI and the NREGA, can only ever be realized through a reliance on and strengthening of precisely those practices that formed the lynchpin of empire.

There is of course a staggering irony to my claim that a transparent contemporary India in effect strengthens those practices that allowed Mill to declare it an ideal colony. Leaving righteous post-colonial dismay aside, let us not forget that new forms of government or rule, of necessity, build upon extant ones with their attendant histories. This would appear obvious but the ruination of the past that is rhetorically declared by new regimes often obscures this fact. This can be true of newly elected political parties to Parliament or newly formed states, and holds water even for progressive laws such as NREGA that predicate their legitimacy on effecting a radical rupture from the (disappointing) past. This is not to say that the new is just more of the same old. Rather, it is to draw attention to the discourse of the new and to be aware that it cannot but engage with the past and build from that. It is for this reason that the NREGA presents such an interesting case – it builds upon a long tradition of public works and rural employment programmes in India but, through its critical engagement with current modalities of rule, it is able to perturb this history. The fact that the perturbances can be caused by what is often thought of as 'mere paper' is crucial to note. In the current environment when talk of 'new technologies' and their capacity to somehow recreate the art and practice of government abounds, it is worth underlining a point that *Paper Tiger* makes: small and seemingly simple modifications or tweaks in the existing system can have startling effects. Thus the introduction of job cards as an ID for NREGA labourers would appear to be a straightforward accounting procedure, but I hope to have shown its potency. Changes can, in other words, be introduced without necessarily dropping the entire apparatus of the previous system. Yet organizations constantly articulate the desire to abandon extant technologies and modernize themselves through the adoption of something that is considered newer. In a study entitled *The Myth of the Paperless Office*, Sellen and Harper write: 'paper has always been a symbol of old-fashioned practices and old-fashioned technology. New technologies, as long ago as the mid-1800s, were offering something 'better'' (2002, p. 5). Interestingly, they note that ever since the invention of the World Wide Web, which is supposed to have allowed for the paperless office, the consumption of paper has actually gone up. In fact, they argue that what has enhanced interest in new technologies of communication such as the web is 'the fact that technologies are beginning to look and feel more paperlike' (8).

The techno-fantasy of the British colonial state once hoped to produce paper-based reports that were akin to photographs in the way in which they represented social facts (Saumarez-Smith, 1985). Today the techno-fantasy has shifted to the use of new technologies like biometrics or mobile phones and on inclusion into the warm embrace of supposedly modern institutions like banks. I want to end by inserting a cautionary note into the jubilant discourse of new technologies as the route to 'good' government on the basis of one final NREGA observation.

During the majority of my stay in Uttarakhand, NREGA wages were being paid in cash by the village headperson. This mode of operation keeps evidence of payment of wages through the means of the labourer's thumb impression or signature, both of which are very easily forged. It is, therefore, considered to leave behind no trace that is fully verifiable, making it an un-transparent aspect of the NREGA in the eyes of the state. New Delhi accordingly ordered that all wages be paid through bank accounts. This created huge problems in Chamoli because there are very few bank branches in the region, the ones that exist are located miles away from most villages, and villagers don't have either the wherewithal or the documents to open bank accounts. Most problematically, women (who were certainly the ones undertaking most of the labour under NREGA works) feared losing control over their own wages in becoming dependent either on middlemen or on male relatives to operate their bank account for them. They were also befuddled by this new directive from New Delhi as, even leaving aside the inconvenience of trekking hours on end to get to a bank and then further waiting hours to, hopefully, get your cash, this new policy shows a complete lack of awareness of systems of social networks and the operation of trust in rural India. It was much more convenient to have your wages paid in cash by someone who visits your village. While sometimes this would not happen for reasons ranging from caste or gender discrimination to feuds to sheer incompetence, there are ways in which social pressure to pay up does build on officials and elected representatives. Furthermore, there are other ways in which one could organize payment of wages in a transparent manner, such as publically speaking aloud the wages or pinning up final payments in Panchayat Houses, or separating the agencies/officials who implement the programme from those that pay out the wages.

The result of this Central push for bank accounts was that the figure of 'the number of bank accounts opened' became a target for development bureaucrats. This banking push, which is often patronisingly described as imparting 'financial literacy', created an extreme and peculiar form of pressure on the district bureaucracy. The peculiarity stemmed from the fact that they were ordered to create something for which the institutional and material resources were not yet available. The banking system in this remote Himalayan district is skeletal, yet the official picture had to depict that bank accounts were being opened rapidly. The exigencies of the state structure required that lower-level bureaucrats produce evidence – on paper – of having met the targets. In reality, though, the bank accounts were either fictitious or, even more dangerously, completely in the control of middlemen or other sorts of brokers who dictated how the actual bank account holder dealt with the money that was being transferred in. Yet, the assumption was that the bank account had, automatically and in and of itself, rendered the payment of wages transparent. In reality, a strikingly gender-biased – almost flagrantly anti-women – structure was being set up which, arguably, left equal if not more space for the 'eating' of money and the denial of wages, by facilitating the wresting away of control over the bank account from the labourer's hands (cf. Vanaik, 2009). Furthermore, the assumption is that once the worker has a bank account, no more monitoring of the scheme is required as it is now self-evidently transparent – a deeply disturbing assumption given what was unfolding in the villages; which is why this idea could have extremely grave consequences for the labourers (see Khera and Dreze, 2009). Similarly, the move to introduce biometric-based IDs and link it to the NREGA not only holds worrying implications of loss of privacy and increased possibilities for surveillance (Ramanathan, 2010) but its practical utility remains questionable and complicated (Khera, 2013). I am arguing, then, that the move to the 'new', be it a technology or an institutionalized service needs to be approached with caution (see Bear and Mathur, 2015). As *Paper Tiger* shows, the effect of the 'new', be it an ideological shift in technique such as 'transparency' or the insertion of something material such as an ID, is never quite what one expects it to be.

I can just see my interlocutors in Uttarakhand rolling their eyes when they read my statement on the unexpected results of state interventions or welfare programmes. For they know what the results unwaveringly are: progress 'on paper' but nothing in reality other than an unremitting lack of succour or advancement and, in some cases, active persecution. This book is written from a position of the deepest solidarity with my *pahari* friends such as S & K in the erstwhile bamboo-weavers' federation, and the serial petition writer who would so hopefully come to the district headquarters only to find his letters 'never arrived' or had gotten 'lost' (read: binned) and hence no action by *sarkar* was possible. What can I even say of the victims of the maneaters that haunt Uttarakhand, and who but rarely receive compensation for injuries or for the deaths of their kin even as their daily lives must be conducted in fear of further attacks. The same applies to the many who could not physically hold on to their job cards, or who enter the NREGA system without their knowledge as mere names on muster rolls, or those who were never paid the wages due to them or even given employment in the first place. What the papers say (*kaghaz kya kehte hai*) can, for varying reasons, be experienced most cruelly by the people who are most dependent upon them. It is with good reason that so much of the extremely accomplished literature on the state and bureaucracy in India has explicitly worked through a focus on violence (e.g. Das, 2007; Gupta, 2012; Shah, 2011; Hansen, 2001). My own ethnographically derived stance, though inspired by much of this fine work, has taken me down a less-travelled path. What I find striking and in need of detailed analysis is not so much the violence (in whatever form) of the Indian state bureaucracy, but rather its quotidian laborious struggle with the material overcoming of illegibilities and the mediation of differing social times.

The ethnographic approach to law, state, and bureaucracy that I have adopted here has allowed me to show how a law aimed at providing employment to an impoverished region beset with high levels of unemployment can be rendered 'unimplementable'. I have also described how a reign of terror could be established by a non-human entity such as a big cat and why it appeared to go unchallenged by the state for an inordinately long period. In both these cases, I have not located the causes within intentionality, indifference, dysfunctionality, incapacity, or forms of violence. Instead, I have shown the specific effects of particular laws in named places and within a definitive time. This attention to detail compels me to radically question standard accounts of 'waiting' as well as to eschew normative answers to the question of the performance of an anti-poverty legislation. Studies of NREGA are almost always derived from and based upon sociological constructs such as caste, gender, geographic terrain, or temperament of labourers and emerging from surveys undertaken, statistics analysed or official records inspected. An ethnography of law and bureaucracy allows me, instead, to spell out the difficulties experienced in getting the law off the ground in the first place, and to express a caution against a historic over-attachment to those papery artefacts that are believed to make-transparent the state, its actions, and its intentions. At the same time, I refrain from a wholehearted rejection of state documents and statistics as sheer artifice. Instead, I have tried to show the complexities and layers of entanglement between the *sarkari* and the real, and the sheer vexedness of implementing utopian plans and deeply desired reforms. In lieu of reproach, quantitative analyses, or theoretical exegeses, I have chosen to ethnographically work through a mocking phrase – 'paper tiger' – that is believed to be a particularly apt descriptor of the regularly reported and much puzzled-over peculiarities of the faltering Indian state. By highlighting the logic, practice, and materiality of contemporary state bureaucracy in India, emerging as it does from its particular historically sedimented system of rule, I hope to have shown this phrase's capacity to acquire popular currency but also its inherent inadequacy to function, in and of itself, as an instrument of critique.

References

Abrams, Philip. 2006. 'Notes on the Difficulty of Studying the State.' In *The Anthropology of the State: A Reader*, edited by Aradhana Sharma and Akhil Gupta, 112–130. Oxford: Blackwell Press.

Abram, Simone, and Giza Weszkalnys. 2011. 'Introduction: Anthropologies of Planning—Temporality, Imagination, and Ethnography.' *Focaal—Journal of Global and Historical Anthropology* 61: 3–18.

Adams, Vincanne, Murphy, Michelle, and Adele E. Clarke. 2009. 'Anticipation: Techno-science, Life, Affect, Temporality.' *Subjectivity* 28 (1): 246–65.

Aiyar, Yamini and Soumya Mehta. 2015. 'Spectators or Participants? Effects of Social Audits in Andhra Pradesh'. *Economic and Political Weekly* 50 (7): 66–71.

Althusser, Louis. 2006. 'Ideology and Ideological State Apparatuses (Notes Towards an Investigation).' In *The Anthropology of the State: A Reader*, edited by Aradhana Sharma and Akhil Gupta, 86–111. Oxford: Blackwell.

Appadurai, Arjun. 1988. *The Social Life of Things: Commodities in Cultural Perspective*. Cambridge: Cambridge University Press.

Anderson, Clare. 2003. 'The Politics of Convict Space: Indian Penal Settlements and the Andaman Islands.' In *Isolated: Places and Practices of Exclusion*, edited by Carolyn Strange and Alison Bashford, 40–55. London: Routledge.

Anjaria, Jonathan S. 2011. 'Ordinary States: Everyday Corruption and the Politics of Space in Mumbai.' *American Ethnologist* 38 (1): 58–72.

Aretxaga, Begona. 2003. 'Maddening States.' *Annual Review of Anthropology* 32: 393–410.

Arnold, David. 2005. *The Tropics and the Traveling Gaze: India, Landscape, and Science, 1800-1856*. Delhi: Permanent Black.

Atkinson, E. T. 2002. *The Himalayan Gazeteer or the Himalayan Districts of the North Western Province of India, Volume II*, 1881. Delhi: Low Price Publication.

Auge, Marc. 2009. *Non-Places: An Introduction to an Anthropology of Supermodernity*. London: Verso.

Auyero, Javier. 2012. *Patients of the State: The Politics of Waiting in Argentina*. Durham: Duke University Press.

Ballestero, Andrea S. 2012. 'Transparency in Triads'. *Political and Legal Anthropology Review* (PoLAR) 35 (2): 160–66.

Banerjee, Sarnath. 2011. *The Harappa Files*. New Delhi: Harper Collins.

Barry, Andrew, Thomas Osborne, and Nikolas Rose. 1996. 'Introduction.' In *Foucault and Political Reason: Liberalism, Neo-liberalism and Rationalities of Government*, edited by Andrew Barry, Thomas Osborne and Nikolas Rose, 1–18. London: University of Chicago Press.

Baru, Sanjaya. 2014. *The Accidental Prime Minister: The Making and Unmaking of Manmohan Singh.* New Delhi: Penguin

Baviskar, Amita. 2006. '*Is Knowledge Power? The Right to Information Campaign in India.*' Draft Paper, 1–24. New Delhi: Institute of Economic Growth.

Bear, Laura. 2007. *Lines of the Nation: Indian Railway Workers, Bureaucracy, and the Intimate Historical Self.* New York: Columbia University Press.

Bear, Laura and Nayanika Mathur. 2015. 'Introduction: Remaking the Public Good: A New Anthropology of Bureaucracy'. *The Cambridge Journal of Anthropology* 33 (1): 18–34.

Berdahl, Daphne. 1999. *Where the World Ended: Re-unification and Identity in the German Borderland.* Berkeley and Los Angeles: University of California Press.

Berreman, Gerald. 1972. *Hindus of the Himalayas: Ethnography & Change.* Berkeley & Los Angeles: University of California Press.

Bhalla, Surjit. 2004. 'Corruption with a Human Face'. *Business Standard.*

Bhatt, Chandi P., and Kunwar, S. S. 1982. *Hugging the Himalaya: the Chipko Experience.* Gopeshwar: DGSS Press.

Boomgaard, Peter. 2001. *Frontiers of Fear: Tigers and People in the Malay World, 1600–1950.* New Haven: Yale University Press.

Bourdieu, Pierre. 2000. *Pascalian Meditations.* Cambridge: Polity Press.

Brennan, Lance. 1984. 'The Development of the Indian Famine Code'. In *Famine as a Geographical Phenomenon,* edited by Bruce Currey and Graeme Hugo, 91–112. Dordrecht: D. Reidel Publishing Company.

Brittlebank, Kate. 1995. 'Sakti and Barakat: The Power of Tipu's Tiger, An Examination of the Tiger Emblem of Tipu Sultan of Mysore'. *Modern Asian Studies* 29 (2): 257–69.

Brown, Wendy. 1995. *States of Injury: Power and Freedom in Late Modernity.* Princeton, NJ: Princeton University Press.

_____. 2005. *Edgework: Critical Essays on Knowledge and Politics.* Princeton: Princeton University Press.

Burton, Richard G. 1933. *The Book of the Tiger with a Chapter on the Lion in India.* London: Hutchinson & Co.

Centre for Science and Environment (CSE). 2008. *NREGA: Opportunities and Challenges.* New Delhi: Natural Resource Management and Livelihood Unit, CSE.

Chandrasekhar, C. P., and Jayati Ghosh. 2004. 'How Feasible is a Rural Employment Guarantee?' *Hindu Business Line.*

Chatterjee, Partha. 2004. 'Development Planning and the Indian State'. In *State and Politics in India,* edited by Partha Chatterjee, 271–97. New Delhi: Oxford University Press.

Chatterjee, Upamanyu. 1988. *English, August: an Indian Story.* London: Faber & Faber.

Chatterji, Aditi. 2002. 'Landscapes of Power: The Indian Hill Stations'. Research Paper. Department of Geography, University of Oxford.

Chatterji, Roma and Mehta, Deepak. 2007. *Living with Violence: An Anthropology of Events and Everyday Life.* New Delhi: Routledge.

Chowdhury, Shovon. 2013. *The Competent Authority.* New Delhi: Aleph

Cody, Francis. 2009. 'Inscribing Subjects to Citizenship: Petitions, Literacy Activism, and the Performativity of Signature in Rural Tamil India'. *Cultural Anthropology* 24 (3): 347–80.

_____. 2013. *The Light of Knowledge: Literary Activism and the Politics of Writing in South India.* Hyderabad: Orient BlackSwan.

Coetzee, John M. 2004. *Waiting for the Barbarians.* London: Vintage Books.

Collier, Stephen J., and Aihwa Ong. 2005 'Global Assemblages, Anthropological Problems.' In *Global Assemblages: Technology, Politics, and Ethics as Anthropological Problems,* edited by Aihwa Ong and Stephen J. Collier, 3–21. Malden, MA: Blackwell.

Cooke, Bill and Kothari, Uma. 2001. *Participation: The New Tyranny?* London: Zed Books.

Corbett, Jim. 2007. *The Man-Eating Leopard of Rudraprayag.* New Delhi: Oxford University Press.

Corbridge, Stuart. 2004. 'Waiting in Line, or the Moral and Material Geographies of Queue-jumping.' In *Geographies and Moralities: International Perspectives on Development, Justice, and Place,* edited by Roger Lee and David M. Smith, 183–98. Oxford: Blackwell.

Corbridge, Stuart, Williams, Glyn, Srivastava, Manoj, and Veron, Rene. 2005. *Seeing the State: Governance and Governmentality in India.* Cambridge: Cambridge University Press.

Corngold, Stanley. 2009. 'Kafka and the Ministry of Writing.' In *Franz Kafka: The Office Writings,* edited by Stanley Corngold, Jack Greenberg, and Benno Wagner, 1–18. Oxford: Princeton University Press.

Crapanzano, Vincent. 1985. *Waiting: the Whites of South Africa.* London: Random House.

Damania, Richard, Seidensticker, John, Witten, Anthony, et al. 2008. *A Future for Wild Tigers.* Washington, D.C: The World Bank.

Das, Veena. 2004. 'The Signature of the State: The Paradox of Illegibility.' In *Anthropology in the Margins of the State,* edited by Veena Das and Deborah Poole, 225–52. New Delhi: Oxford University Press.

_____. 2007. *Life and Words: Violence and the Descent into the Ordinary.* New Delhi: Oxford University Press.

Das, Veena and Poole, Deborah. 2004. 'State and Its Margins: Comparative Ethnographies.' In *Anthropology in the Margins of the State,* edited by Veena Das and Deborah Poole, 3–34. New Delhi: Oxford University Press.

Dasgupta, Swapan. 2005. 'Rename REGA as Corruption Guarantee Scheme.' *Pioneer.*

de Certeau, Michel. 1988. *The Practice of Everyday Life.* Berkeley: University of California Press.

Derrida, Jacques. 1988. *Limited Inc.* Evanston, IL: Northwestern University Press.

_____. 2005. *Paper Machine.* Stanford: Stanford University Press.

Dery, David. 1998. 'Papereality' and Learning in Bureaucratic Organisation'. *Administration and Society* 29(6):677–89

Desai, Kiran. 2006. *The Inheritance of Loss.* London: Hamish Hamilton.

Dirks, Nicholas B. 2008. *Castes of Mind: Colonialism and the Making of Modern India.* Delhi: Permanent Black.

Dreze, Jean. 2004. 'Employment as a Social Responsibility.' *The Hindu,* November 22.

_____. 2005. 'Time to Clean Up.' *The Times of India,* August 13.

_____. 2007. 'NREGA: Dismantling the Contractor Raj.' *The Hindu,* November 20.

Dreze, Jean and Reetika Khera. 2008. From Accounts to Accountability. *The Hindu,* December 6.

Dreze, Jean and Siddhartha. 2009. 'Flaws in the System.' *Frontline* 26 (1).

Englund, Harri. 2006. *Prisoners of Freedom: Human Rights and the African Poor.* Berkeley: University of California Press.

Escobar, Arturo. 1995. *Encountering Development: The Making and Unmaking of the Third World.* Princeton, NJ: Princeton University Press.

Fassin, Didier. 2009. 'Another Politics of Life is Possible.' *Theory, Culture & Society* 26 (5): 44–60.

Fehervary, Krisztina. 2009. 'Goods and States: The Political Logic of State Socialist Material Culture.' *Comparative Studies in Society and History* 51 (2): 426–59.

Feldman, Ilana. 2008. *Governing Gaza: Bureaucracy, Authority, and the Work of Rule, 1917–1967.* Durham & London: Duke University Press.

Ferguson, James. 1994. *The Anti-politics Machine: 'Development', Depoliticisation and Bureaucratic Power in Lesotho.* Cambridge: Cambridge University Press.

_____. 2006. *Global Shadows: Africa in the Neoliberal World Order.* Durham & London: Duke University Press.

_____. 2009. 'The Uses of Neoliberalism.' *Antipode* 41: 166–84.

Ferguson, James and Akhil Gupta. 2005. 'Spatializing States: Toward an Ethnography of Neoliberal Governmentality.' In *Anthropologies of Modernity: Foucault, Governmentality, and Life Politics*, edited by Javier. X. Inda, 105–34. Malden, MA: Blackwell.

Forster, Ernest. M. 1953. *The Hill of Devi: Being Letters from Dewas State Senior.* London: E. Arnold.

Foucault, Michel. 1995. *Discipline and Punish: The Birth of the Prison.* New York: Random House.

_____. 2008. *The Birth of Biopolitics: Lectures at the College de France, 1978–1979.* New York: Palgrave Macmillan.

_____. 1991 'Questions of Method.' In *The Foucault Effect: Studies in Governmentality*, edited by Graham Burchell, Colin Gordon and Peter Miller, 73–86. Chicago: University of Chicago Press.

Fuller, Chris J. and Harris, John. 2000. 'For an Anthropology of the Modern Indian State.' In *The Everyday State and Society in Modern India*, edited by Chris J. Fuller and Veronique Benei, 1–30. New Delhi: Social Science Press.

Geertz, Clifford. 1980. *Negara: The Theatre State in Nineteenth-Century Bali.* Princeton: Princeton University Press.

Ghosh, Jayati. 2004. 'Rural Employment as Policy Priority.' *Frontline* 21 (14).

Goodsell, C. B. 1984. 'Welfare Waiting Rooms.' *Journal of Contemporary Ethnography* 12 (4): 467–77.

Goswami, Manu. *Producing India: From Colonial Economy to National Space.* Chicago & London: University of Chicago Press, 2004.

Gould, William. 2012. "That Venerable and Wonderful Institution *Dustooree*:' Custom, *Daalii* and Influence in the Bureaucracy of Late Colonial/Early Independent North India.' Paper presented at 'The New Public Good' conference, Cambridge, March 23–24.

Government of India. 1972. The Wildlife (Protection) Act, 1972. New Delhi: GoI. Accessed November 10, 2008. http://envfor.nic.in/legis/wildlife/wildlife1.html.

Government of India, Ministry of Rural Development. 2005. Operational Guidelines for the Implementation of the National Rural Employment Guarantee Scheme (NREGS), First Edition. New Delhi: GoI.

_____. 2008. Operational Guidelines for the Implementation of the National Rural Employment Guarantee Scheme (NREGS), Third Edition. New Delhi: GoI.

Government of Uttar Pradesh. 1995. Chamoli-Gopeshwar Mahayojana Praroop (1995–2016). Municipal Corporation. Gopeshwar: Government of UP.

Graeber, David. 2012. 'Dead Zones of the Imagination: On Violence, Bureaucracy, and Interpretive Labour.' *HaU: Journal of Ethnographic Theory* 2 (2): 105–28.

Gramya Vikas Vibhag Chamoli. 2006. *Soochna Ka Adhikar Adhiniyam 2005–06*. Rural Development Department. Gopeshwar: Government of Uttarakhand.

Gray, John. N. 2000. *At Home in the Hills: Sense of Place in the Scottish Borders*. New York and Oxford: Berghahn Books.

Greenhouse, Carol. 1989. 'Just in Time: Temporality and the Cultural Legitimation of Law.' *The Yale Law Journal* 98: 1631–51.

Guha, Ramachandra. 2001. *The Unquiet Woods: Ecological Change and Peasant Resistance in the Himalaya*. New Delhi: Oxford University Press.

_____. 2005. 'The Authoritarian Biologist and the Arrogance of Anti-humanism: Wildlife Conservation in the Third World.' In *Battles over Nature: Science and the Politics of Conservation*, edited by Vasant Saberwal and Mahesh Rangarajan, 139–57. New Delhi: Permanent Black.

Gupta, Akhil. 1995. 'Blurred Boundaries: The Discourse of Corruption, the Culture of Politics, and the Imagined State.' *American Ethnologist* 22 (2): 375–402.

_____. 1998. *Postcolonial Developments: Agriculture in the Making of Modern India*. Durham: Duke University Press.

_____. 2012. *Red Tape: Bureaucracy, Structural Violence, and Poverty in India*. Durham: Duke University Press.

Gupta, Akhil and Ferguson, James. 1992. 'Beyond "Culture": Space, Identity, and the Politics of Difference.' *Cultural Anthropology* 7 (1): 6–23.

Gupta, Akhil and Sharma, Aradhana. 2006. 'Globalization and Postcolonial States.' *Current Anthropology* 47 (2): 277–93.

Gupta, Smita. 2005. 'A Very Significant Legislation.' *People's Democracy* 29 (35).

Guyer, Jane. 2007. 'Prophecy and the Near Future: Thoughts on Macroeconomic, Evangelical and Punctuated Time.' *American Ethnologist* 34 (3): 409–21.

Hansen, Thomas B. 2001. *Wages of Violence: Naming and Identity in Postcolonial Bombay*. Princeton: Princeton University Press.

Hansen, Thomas B. and Finn Stepputat. 2001. 'Introduction: States of Imagination.' In *States of Imagination: Ethnographic Explorations of the Postcolonial State*, edited by Thomas B. Hansen and Finn Stepputat, 1–40. Durham: Duke University Press.

Harper, Richard. 1997. *Inside the IMF: An Ethnography of Documents, Technology, and Organizational Action*. San Diego: Academic Press.

_____. 2000. 'The Social Organisation of the IMF's Mission Work: An Examination of International Auditing.' In *Audit Cultures: Anthropological Studies in Accountability, Ethics, and the Academy*, edited by Marilyn Strathern, 21–54. New York: Routledge.

Harris-White, Barbara. 1997. 'Informal Economic Order: Shadow States, Private Status States, States of Last Resort and Spinning States—A Speculative Discussion on South Asian Case Material.' Oxford: Queen Elizabeth House. Oxford Department for International Development Working Paper Series.

Harrison, Elizabeth. 2003. 'The Monolithic Development Machine?' In *A Moral Critique of Development: In Search of Global Responsibilities*, edited by P. Quarles van Ufford and A. K. Giri, 101–17. London and New York: Routledge.

Harvey, David. 2005. *A Brief History of Neoliberalism*. New York: Oxford University Press.

Harvey, Penny. 2005. 'The Materiality of State Effects: An ethnography of a Road in the Peruvian Andes.' In *State Formation. Anthropological Explorations*, edited by Christian Krohn-Hansen and Knut G. Nustad, 216–47. Cambridge: Pluto Press.

Hasan, Zoya. 2005. 'EGA: Needed, a Government Guarantee Act.' *Indian Express*, 6.

Herzfeld, Michael. 1992. *The Social Production of Indifference: Exploring the Symbolic Roots of Western Bureaucracy*. Chicago and London: The University of Chicago Press.

Hetherington, Kregg. 2011. *Guerilla Auditors: The Politics of Transparency in Neoliberal Paraguay*. Durham & London: Duke University Press.

_____. 2012. 'Promising Information: Cadastral Reform and Development Expertise in Latin America.' *Economy and Society* 41 (2): 127–50.

Highmore, Ben. 2002. 'Introduction: Questioning Everyday Life.' In *The Everyday Life Reader*, edited by Ben Highmore, 1–36. London: Routledge.

Holston, James. 1989. *The Modernist City: An Anthropological Critique of Brasilia*. London: The University of Chicago Press.

Hull, Matthew S. 2008. 'Ruled by Records: The Expropriation of Land and the Misappropriation of Lists in Islamabad.' *American Ethnologist* 35 (4): 501–18.

_____. 2012a. *Government of Paper: The Materiality of Bureaucracy in Urban Pakistan*. Berkeley: University of California Press.

_____. 2012b. 'Documents and Bureaucracy.' *Annual Review of Anthropology* 41: 251–67.

Hussain, Shafqat. 2012. 'Forms of Predation: Tiger and Markhor Hunting in Colonial Governance.' *Modern Asian Studies* 46 (5): 1212–38.

Jalais, Annu. 2005. 'Dwelling on Morichjhanpi: When Tigers Became "Citizens", Refugees "Tiger-Food".' *Economic and Political Weekly* 40 (17): 1757–62.

_____. 2008. 'Unmasking the Cosmopolitan Tiger.' *Nature and Culture* 3 (1): 25–40.

Jauregui, Beatrice. 2014. 'Provisional Agency in India: Jugaad and the Legitimation of Corruption.' *American Ethnologist* 41 (1): 76–91.

Jayal, Niraja G. 2000. 'Uttaranchal: Same Wine, Same Bottle, New Label?" *Economic and Political Weekly* 23 (1): 16–24.

Jeffrey, Craig. 2008. 'Waiting.' *Environment and Planning D: Society and Space* 26: 954–8.

_____. 2011. *Timepass: Youth, Class and the Politics of Waiting in India*. Stanford: Stanford University Press.

Jhala, Y. V., Gopal, R., et al. 2008. *Status of the Tiger, Co-predators, and Prey in India*. Dehradun: National Tiger Conservation Authority and Wildlife Institute of India.

Kafka, Ben. 2012. *The Demon of Writing: Powers and Failures of Paperwork*. New York: Zone Books.

Kafka, Franz. 2000. *The Trial*. London: Penguin Books, 2000.

Kanwar, Pamela. 1990. *Imperial Simla: The Political Culture of the Raj*. Delhi: Oxford University Press.

Karat, Brinda. 2004. 'No Jobs Ahead: Dilution in Unemployment Law.' *The Times of India*.

Kaviraj, Sudipto. 1984. 'On the Crisis of Political Institutions in India.' *Contributions to Indian Sociology* 18: 223–43.

Kennedy, Dane K. 1996. *The Magic Mountains: Hill Stations and the British Raj*. London: University of California Press.

Khan, Panchkouree. 1866. *The Revelations of an Orderly: Being an Attempt to Expose the Abuses of Administration by Relation of Every-day Occurrences in Mofussil Courts*. Benares: E. J. Lazarus & Co.

Khera, Reetika. 2011. *The Battle for Employment Guarantee*. New Delhi: Oxford University Press.

_____. 2013. 'A 'Cost-Benefit' Analysis of UID.' *Economic and Political Weekly* XLVIII (5): 13–5.

King, Anthony. 1976. *Colonial Urban Development: Culture, Social Power and Environment*. London: Routledge.

Kipnis, Andrew. 2008. 'Audit Cultures: Neoliberal Governmentality, Socialist Legacy, or Technologies of Governing.' *American Ethnologist* 35 (2): 275–89.

Kumar, Nita. 2006. 'Provincialism in Modern India: The Multiple Narratives of Education and their Pain.' *Modern Asian Studies* 40 (2): 397–423.

Kumar, Pramod. 2000. *The Uttarakhand Movement: Construction of a Regional Identity*. New Delhi: Kanishka Publishers.

Lakoff, Andrew. 2006. 'Preparing for the Next Emergency.' *Public Culture* 19 (2): 247–71.

Lakin, Jason and N. Ravishankar. 2006. 'Working for Votes: the Politics of Employment Guarantee in India.' Paper presented at the American Political Science Association Annual Meeting, Philadelphia.

Larner, Wendy. 2000. 'Neoliberalism: Policy, Ideology, Governmentality.' *Studies in Political Economy* 63: 5–25.

Latour, Bruno. 2000. 'When Things Strike Back: a Possible Contribution of 'Science Studies' to the Social Sciences.' *British Journal of Sociology* 51 (1): 107–23.

_____. 2002. *Aramis or the Love of Technology*. Cambridge & London: Harvard University Press.

_____. 2005. *Reassembling the Social: An Introduction to Actor-Network-Theory*. Oxford: Oxford University Press.

_____. 2009. *The Making of Law: An Ethnography of the Conseil D'Etat*. Cambridge: Polity Press.

Lazar, Sian. 2008. *El Alto, Rebel City: Self and Citizenship in Andean Bolivia*. Durham & London: Duke University Press.

Lefebvre, Henri. 1991. *The Production of Space*. Oxford: Blackwell.

Li, Tania M. 2001. 'Relational Histories and the Production of Difference on Sulawesi's Upland Frontier.' *The Journal of Asian Studies* 60 (1): 41–66.

_____. 2007. *The Will to Improve: Governmentality, Development, and the Practice of Politics*. Durham & London: Duke University Press.

Low, Setha M., and D. Lawrence-Zuniga. 2003. *The Anthropology of Space and Place: Locating Culture*. Oxford: Blackwell.

Ludden, David. 2000. 'India's Development Regime.' In *Colonialism and Culture*, edited by Nicholas B. Dirks, 245–87. Ann Arbor: University of Michigan Press.

_____. 2012. 'Imperial Modernity: History and Global Inequity in Rising Asia.' *Third World Quarterly* 33 (4): 581–601.

Macauslan, Ian. 2007. 'Working the System: Elites and the Passage of India's National Rural Employment Guarantee Act.' Draft Paper.

Mackenzie, John M. 1988. *The Empire of Nature: Hunting, Conservation and British Imperialism*. Manchester: Manchester University Press.

Mamgain, R. P. 2008. 'Growth, Poverty, and Employment in Uttarakhand.' *Labour and Development* 13 (2): 234–61.

Mander, Harsh. 2005. 'The Battle Against Hunger.' *Indian Express*, 18 August.

Mathur, Nayanika. 2012a. 'Transparent-Making Documents and the Crisis of Implementation: A Rural Employment Law and Development Bureaucracy in India.' *Political and Legal Anthropology Review (PoLAR)* 35 (2): 167–85.

_____. 2012b. 'Effecting Development: Bureaucratic Knowledges, Cynicism, and the Desire for Development in the Indian Himalaya.' In *Differentiating Development: Beyond an Anthropology of Critique,* edited by Soumhya Venkatesan and Thomas Yarrow, 193–209. London: Berghahn.

_____. 2013. 'State Debt and the Rural: Two Historical Moments in India.' *Anthropology News* 54 (5): e12–21.

_____. 2014. 'The Reign of Terror of the Big Cat: Bureaucracy and the Mediation of Social Times in the Indian Himalaya.' *Journal of the Royal Anthropological Institute* 20 (1): 148–65.

Mathur, Nayanika (forthcoming) 'Eating Money: A Questioning of the Villainy of Corruption in the Leaky Indian State'.

Mawdsley, Emma. 1996. 'The Uttarakhand Agitation and Other Backward Classes.' *Economic and Political Weekly* 31 (4): 205–10.

_____. 1997. 'Nonsecessionist Regionalism in India: the Uttarakhand Separate State Movement.' *Environment and Planning A* 29 (12): 2217–35.

_____. 1998. 'After Chipko: From Environment to Region in Uttaranchal.' *The Journal of Peasant Studies* 25 (4): 36–54.

Mazzarella, William. 2009. 'Affect: What is it Good for?" In *Enchantments of Modernity: Empire, Nation, Globalisation,* edited by Saurabh Dube, 291–309. New Delhi: Routledge.

Messick, Brinkley. 1997. *The Calligraphic State: Textual Domination and History in a Muslim Society.* California: University of California Press.

Ministry of Rural Development. 2001. Operational Guidelines for the Sampoorna Grameen Rozgar Yojana (SGRY). New Delhi: Government of India. Accessed December 6, 2005. http://www.rural.nic.in/SGRY%20Guidelines%20-%20Final.htm.

Mishra, Pankaj. 1995. *Butter Chicken in Ludhiana: Travels in Small Town India.* New Delhi: Penguin.

Mitchell, Nora. 1972. 'The Indian Hill Station: Kodaikanal.' Research Paper Chicago, Department of Geography, University of Chicago.

Mitchell, Timothy. 1999. 'Society, Economy, and the State Effect.' In *State/Culture: State-Formation After the Cultural Turn,* edited by George Steinmetz, 76–97. Ithaca: Cornell University Press.

Mody, Perveez. 2002. 'Love and the Law: Love-Marriage in Delhi.' *Modern Asian Studies* 36 (1): 223–56.

Moir, Martin. 1993. 'Kaghazi Raj: Notes on the Documentary Basis of Company Rule: 1783–1858.' *Indo-British Review* 21 (2): 185–93.

Moore, Donald S. 2005. *Struggling for Territory: Race, Place, and Power in Zimbabwe.* Durham & London: Duke University Press.

Mosse, David. 2004. 'Is Good Policy Unimplementable? Reflections on the Ethnography of Aid Policy and Practice.' *Development and Change* 35 (4): 639–71.

_____. 2005. *Cultivating Development: An Ethnography of Aid Policy and Practice.* London: Pluto Press.

Murgai, Rinku and Ravallion, Martin. 2005. 'Employment Guarantee in Rural India: What Would it Cost and How Much Would it Reduce Poverty.' *Economic and Political Weekly* 40 (31): 3450–5.

Navaro-Yashin, Yael. 2007. 'Make-Believe Papers, Legal Forms, and the Counterfeit: Affective Interactions Between Documents and People in Britain and Cyprus.' *Anthropological Theory* 7 (1): 79–96.

_____. 2012. *The Make-Believe Space: Affective Geography in a Post-War Polity*. Durham: Duke University Press.

Ogborn, Miles. 2007. *Indian Ink: Script and Print in the Making of the English East India Company*. Chicago: University of Chicago Press.

Ong, Aihwa and Zhang, Li. 2008. 'Introduction: Privatizing China: Powers of the Self, Socialism from Afar.' In *Privatizing China: Socialism from Afar*, edited by Aihwa Ong and Li Zhang, 1–120. New York: Cornell University Press.

Orwell, George. 1948. *Burmese Days*. London: Secker & Warburg.

_____. 1950. *Shooting an Elephant and Other Essays*. London: Secker & Warburg.

Pahari, Ramesh. 1997. *Dasholi Gram Swarajya Mandal (DGSM)*. Dehar Dun: Micro Mint.

_____. 2005. *Aniket: Janpad Chamoli Ank*. Dehra Dun: Valley Offest Press.

Pandian, Anand. 2001. 'Predatory Care: The Imperial Hunt in Mughal and British India.' *Journal of Historical Sociology* 14 (1): 79–107.

Parry, Jonathan. 'The 'Embourgeoisement' of a 'Proletarian Vanguard'?" Unpublished Paper.

Pathak, Shekhar. 2005. 'Submergence of a Town, Not of an Idea.' *Economic and Political Weekly* LX (33): 3637–9.

_____.1997. 'State, Society and Natural Resources in Himalaya: Dynamics of Change in Colonial and Post-colonial Uttarakhand.' *Economic and Political Weekly* XXX (17): 908–12.

Pels, Peter. 2000. 'The Trickster's Dilemma: Ethics and the Technologies of the Anthropological Self.' In *Audit Cultures: Anthropological Studies in Accountability, Ethics and the Academy*, edited by Marilyn Strathern, 135–72. New York: Routledge.

Pigg, Stacey L. 1992. 'Inventing Social Categories through Place: Social Representations and Development in Nepal.' *Comparative Studies in Society and History* 34 (3): 491–513.

Power, Michael. 1999. *The Audit Society: Rituals of Verification*. Oxford: Oxford University Press.

Radcliffe-Brown, Alfred R. 1940. 'Preface.' In *African Political Systems*, edited by Meyer Fortes and E. E. Evans-Pritchard, xi–xxii. Oxford: Oxford University Press.

Rai, P. *The Great Job Robbery: Rs 2100 Crore NREGS Scam in Madhya Pradesh*. New Delhi: Centre for Environment and Food Security (CEFS), 2008.

Raman, Bhawani. 2012. *Document Raj: Writing and Scribes in Early Colonial South India*. Chicago: Chicago University Press.

Ramanathan, Uma. 2010. 'A Unique Indentity Bill.' *Economic and Political Weekly* XLV (30): 10–14.

Ramble, Charles. 1997. 'Tibetan Pride of Place; Or, Why Nepal's Bhotiyas are Not an Ethnic Group.' In *Nationalism and Ethnicity in a Hindu Kingdom: The Politics of Culture in Contemporary Nepal*, edited by David Gellner, J. Pfaff-Czarnecka, and J. Whelpton, 379–413. Amsterdam: Harwood Academic.

Rangan, Haripriya. 2000. *Of Myths and Movements: Rewriting Chipko into Himalayan History*. London: Verso.

Rangarajan, Mahesh. 1996. 'The Politics of Ecology: The Debate on Wildlife and People in India, 1970–95.' *Economic and Political Weekly* 31: 2391–409.

_____. 2005. *India's Wildlife History*. New Delhi: Permanent Black.

Reeves, Madeleine. 2011. 'Fixing the Border: On the Affective Life of the State in Southern Kyrgyzstan.' *Environment and Planning D: Society and Space* 29: 905–23.

Reith, Gerda. 2004. 'Uncertain Times: The Notion of 'Risk' and the Development of Modernity.' *Time & Society* 13 (2/3): 383–402.

Riles, Annelise. 2001. *The Network Inside Out.* Ann Arbor: University of Michigan Press.

_____. 2006a. 'Anthropology, Human Rights, and Legal Knowledge: Culture in the Iron Cage.' *American Anthropologist* 1: 52-65.

_____. 2006b. '[Deadlines]: Removing the Bracket on Politics in Bureaucratic and Anthropological Analysis.' In *Documents: Artifacts of Modern Knowledge,* edited by Annelise Riles, 71–92. Ann Arbor: University of Michigan Press.

Rose, Nikolas. 1996. 'Governing 'Advanced' Liberal Democracies.' In *Foucault and Political Reason: Liberalism, Neo-liberalism and Rationalities of Government,* edited by Andrew Barry, Thomas Osborne and Nikolas Rose. London: University of Chicago Press.

Roy, Aruna and Dey, Nikhil. 2005. 'Guaranteeing Action for Employment.' *The Hindu,* 15 August.

Saberwal, Vasant, Rangarajan, Mahesh and Kothari, Ashish. 2001. *People, Parks and Wildlife: Towards Coexistence.* New Delhi: Orient Longman.

Sainath, Palagummi. 2000. *Everybody Loves a Good Drought: Stories from India's Poorest Districts.* New Delhi: Penguin.

Saumarez-Smith, Richard. 1985. 'Rule-by-Records and Rule-by-Reports: Complementary Aspects of the British Imperial Rule of Law.' *Contributions to Indian Sociology* (n.s.) 19 (1): 153–76.

Schwegler, T. A. 2008. 'Taking it from the top (down)? Rethinking Neoliberalism and Political Hierarchy in Mexico.' *American Ethnologist* 35 (4): 682–700.

Schwarz, B. 1974. 'Waiting, Exchange and Power: The Distribution of Time in Social Systems.' *American Journal of Sociology* 79: 841–71.

Scott, James C. 1998. *Seeing Like a State: How Certain Schemes to Improve the Human Condition Have Failed.* New Haven and London: Yale University Press.

Sellen, Abigail J., and Harper, Richard. 2002. *The Myth of the Paperless Office.* Cambridge: The MIT Press.

Shah, Alpa. 2010. *In the Shadows of the State: Indigeous Politics, Environmentalism, and Insurgency in Jharkhand, India.* Durham: Duke University Press.

Sharma, Aradhana. 2006. 'Crossbreeding Institutions, Breeding Struggle: Women's Empowerment, Neoliberal Governmentality, and State (re)formation in India.' *Cultural Anthropology* 21 (1): 60–95.

_____. 2008. *Logics of Empowerment: Development, Gender, and Governance in Neoliberal India.* Minneapolis & London: University of Minnesota Press.

Sharma, Aradhana and Gupta, Akhil. 2006. 'Introduction: Rethinking Theories of the State in an Age of Globalisation.' In *The Anthropology of the State: A Reader,* edited by Aradhana Sharma and Akhil Gupta, 1–42. Oxford: Blackwell Publishing.

Sharma, Prashant. 2015. *Democracy and Transparency in the Indian State: The Making of the Right to Information Act.* London: Routledge

Shore, Cris and Wright, Susan. 2000. 'Coercive Accountability: The Rise of Audit Culture in Higher Education.' In *Audit Cultures: Anthropological Studies in Accountability, Ethics, and the Academy,* edited by Marilyn Strathern, 57–89. New York: Routledge.

Simmel, Georg. 1950. 'The Secret and the Secret Society.' In the *The Sociology of Georg Simmel*, edited by K. H. Wolff. New York: The Free Press.

Smith, Dorothy E. 1987. *The Everyday World as Problematic: A Feminist Sociology*. Boston: Northeastern University Press.

Sneath, David. 2007. *The Headless State: Aristocratic Orders, Kinship Society, and Misrepresentation of Nomadic Inner Asia*. New York: Columbia University Press.

_____. 2006. 'Transacting and Enacting: Corruption, Obligation and the Use of Monies in Mongolia.' *Ethnos* 71 (1): 89–112.

Ssorin-Chaikov, Nikolai. 2006. 'On Heterochrony: Birthday Gifts to Stalin, 1949.' *Journal of the Royal Anthropological Institute* 12: 355–75.

Subramanian, T.S.R. 2004. *Journeys Through Babudom and Netaland: Governance in India*. Delhi: Rupa

Stoler, Laura Ann. 2009. *Along the Archival Grain: Epistemic Anxieties and Colonial Common Sense*. Princeton and Oxford: Princeton University Press.

Strathern, Marilyn. 2000. 'Introduction: New Accountabilities.' *Audit Cultures: Anthropological Studies in Accountability, Ethics and the Academy*, edited by Marilyn Strathern, 1–18. New York: Routledge.

_____. 2006. 'Bullet-Proofing: A Tale from the United Kingdom.' In *Documents: Artifacts of Modern Knowledge*, edited by Annelise Riles, 181–205. Ann Arbor: University of Michigan Press.

Tarlo, Emma. 2000. 'Paper Truths: the Emergency and Slum Clearance through Forgotten Files.' In *The Everyday State and Society in Modern India*, edited by Chris Fuller and Veronique Benei, 68–90. Delhi: Social Science Press.

Taussig, Michael. 1997. *The Magic of the State*. New York: Routledge.

The Gazette of India. 2005. The National Rural Employment Guarantee Act, 2005. D L-(N) O4/000/72 003~5. Ministry of Law and Justice. New Delhi: Government of India.

The Tiger Task Force. 2005. *The Report of the Tiger Task Force: Joining the Dots*. New Delhi: Project Tiger, Government of India.

Thrift, Nigel and Jon May. 2001. *Timespace: Geographies of Temporality*. London: Routledge.

Tsing, Anna. 1994. 'Further Inflections: Towards Ethnographies of the Future.' *Cultural Anthropology* 9 (3): 279–97.

Turem, Ziya Umut and Ballestero, Andrea. 2014. 'Regulatory Translations: Expertise and Affect in Global Legal Fields (Symposium Introduction).' *Indiana Journal of Global Legal Studies* 21(1): 1–25.

Vanaik, Anish. 2009. 'Accounts of Corruption.' *Frontline* 26 (1).

Wade, Robert. 1985. 'The Market for Public Office: Why the Indian State is Not Better at Development.' *World Development* 13 (4): 467–97.

Walton, H. G. 1910. *A Gazetteer of the Garhwal Himalaya*. Dehradun: Natraj Publishers, 1889.

Wacquant, Loic. 2009. *Punishing the Poor: the Neoliberal Government of Social Insecurity*. Durham & London: Duke University Press.

Weber, Max. 2006. 'Bureaucracy.' In *The Anthropology of the State: A Reader*, edited by Aradhana Sharma and Akhil Gupta, 49–70. Oxford: Blackwell.

West, Harry G. and Todd Sanders. 2003. 'Introduction: Power Revealed and Concealed in the New World Order'. In West, Harry G. and Sanders, Todd (eds.) *Transparency and Conspiracy: Ethnographies of Suspicion in the New World Order*. 51–90. Durham: Duke University Press

Woodman, Dorothy. 1969. *Himalayan Frontiers: A Political Review of British, Chinese, Indian, and Russian Rivalries*. London: Barrie and Rockliff the Cresset Press.

Yarrow, Thomas and Soumhya Venkatesan. 2012. 'Introduction: Anthropology and Development - Critical Framings.' In *Differentiating Development: Beyond an Anthropology of Critique*, edited by Soumhya Venkatesan and Thomas Yarrow, 1–22. New York: Berghahn.

Yurchak, Alexei. 2006. *Everything Was Forever, Until It Was No More: The Last Soviet Generation*. Princeton: Princeton University Press.

Websites accessed

www.gov.ua.nic.in (Accessed on 02/07/2014)
(Uttarakhand's official website)
http://chamoli.nic.in/ (Accessed on 02/07/2014)
(Chamoli district's official website)
http://nrega.nic.in/Planning_Commision.pdf (Accessed on 02/07/2014)
(Planning Commission's list of 200 most backward districts)
http://www.nrega.nic.in/ (Accessed on 02/07/2014)
(The official NREGA website with regular updates on wages, working day, rules and changes to name, etc.)
http://rural.nic.in/speeches/pm_speech.pdf (Accessed on 02/07/2014)
(Prime Minister's speeches on the NREGA including the inaugural one on 2nd February 2006)
http://nrega.nic.in/Nrega_guidelines.pdf: (Accessed on 02/07/2014)
(The NREGA guidelines online—most updated versions)
http://righttoinformation.gov.in/ (Accessed on 02/07/2014)
(The official Right to Information website)
http://rural.nic.in/SGRY%20Guidelines%20-%20Final.htm (Accessed on 02/07/2014)
(The guidelines for the *Sampoorna Grameen Rozgar Yojana*)
http://www.righttofoodindia.org/ (Accessed on 02/07/2014)
(Resources maintained by the NREGA activists)
http://www.kalahandi.nic.in/ (Accessed on 02/07/2014)
(Kalahandi district's official website carrying details of poverty estimates and development schemes)
http://www.censusindia.net/ (Accessed on 02/07/2014)
(All Census of India 2001 figures have been taken from this official website)
Debate in Parliament on NREGA available at
http://164.100.47.134/newls/textofdebatedetail.aspx?sdate=08/18/2005 (Accessed on 04/04/09)
The Story in Outlook magazine on petitions to Golu *devata* (god)
http://www.outlookindia.com/article.aspx?232117 (Accessed on 18/09/2006)
Categorisation of endangered animals by the IUCN
http://www.iucnredlist.org/ (Accessed on 16/06/2009)

Index

CPSIA information can be obtained
at www.ICGtesting.com
Printed in the USA
LVHW052046131118
596987LV00017B/380